M000266724

MARCOS RIVERA

Copyright © 2022 by Marcos Rivera

All rights reserved. No part of this publication may be reproduced, distributed, or transmitted in any form or by any means, including photocopying, recording, or other electronic or mechanical methods, without the prior written permission of the publisher, except in the case of brief quotations embodied in critical reviews and certain other noncommercial uses permitted by copyright law. For permission requests, write to the author, subject line "Attention: Permissions" at info@pricingio.com. For ordering details, contact info@pricingio.com.

All song titles, lyrics, and logos are registered and copyrighted by their respective owners. This publication has not been authorized, prepared, or sponsored by the artists referenced in this book.

Hardcover ISBN: 978-1-7375280-0-5
Paperback ISBN: 978-1-7375280-1-2
eBook ISBN: 978-1-7375280-2-9

Library of Congress Control Number: 2022905518

Printed in the United States of America
First Edition

To my loving family: Melanie, Tiago, and Dahlia. You are the momentum that keeps me moving, the gravity that keeps me grounded, and the center of my world that keeps me focused. And to Gloria Rivera, in loving memory. I hope this book will make you proud, Mom. I miss you every day!

PRAISE FROM AROUND THE BLOCK

Very few people can explain complex pricing strategies with the graceful clarity of Marcos Rivera.

SYED BALKHI ▪ CEO AT AWESOME MOTIVE

Marcos' advice has been invaluable to me over the last several years. His experience and expertise makes him one of the most important thought leaders in the area of optimally pricing software products and services. For any executive interested in using pricing as a strategic lever to drive business growth, this book is an invaluable resource and an insightful read.

ARNAB MISHRA ▪ CHIEF PRODUCT OFFICER AT XACTLY CORPORATION

Most SaaS pricing advice is theoretical bullshit that takes forever to apply. Marcos' Street Pricing *takes a different approach. You can make an impact at your company in weeks, not quarters. I can attest. Marcos' pricing strategies have been one of the highest ROI for our company. Nothing else comes close.*

ALI MAMUJEE ▪ HEAD OF PRODUCT STRATEGY AT MERCATUS, A STATE STREET COMPANY

Marcos made it easy to capture a once underserved enterprise market and reclaim value across the board. His book is a must-read for PLG companies looking to go upmarket.

TOPE AWOTONA ▪ CEO OF CALENDLY

Marcos nailed the art and science of pricing in this book. With his invaluable experiences in a variety of businesses from startups to fast growth, Marcos has demystified the pricing game once for all. This book should be a great reference for every founder and executive in SaaS.

RAVI ADUSUMILLI ▪ SENIOR VICE PRESIDENT OF PARTNERSHIPS AT AIRWALLEX

Understanding how best to package and price a company's product(s) is a key component to any Private Equity value creation plan. Marcos' thoughtful and data-driven approach really gets to the heart of how best to do so. A highly recommended read!

SUSAN CLARK ▪ MANAGING DIRECTOR AND HEAD OF TECHNOLOGY VALUE CREATION AT SUN CAPITAL PARTNERS

If you want to learn a little bit about hip-hop, and a lot about pricing, this is the book for you! Marcos breaks down some of the things SaaS leaders need to know (and avoid) in an enjoyable and accessible way.

JAMES WOOD ▪ SENIOR VICE PRESIDENT OF PRICING ADVISORY AT INSIGHT PARTNERS

Getting price right is a huge driver of value creation for SaaS companies. Price too low and you're tanking your potential value, price too high and you can slow down deals or even drive up churn, make your pricing too complex and you put a big headwind on sales. Marcos is a true genius when it comes to SaaS pricing, and this book provides invaluable insight into getting SaaS pricing right.

SHAM SAO ▪ FOUNDER OF GROWTH II, BOARD MEMBER, ALUM OF MCKINSEY & COMPANY

Pricing is one of the hardest and least understood areas of business in my experience. It's also one of the most valuable levers a company has. In Street Pricing, *Marcos uses his extensive experience to lay out a simple framework that anyone can apply, points out the pitfalls to avoid, and clears the fog of how to price. Every growing business should read this book.*

GEOFFREY BAIRD ▪ TECH INVESTOR AND BOARD MEMBER

Marcos has been a fantastic partner with pricing and product strategy for many years now. This book exhibits his ability to provide a fresh perspective on what could otherwise be a mundane topic, deliver recommendations and guidance that can have rapid impact, and communicate sound advice for earlier stage and mature B2B SaaS companies alike.

NEIL CAREW ▪ OPERATING PARTNER TO PE-BACKED SAAS BUSINESSES

SaaS Founders and CEOs: If driving revenue growth is top of mind then you must read Marcos' book. Most companies try to do more at the top of the funnel–more leads, more marketing, work on sales velocity–but pricing and packaging is hands-down one of the highest impact ways to accelerate and start ramping up your revenue. You'll see the benefits across both new business and upsell as ASP and ARPA start to increase, without working harder. We made most of the mistakes in Marcos' book before working with him at GatherContent! What followed was a strategic overhaul of the entire business, huge strides in product-led growth and a data culture that we're constantly reaping rewards from. My advice would be to get a pricing initiative into your priorities for the quarter, if you haven't already. Before you kick things off, sit down with Street Pricing. *It's the ultimate guide to doing pricing right.*

ALICE DEER ▪ CO-FOUNDER AND CEO OF GATHERCONTENT

Succeeding at pricing strategy for a growth stage company is a crucible that melds product strategy with go-to-market strategy. That is, the stakes could not be higher. But, it's also a deliberative process that, if done correctly, can bend the arc of the company's trajectory in an incredibly profound way. Working with Marcos and Pricing I/O was just that and their work continues to amplify our product's impact the world over. His meticulous framework approach was remarkable in balancing the organization's competing priorities while teaching us and our stakeholders to think about future growth at scale. Priceless really!

PAROON CHADHA ▪ CO-FOUNDER AND CEO OF ONBOARD

Marcos takes the mystery out of pricing strategy, and provides a very effective roadmap for helping teams journey through important pricing and packaging decisions. His approach not only anchored our pricing exploration to the company's product and GTM strategies, it helped us align around and refine them.

DAVID KAREL ▪ CMO AT ZENPUT

Our fund invests in high-growth B2B SaaS companies and we have partnered with Marcos on pricing projects across our portfolio. Street Pricing *captures Marcos' wealth of experience in an easy to consume but impactful book for all of us to benefit from and is a great way to get up the learning curve, avoid pitfalls and tap into a key, but complex, growth lever.*

TODD MARKSON ▪ OPERATING PARTNER AT BAIN CAPITAL

Having worked with Marcos, I can tell you he knows his stuff! Marcos brings a fresh and, dare I say it, fun take on the complicated and complex world of pricing. A must-read for anyone wanting a practical, effective and hip guide into the world of SaaS pricing.

VIDYA DINAMANI ▪ FOUNDER AT PRODUCT REBELS, PRODUCT COACH AND AUTHOR OF *GROUNDWORK: GET BETTER AT MAKING BETTER PRODUCTS*

The Street Pricing *framework provides product leaders with a proven toolkit to maximize value capture, using an agile approach to SaaS pricing. It is the culmination of decades of first-hand experience in product management, exceptional pricing thought-leadership, and extensive consulting work with SaaS companies.*

CYNTHIA WILLIAMSON ▪ SENIOR VICE PRESIDENT OF PRODUCT MANAGEMENT AT JAMF

Pricing, a powerful value driver, can quickly become complex when you are unsure of how best to align with the needs of your customer base. Marcos makes it faster and easier to identify how to use pricing as a lever to scale your company's growth.

KRISHNA POTARAZU ▪ OPERATING PARTNER AT JMI EQUITY

CONTENTS

FOREWORD

I met Marcos when he worked with Vista Equity Partners. He was tasked with creating product strategy and product management best practices for Vista's portfolio companies. I vividly remember the first time he visited us onsite. The team was a little intimidated by him because he was in a suit whereas the team was in "California Tech Attire," which translates to whatever feels comfortable that day. He was very articulate and spoke very convincingly about his perspectives and recommendations. There were a lot of questions and good discussions between him and the team. At the end of the first day of our interactions, the team and I decided that despite the initial trepidation about him being "corporate" (the suit!) that we respected his perspectives, and we liked him. In subsequent interactions, I realized that there was a lot more to Marcos and a lot more to like and respect. First off, his origin story is incredible and inspiring. He has made it to the higher echelons in the corporate world despite the odds being stacked against him. He is a family man who makes decisions that optimize for his family first, which I respect tremendously.

When I heard from Marcos that he was looking to open up his own pricing firm, I was sad to see him leave, but that turned to happiness when we were able to sign up as his first customer to help us with our pricing effort. I have worked with multiple pricing consulting companies in the past. Pricing is a complex area. It is an underappreciated function, and most companies wing it and go with their gut, which is exactly the wrong way to go about it. It is also one of those areas where ownership is not clear across the different functions, and it ends up with a lot of different cooks in the kitchen and a lot of cooks with a lot of different opinions. Even those who have a dedicated function and people allocated to pricing often struggle with their pricing strategy and execution. There are a lot of different ways to go about it. Marcos educated the team on the art and science of pricing starting with understanding the value that you are providing as the beginning point. Pricing is not just about revenue maximization in the short term but getting "paid" for the real value that you are providing your customers and creating a win-win for the longer term. He laid out a repeatable framework that we have been using ever since his engagement. I repeatedly engage with companies where I see the same anti-patterns with pricing over and over again. I am glad that Marcos wrote this book to capture his framework and best practices on pricing. I can see a lot of companies benefiting from it.

SUNIL RAJASEKAR ▪ PRESIDENT OF MINDBODY

INTRODUCTION

Two out of three SaaS founders I work with are leaving money on the table and limiting their growth potential by overlooking one of the most powerful levers in business: pricing. Why would they leave money for someone else to grab? Well, it's because they don't know any better. They need some street smarts when it comes to pricing.

Welcome to the street. Street pricing, that is. I use the word "street" as my euphemism for unfiltered reality. And to deal with the sometimes brutal reality of street life, I learned that you need to quickly notice signals, you must read people and situations, and you must know what not to do by using intuition, instincts, and the information you have at hand. You have to cut through the theory and rely on the practical to make things work. That's true in life and in business, especially when it comes to leveraging your pricing.

Turns out, a lot of what I learned growing up applies to my pricing work today in the SaaS industry. This book connects those two worlds and (I hope) helps illustrate the concepts of pricing in bold relief. To properly represent street life and pay homage to my upbringing on the streets of New York City, each chapter is influenced by a head-bobbing, booty-shaking, crowd-cheering hip-hop song from the 90s. I believe the 90s were arguably the most entertaining era of urban music and the decade heavily influenced me as a kid growing up in the Bronx. I asked myself, "Can I use ear-catching music to embellish a topic that is notoriously boring, dense, and intimidating?"

I answered myself, "Why not?"

Hip-hop music naturally has inspirational messages woven into the lyrics. Based on my unique background, I couldn't help but draw the parallels between what I learned growing up listening to hip-hop and in my lessons from my extensive career with pricing.

But make no mistake. This is not another book about pricing theory. And do you know what else? I'm not going to tell you that all your dreams will come true if you simply "price to value." I'm going to keep it real.

Why? Because I'm tired of talking about value, and I bet you are, too. We should be talking about how to capture it!

From my point of view, value is like love. Most people know when they have it, and most know when they don't. But even still, it's crazy hard to measure! And like love, people enjoy giving you countless tips and advice for how to get it ... advice that falls short of showing you how to do anything. That's because pricing has many convenient principles that are inherently easy to talk about, but invariably hard to practice in the messy world we live in.

For the well-googled brainiacs out there, it is easy to find plenty of pricing theory, platitudes, and clever expressions that can give you a general clue about what to do. But if you are anything like I was or like the majority of coffee-infused "SaaSletes"—entrepreneurs and business athletes who play in the wild sport of Software as a Service out there pitching, coding, and hustling their way to a lucky break—you don't know where to start with pricing. And you are not alone!

WHY I WROTE THIS BOOK

I wrote *Street Pricing* to make the topic of monetization real to the touch. In other words, to make it approachable and tangible for all the hard-working leaders in software who are changing the world one line of code at a time.

I wrote this book for those who want to grow a Software as a Service business but aren't sure of the right path to take or where to start with monetizing their value.

In other words, for those who are guessing their way through it.

Pause for dramatic effect.

But before we get started, my first question is whether this book is right for you. Here's a quick litmus test:

- If you copied your competitor's pricing model, this book is for you.
- If you have a tough time expressing and measuring your product's value, this book is for you.
- If you are looking for new ways to unlock revenue growth, this book is for you.
- If you're wondering if your B2B SaaS product is too cheap or too expensive, this book is for you.
- If you enjoy head-bobbing hits punctuated by 90s hip-hop, this book is especially for you!

And last, I wrote this book for the curious, open-minded, and action-oriented reader. If that describes you, then you are my people, and you are reading the right book!

There are many struggles in the SaaS world. Among the most dangerous is failing to capture the value created that leads to cash flow pains, which fuels desperation and opens the door to suboptimal decision-making and failure. This is the quicksand trap of under-monetizing. If I achieve my goal with this book, here is what will happen instead of the quicksand trap:

- More value created by SaaS companies will be captured.
- The captured value will lead to more profits and growth.
- More growth will lead to even more value created for consumers (starting a virtuous cycle).
- More value created for consumers will accelerate innovation, commerce, economics, quality of life, and yes, even humankind!

Cue the lights and confetti drop.

WHY FOCUS ON B2B SAAS?

The reality is that a good pricing framework will transcend across sectors and business models. So anyone working in tech, whether they're in B2C or B2B, vertical or horizontal platforms, marketplaces or APIs, will benefit from the pricing principles in this book. The thing with B2B that I find intriguing is the pronounced tension between the need for simplicity and flexibility in a world that demands the promise of software the most.

In B2B, packaging and segmentation can be trickier when trying to shift from personas to "orgsonas" (organization persona). The sales cycle is longer, more convoluted, and riddled with landmines. The implementation of the software is deeper and more complex. A B2B SaaS company must factor in the commonalities and sharp contrasts between a small business getting off the ground and a global conglomerate like Honeywell in order to serve them well.

Solving these complexities leads to undeniable business value in massive quantities and a one-to-many flywheel of impact across legions of constituents. One B2B software platform can generate value to thousands of businesses, which in turn can help millions of people.

Last but not least, most of my experience in monetization involved simplifying pricing models in complex B2B software environments. I have seen the inner workings of over 200 software businesses, from startups to global enterprises and how they attempted to capture value with pricing, super-charging my pattern-recognition engine. Assuming the average stint in a tech job is about three years per company, you'd have to work for 600 years to see what I've seen.

But today is your lucky day. I've packed this book with 600 working years of patterns and goodies to give you a leg up and shorten your path to success! How's that for having your back?

WHAT TO EXPECT

Going back to my "street" euphemism, you have to cut through the pricing theory and rely on practical frameworks, toolkits, and best practices to nail your ideal pricing model.

To help us dig deeper into useful best practices, I included small excerpts called **INTERLUDES** throughout the book to focus in on a pricing-specific topic demonstrated by a real case study or interview. To protect the guilty, I masked real business names and data while still staying true to the message. These interludes help you visualize the lesson in action in a "near-real" scenario, helping to quickly connect the dots.

I include what I call **PLAYBACK EXERCISES** throughout the book to give you a chance to stop, think, and apply what you learned. Some of these exercises can be done in five minutes at your desk but can also be taken much further for the ambitious (you know who you are). And to help you scan pearls of wisdom as you read, I've interspersed **PRICING TIPS** in each track and compiled them all in a section I call "High Speed Dubbing" at the end of the book.

WHAT YOU WILL LEARN

I want to give you the courage to go out there and improve your pricing and how you monetize value. I've learned over the years that **pricing is really about confidence**—confidence that you know your value and why people should pay for it, and confidence that your pricing is fair and relevant as the value changes over time. Confidence comes from diligence, practice, and having good data ... three things I want to encourage you to have after you put this book down and try on your own. Here is a quick rundown of what you will learn after reading *Street Pricing*:

- Why most pricing efforts fail
- How to tell if your pricing is working
- How to master the art of packaging
- How to charge for the right value
- How to get better at pricing over time

A few years ago, I was attending a pricing conference in Boston. The conference was full of great speakers and tangible takeaways, but the talking point that stuck with me the most was the following statistic from the keynote speaker: Only one in 10 of attendees would actually put this newly acquired knowledge into action.

I found this both surprising and heartbreaking. I totally get the daily grind, especially as a SaaSlete or business owner. It takes a great deal of discipline to take a step forward in a new direction. Believe me, I feel you!

But for the sake of your product, startup, or company, take these lessons forward! I urge you to take this new knowledge to the streets and get real results within 90 days of reading this book.

Do you accept my challenge?

I thought you would!

So, let's get this party started right with **PART ONE: REWIND**. In this first section, you will learn a little about my background and some of the best and worst pricing advice I've had to learn the hard way. This background will stand up a few pillars that support my pricing perspective and will set the stage for the rest of the book.

Ready? Mic check one-two-one-two.

SEARCH / SKIP

If you are impatient like me, then here is a quick reference list to let you skip ahead to content throughout the book based on a hot topic or specific issue you're grappling with today.

"But Marcos," you might ask, "Why do you want to encourage skipping around? Don't you want us to read the entire book?"

If you want to maximize the ROI from buying this book, then read the whole thing from front to back. That's why I decided to keep it shorter in text than your average pricing book and richer with images, checklists, and tables.

But I promised to keep things real with you. I know that real people buy a book with burning questions in their minds and a strong yearning to find the answers. Once we extinguish a few fires in your brain, you'll be in a better mental state to absorb all the lessons necessary to master pricing.

And let's face it, we don't have all day. So, enjoy my quick reference table on the following page to scratch the itch, and the surface.

FIGURE A: SHORTCUT TO TOP PRICING QUESTIONS

How do I know if I am charging enough?	TRACK 5 KILLING ME SOFTLY TRACK 6 CHECK YO SELF TRACK 11 CASH RULES EVERYTHING
What should I do if I want to raise my prices?	TRACK 6 CHECK YO SELF TRACK 11 CASH RULES EVERYTHING TRACK 14 MO MONEY, MO PROBLEMS
How do I know if my pricing model is the best one?	TRACK 5 KILLING ME SOFTLY TRACK 7 I GOT 5 ON IT TRACK 12 THIS IS HOW WE DO IT
What is the best way to package my features?	TRACK 6 CHECK YO SELF TRACK 9 MY PEOPLES COME FIRST TRACK 10 THE CHOICE IS YOURS
How can I simplify my pricing model?	TRACK 5 KILLING ME SOFTLY TRACK 6 CHECK YO SELF TRACK 7 I GOT 5 ON IT
How do I price a new product or startup?	TRACK 7 I GOT 5 ON IT TRACK 11 CASH RULES EVERYTHING TRACK 13 SO FRESH, SO CLEAN
How should I approach pricing during a crisis?	TRACK 5 KILLING ME SOFTLY TRACK 8 NUTHIN' BUT A "G" THANG TRACK 15 KEEP YA HEAD UP

PART ONE: REWIND

You can learn a lot by paying attention to the past. In the next four chapters (or, as I like to call them, **TRACKS**), we're going to **REWIND** time and take an inside look at how I developed my pricing point of view and the biggest B2B SaaS lessons that shaped the 5Q Pricing framework you will learn in the later tracks.

YOU WILL LEARN	TRACK
HOW TO GET STARTED WITH PRICING	1
HOW TO AVOID THE BIGGEST PRICING MISTAKES	2
WHY YOU SHOULD PRICE FOR ENTERPRISE VALUE	3
WAYS TO PRICE FOR REALITY, NOT FANTASY	4

STEP INTO A WORLD

HOW A SKINNY KID FROM THE BRONX DISCOVERED THE POWER OF PRICING

NO ONE IS BORN KNOWING BEST PRACTICES IN MONETIZING B2B TECHNOLOGY ...

... and there are no universities offering a major in SaaS pricing the last time I checked. Pricing skills are not gained but earned through experience in building, communicating, and capturing value in the real world. Anyone can learn how to price to value, and to prove it, I want to share my journey in learning the art of pricing.

"Step Into a World," released in 1997 by KRS-One, really captures my mental state as I broke my way into pricing. It's a single on his third solo studio album, *I Got Next*, and is a clever remake of the Blondie classic "Rapture" featuring new singer Keva cooing the Deborah Harry lead. It represents KRS-One at his most lyrically ferocious. It's that ferocity and commitment to being "strictly about skills" that embodies my point of view on pricing.

Before I tell you how I got my start, let me ask you a question. You guessed when you produced your current pricing and packaging, didn't you? No shame or judgment if you did, and if I'm being honest here, you would be in good company. A staggering 75 percent of SaaS companies I've worked with have completely guessed on their pricing. That's three out of four, y'all. And those guessers are leaving crazy amounts of money on the table and holding back their growth potential!

It's okay. I'm here to help in a way that will keep things simple and actionable.

Pricing is a major blind spot for B2B SaaS businesses today. But if you think you nailed it and know everything there is to know about pricing to value, then sorry, this book is not for you.

I've been obsessed with building and capturing value in SaaS for over 20 years and across 200 technology companies. I have learned about trends, observed patterns, and made every mistake possible on the path to impactful and innovative monetization.

But to learn more about how I've helped hundreds of SaaSletes monetize their products, you need to understand where I'm coming from, and where I *came* from.

BRONX BOY DIARY

Over the years of working with hundreds of pricing models across all types of B2B SaaS products, I've learned more than my fair share of useful adages about pricing to capture value:

- Your pricing and packages will become stale and disconnect with value after two years.
- You should aim to capture up to 40 percent of your net positive differentiated value.
- Avoid giving away too much value by ensuring less than 20 percent of active customers are in your entry package.

These general truths are not learned in a college lecture hall. They accumulate through experimentation with real customers, real money exchanging hands, and real risk. Many SaaSletes out there are not ready or in a position to take this risk. But I'm betting that if you learn how I took risks, you will be one step closer to taking the steps necessary to build your own general truths that will unlock millions for your SaaS business.

So how did a skinny Puerto Rican kid from the Bronx end up as a respected authority in SaaS monetization?

Let's take you back to the beginning.

They said it was the worst black out in the history of New York. During the 1977 power outage that hit on July 14th as a result of lightning, my mother, Gloria, was already at the hospital experiencing contractions. The hospital was running on backup generators and the medical staff were all on edge about the citywide looting and arson happening outside.

A piercing beeping sound filled through the room as the unborn baby's heart rate dropped to dangerously low levels. Doctors had to act fast in the moment. Who knew if lightning would strike twice, or if the looters would grow even more lawless, or if the backup generators would fail? They decided to perform a C-section and remove the baby quickly before it was too late.

Around 2 a.m., July 16th, the baby's cry filled the room and the doctors exhaled in relief.

"That was a close one," sighed a nurse as she wrapped me up like a little bean burrito with a blue beanie (try saying that five times fast) and handed me over to my exhausted, but elated, mother.

"You made it!" she cried out. As a 22-year-old single mom from Puerto Rico and living in the Bronx, life was scary and uncertain, but my wailing cry gave her hope that we would survive living in the concrete jungle, and that we'd be okay.

Fast forward 10 years.

Life was about getting by and surviving as a kid in the Bronx. Fortunately for me, hip-hop music found its voice during my early childhood years. During the day, I filled the air from my boom box playing a mix tape of dubbed jams from Hot 97's Funkmaster Flex, and at night I enjoyed the playful banter, freestyle battles, and eye-catching videos from *Yo! MTV Raps*, hosted by Ed Lover and Doctor Dre.

The rap game was young and raw. The lyrical poetry from the MCs planted seeds in my mind; seeds that grew into ideas that life was more than the struggle, more than white rice with corned beef for dinner, more than the shame of paying with food stamps, and more than wondering if Con Edison would turn off our heat.

Life was cozy with the four of us living in a 500-square-foot apartment, so getting outside was an everyday norm. In New York, our world was "the block." We knew everyone who lived there like a big family and people looked out for one another. Living under the warm arms of my block on

205th Street and Bainbridge made life more palatable growing up in a single-parent household with three young kids. And being the first born, I had to grow up fast to help out.

I woke up every morning with ideas on how I can be helpful. My mom and younger siblings needed me. I was proud to be her sidekick. It didn't matter what the task was: carrying groceries, running to the store, changing diapers, cooking, cleaning ... whatever it took to help out and make my mom's life a little easier. I guess that's why I naturally like to help people; it was ingrained from an early age.

Life is full of shocking moments that spew out different paths like a fractal. Mom passed away suddenly when I was 11 years old. I was a sidekick who lost his superhero, so how was I supposed to move on? I felt as if fear, sadness, loneliness, and insecurity chased me into a dark alley, cornered me, and kicked the shit out of me!

They say hardship builds character. I needed to stay strong for my little brother and baby sister. I needed to set the stage and be a role model. I needed to prove that we could fight our way out of poverty. And here is where the seeds from hip-hop music began to grow into powerful and life-changing ideas.

It was time to decide.

My grandmother uprooted her life in San Diego to watch over us in the Bronx. I'd visited California a few times to see her along with aunts, uncles, and cousins. Cali trips were nerve-wracking due to my healthy paranoia of earthquakes. If I ever go back, it will be too soon.

Grandma spent most of her days in court battling for custody against my father. After the dust settled, I had two options. Option A: Move to Florida with my sharp-tongued, critical, absentee father, a man whom I didn't meet for the first time until I was six years old due to his prison sentence for drug trafficking cocaine in the seventies. Or I could choose Option B: Move to San Diego with my tough-love and no-nonsense abuela and potentially get swallowed up in an earthquake.

So I decided I was "going-going back-back to Cali-Cali." And that was when things got interesting.

PASSION FOR PRICING

Despite my paralyzing fear of earthquakes, the choice was easy. I was off to San Diego at age 13 where I have lived and discovered three very important passions in life (And no, not fish tacos, flip flops, and avocados. Well, okay. You got me on the tacos.).

My first passion is analysis. I was always good with numbers and aced every math test I took as a kid; I was ahead of the curve and that thrust me into calculus and linear algebra as a first-year student in high school. To me, it was all about hunting for the right answer, and I loved the pursuit. I learned at an early age that numbers make the world of business go around and understanding the ins and outs of equations makes it easier to grasp the ins and outs of business.

My second passion is something that fed the other half of my brain. I was keenly interested in psychology and human behavior. I never studied formally, but they were always topics I chose to dig into for pleasure reading. I enjoy how the brain thinks, how people make decisions, and how truly flawed our logic really is. Conditioning of the human brain was a lot of fun to learn about, but I never realized how relevant this information would be years later. Pricing involves humans sharing value with other humans, and therefore, is heavily psychological.

My third passion is technology. I was the kid who my abuela routinely asked to fix that blinking 12:00 on the VCR (Video Cassette Recorder. Look it up. Yes, I'm old.). I loved fiddling with new gizmos, and I was in constant awe as the internet grew from this "information superhighway" to the global connected tissue that flattened the world and evolved our way of life. I went from *Pac-Man* and pagers to Facebook and *Fortnite*. What a ride! Technology creates and distributes value faster and more dynamically than

PRICING TIP

Understand the language of numbers in business.
Understand how people behave.
Understand the technology in order to understand the value to price.

any other industrial revolution and capturing that value with pricing is a challenge that energizes me every day.

These three passions were my gravitational pull towards pricing, but everyone has different passions and that's okay. The idea is to open your mind to the key areas that will help you absorb and excel in pricing your technology. Here is my checklist to ramp up and learn about pricing without being bored to tears:

- **BUSINESS ANALYSIS.** You can't learn pricing without being comfortable with math. I'm not saying you need to be a statistician, but numbers play a major role in commerce, monetization, and growth.
- **PSYCHOLOGY**, or the understanding of human behavior, is more important than math. As long as people are assessing value and buying things, you need to be open to understanding the inner workings of the human mind and what drives decisions.
- **TECHNOLOGY**, which in our case is the source of value and the core of what we are trying to monetize. We want to solve problems with technology, create new opportunities that were once impossible, and change the world one line of code at a time. If you don't buy into this, learning how to capture the value of it will be a steep mountain climb.

If you check all three boxes, then we have a winner! If you checked two out of three, then you'll extract some but not the maximum benefit, and if you checked one or none, then it's best to put down this book now because connecting the dots will be harder than putting socks on an angry chicken (I'm speaking from experience. It's a long story.).

GETTING SOME PERSPECTIVE

I loved growing up in the past two decades and witnessing the exciting evolution of technology. I truly appreciated the progress differently because I know what it was like before the new tech arrived on the scene. Fax machines, encyclopedias, wired telephones, 56K modems, AOL, Ask

Jeeves, all of it! Some of you will smile as you walk down memory lane with me, and many of you will scratch your heads in bewilderment because you don't know what these things are.

After splitting my childhood between New York and San Diego, I moved on to the University of California at San Diego. Later, I started my career as a financial analyst in the financial services field. It was a great way to sharpen my analytical skills, but it only fed one of my passions. I learned a lot about good and bad data and how to dig deeper to show executives the "So What" from the "What."

PRICING TIP

If you are looking to put someone in charge of pricing, it helps if they have a financial analysis background.

Starting in 2000, my first product manager (PM) job was to build and price an enterprise software platform used to exchange securitized auto loans between financial institutions. Back then, it was a decision engine with an XML exchange between AS400 systems. Do I sound like a dinosaur to you yet? The next year, I was promoted to the product manager role (at a time when the role was still grossly misunderstood). The PM role was a perfect way to pull my passions together.

In 2007, I stepped up and was promoted to a senior PM role and owned a portfolio of on-premise, SaaS, and mobile applications. Building software was fun and fed my three passions equally. But after going round and round with what value to build and which problems to solve, it occurred to me that very little attention was given to how we should price the value we are delivering.

So, I asked around, and here is what I got back in terms of pricing our hard-earned value:

"Just get as much as you can from the customer."

Um, okay.

"Just go and copy the competitors, but charge more if the customer goes for it, or discount if the customer pushes back."

Yeah, that sounds really scientific.

And that was that. We had our price in five minutes flat. Only problem was, it was wrong. Dead wrong.

Here's an example to paint a picture. We decided to "SaaSify" our field workforce dispatching application and charge each license by the user seat. Safe enough, right? Yes, except that it was focused on improving workforce productivity so a business can do more with the same or fewer people on staff.

Do you see the conflict? I didn't at first and neither did senior leadership, which was scary in hindsight. The conflict that we found was that as customers gained value with the software, we were not growing in revenue, and in fact, many paid us less. One customer gained so much efficiency, they reduced their user licenses by half. Yep. We doubled their productivity and halved our revenue as a plump reward for doing so. How does this make any sense? We deliver more value, but get less money for it? Nah, that doesn't add up.

So, I took it upon myself to redefine the entire pricing model. I dove into blogs, books, and courses related to pricing and absorbed as much information as I could.

I was hooked in no time. The discipline of monetizing software fed my trio of passions completely. I devoted every waking hour to learning how to capture value, both in work and in everyday life. I ran random experiments every chance I had, evaluating how I reacted to every price I saw from toothpaste to toilet paper, to TVs. I was priming my brain to recognize the exchange of value. And it wasn't long before I was the de facto pricing expert in the company.

So, what did I do about the lazy pricing we had for the workforce productivity application? I flipped it around to a subscription model based on transaction usage around a key value metric for insurance companies: the number of claims.

The realignment with usage meant we got paid more the more customers used it, whether they adjusted to centralized staffing or not. A claim was a claim.

It was a fairer exchange of value, something I can now see and recognize. It also simplified both purchase and usage by aligning with how our customers accounted for costs. And last, it made more economic sense for our customer since the cost per claim went down as volume went up. It was a win-win proposition, and our revenue tripled over the next two years as a result.

But I wasn't a pricing expert yet. I was just able to figure out ways to capture value better than most using and applying all the knowledge and insights that I've gained in my studies and experiments. The key to getting good at pricing is learning how to apply your knowledge quickly and iteratively. It's a skill that also helps if you want to build great software products.

Some people ask me, "Hey Marcos, how do I get into pricing and learn how to capture value, too?"

We all must take our own path. But the first step is to start reading to tune your antenna. There's a vast amount of material on pricing today. Let me save you time by telling you where to focus your attention, starting with the blogs I've listed in **FIGURE 1.1**.

FIGURE 1.1: TOP BLOGS TO RAISE YOUR PRICING IQ

OpenView Venture Partners → OPENVIEWPARTNERS.COM/BLOG
A growth-stage venture capital firm out of Boston. These guys know how to grow companies and had a hand in major SaaS success stories like DataDog, GitPrime, and Calendly. Their blog is chock full of SaaS growth and monetization goodness (Dang, I sound like such a nerd).

Profitwell → PROFITWELL.COM/RECUR
Formerly known as Price Intelligently, spearheaded much of the best pricing content in the biz. Rebranding to focus on their subscription-based recurring revenue growth platform, they continue to publish solid ebooks and tips to step up your pricing game. I highly recommend their content; it's well worth your time.

Pricing I/O → PRICINGIO.COM/BLOG
C'mon, I know you saw this coming a mile away. In addition to references to some of the great content from the two blogs above, we put out content you can easily understand and put to work right away with no fluff. We also cover B2B and enterprise SaaS deeper than anyone out there right now. (Ooh, shots fired!)

In addition to these blogs, be sure to read *The Strategy and Tactics of Pricing: A Guide to Growing More Profitably* by Thomas T. Nagle, et al. This book started it all for me. The material is foundational in building your pricing knowledge. Buy it using your favorite book source. Trust me, reading the above will give you a leg up on pricing in SaaS. Then once you've absorbed all of this material (and you should keep doing that throughout your career), put something out into the real world by charging for something, then learn by writing down what you observed, and finally, repeat these steps to build up your pattern recognition muscles.

Here is the pricing ramp up process in a nutshell:

- Read up
- Put something out there
- Learn
- Rinse and Repeat

Now that you know a little about how I gained my pricing perspective, and a few nuggets to start building your own point of view, the next track is about some of the worst pricing advice ever dished out by smart people.

And it goes a little something like this ...

LET ME CLEAR MY THROAT

THE WORST PRICING MISTAKES EVER

I CAN'T PUT IT BETTER THAN DJ KOOL.

"Let Me Clear My Throat" is still one of the hypest songs out there to get a party going. This song masterfully mixes samples from a variety of artists, and it inspired me to share a mix of samples from my pricing experience to help you avoid some of the biggest mistakes in monetization. And I've seen a lot of them!

I took the scrappy path to learn how to price, and I made plenty of mistakes. But as you learn and build up your pricing knowledge, you correct these mistakes along the way. And fewer mistakes over the years could result in meaningful boosts in revenue for your SaaS business. I want to save you time and headaches by telling you the deadliest and, unfortunately, most common mistakes in pricing a SaaS product in B2B.

Most pricing mistakes are made in hot pursuit of the appealing subscription-based pricing model that rewards SaaS businesses with a predictable and recurring stream of revenue. Once your customer flips the switch on, you are getting paid repeatedly; some say it's easy money:

- Easy to know your margins and profits.
- Easy to recognize revenue over time.
- Easy to enhance your product and extend that revenue out for years to come.

In my view, it's easy to say, but hard to actually do. *But why is subscription so hard?* you wonder. Although it's worth the effort, a subscription is an ongoing and demanding relationship that needs constant attention and nurturing; it's high maintenance. And high maintenance relationships are hard.

And hard things, like relationships, naturally lend themselves to a trove of advice from your peers, your family, and even random strangers. People just love to give advice.

Some of the time, the advice can be genuine and sincere; simply someone helping their fellow brothers and sisters by offering a pearl of wisdom to guide them in the right direction.

And some of the time, it comes from a need to stroke the ego or show off how smart they are (or think they are). Worse, they might have a habit of grossly oversimplifying complex things and think you should, too.

But most advice is somewhere in the middle, and it can be hard for most people to figure out if they should ignore it or take it.

In 20 years of **#SAASLIFE**, I've seen and heard so much anti-wisdom on pricing that I could write a book (cheap pun, but I couldn't resist).

The following are some of the worst pricing tips I have heard and witnessed in action. I want you to avoid these tactics like the plague if you want to grow and capture value at scale. And you do want to capture value at scale, right?

Here they are in no particular order.

DOUBLE TROUBLE

"Let's double the price and see what happens."

Really? Does someone who says this really have this much disregard to how impactful pricing is across their entire business? Or for their sales pipeline? Or their brand reputation? Or their customers' trust?

Here are a couple reasons why random, uninformed price testing in the form of price doubling is so dangerous.

PRICING TIP

If you have data and observations to back it up, then go right ahead and double your prices.

You are merely throwing darts on the board with no real goal in mind except to grab more money. It's a flat-out guess that won't get you closer to what you should be pricing and figure out what is driving the customer's perception of value. Also, some customers will be upset to learn they are paying double for the same value if compared to another customer, and for no good reason.

Imagine yourself in front of that customer paying two times more than another for the exact same plan. Try to explain your way out of that one.

The better approach is to systematically raise your prices for better offerings to a select group of buyers to test their price sensitivity and elasticity (two different, but related, things I will explain later in **TRACK 11: CASH RULES EVERYTHING**).

Doubling the price without any data or feedback is unnecessary and reckless. It's fine to test higher price points with focused packages, better value, and with specific buyers, but doing it without any data or purpose in mind will lead to random outcomes at best and at worst won't teach you anything.

And yes, you can double your prices after doing the research and realizing you are excessively undercharging for your value. But now that you uncovered this gap in value capture, you need a plan to systematically capture the value over time without impeding your growth trajectory. More on this in **TRACK 14: MO MONEY, MO PROBLEMS**.

To be clear, I don't have a problem with doubling your prices, I have a problem with doubling your prices without data or reasoning. If you want to double your price, here's a quick set of questions to consider:

- *What percentage of sales pushed back on your price?* The lower the better if you want to double your prices.
- *How much is usage and volume compared to expectations?* The higher the better. Make sure that at double the price, the customer still gets a compelling ROI (5X to 10X).
- *How much more are customers buying after the initial purchase?* The more, the better, but at least 20 percent of new dollars are coming from upsell or cross sell.

- *How much churn are you experiencing?* The lower the better. This could suggest you have more pricing power than you think.

But keep in mind that customers talk to each other, so arm yourself and your teams with a good word track. You'll find more on communicating pricing changes also in **TRACK 14**.

INTERLUDE

I witnessed this poor counsel put into action with an $80M ARR SaaS company based in the Bay Area. And do you know what happened? The sales team ended up discounting the price back down from two times to the original price level more than half the time. As they ran back with their tail between their legs, sales lost tons of credibility and had to throw in freebie services and products to close deals and keep customers from leaving, many of whom ended up leaving anyway due to lack of trust.

The backtracking was painful, and even though they sold a few deals at the two times price point, the public relations disaster and eventual churned customers were not worth the experimental guess.

Shift your pricing from guesswork to framework—that's our motto. And soon, it'll be yours, too (completely royalty free, I promise).

PRICING TIP

SaaS models are built on relationships, and relationships are built on trust. You can't build trust with guesswork.

MARGIN OF ERROR

"Let's just slap a margin on our costs and we're done," someone from Finance suggests.

"Great idea. We estimate it will cost us $100 per user to deliver the software, and since our financial projections call for a 50-percent profit margin, we should charge $150 bucks and call it a day," responds someone else from Finance.

PRICING TIP

There is no such thing as an average value to someone, so don't use an average price as your anchor.

Finance types love this one. It's algorithmic, seems fair, and is easy to calculate in Excel. It is the perfect way to monetize, right? Well, there's one problem.

The problem is that this approach is completely disconnected from value.

And in the software game, where value changes constantly and increases over time, you end up leaving hard-earned money on the table taking this approach.

But wondering if you are under-charging for your value today?

If you apply some cost-plus or margin-plus pricing, then the short answer is yes, you are leaving money on the table, especially with larger sized deals.

To give themselves a false sense of scientific accuracy, some companies justify the cost-plus price with an average historical sale price. They take an average of sale prices from the past and use it as a target price when deciding how much margin to tack on (e.g. We sold for an average of $100 last year and our cost is $10, therefore, we should set the price by adding a markup of $90.). The approach seems logical on the surface, but it's not.

From what I've seen, taking this approach ends up in charging everyone the perfectly average and perfectly wrong price.

It is better to look at the distribution of your street prices, aka, the price real people said yes to and paid. This will give you a better idea of how pricing aligns with willingness to pay for different groups of buyers who paid for different types of value.

PRICING TIP

The straight average price is usually the straight wrong price.

I met a mid-sized B2B software company out of Austin that decided to put the finance team in charge of pricing.

As expected, they produced a fancy Excel-based calculator that cranked out a handsome profit margin based on volume inputs like customer size or region. It was beautifully wrong and disconnected from the value the company was selling.

The finance types loved it, though. (No offense to finance types. As you remember from **TRACK 1**, I started my career in finance; much love to y'all.).

Sales found it hard to explain their proposals to customers, who felt the prices were opaque and hard to connect to value. What's worse, the company had trouble raising prices over time to capture the additional value they were delivering.

In the model, price increases were random and ad hoc, reducing their ability to capture the hard work they were putting into the software. They released enhancements weekly, putting out almost 50 updates to value per year.

An internal pricing calculator seems harmless, or even a good idea, on the surface. But beware. Calculators are meant to make the math easier, but it's still up to you to decide the equation and connect it to value.

If your internal pricing model is a "black box" that uses some mix of mysterious "factors" to determine prices, then try again. Black box models make it difficult to explain how prices are right or wrong, and they usually lead to random discounts and difficulty forecasting future prices.

And if your pricing calculator applies across multiple products with different value propositions, then hit the reset button. In most cases, this type of calculator is difficult to maintain as you build out your product value with more functionality, data, and services.

PRICING TIP

If a salesperson cannot explain the pricing calculation to a 10-year-old, then go back to the drawing board.

FASTBALL AND A STRIKE

This is one of the worst mistakes I've seen when it comes to pricing. And it breaks my heart every time I come across this approach.

"Let's hit them with a quick price increase and not tell them until the last minute. We'll give our customers little-to-no notice of the pricing change, so they don't have time to shop the competition. It's genius!"

Well, it's time to cash in your reality check!

Let's get street for this one by asking some hard-hitting questions. Do you really think your customers will love you more after pulling a move like this? Sure, some might renew, but now you've given them a reason to shop around, especially if the new price is not framed or justified well.

It will look like a money grab to your customers and a betrayal of trust; leading them to either churn or at least answer the phone the next time a competitor calls.

If you are asking for a raise, you should have a good story about why you deserve one. Common value proofs that show the "why" of a price increase are latest product enhancements, improvements in the pace of innovation, investments in support or customer success, or improvements to onboarding, training, self-help, performance, or security.

Additional benefits of price increases are sharpening your lead funnel with better prospects and encouraging more annual contracts. At the new price, you attract prospects who better understand the value and are closer to your ideal customer profile. These customers are also more likely to commit to an annual term, and for existing customers, a cadence of annual pricing adjustments conditions them to renew before the pricing changes to save money.

No one likes a price hike, but most customers would understand if you reminded them they are getting more value than they originally purchased.

PRICING TIP

The best approach is giving customers 90 days or more notice for a price increase, along with solid value proof points to justify the new price.

Sometimes a price increase can nudge a customer to use more of the product or service, and in some cases, lead to better retention over time.

But be careful here. In the subscription economy, most customers expect some level of improvement as part of their subscription package. And it's not easy deciding which value to charge extra for and which to include as part of the ongoing subscription. You'll read more on how to think about this in **TRACK 10: THE CHOICE IS YOURS.**

"But Marcos," you interject, "we jack up our prices to signal to everyone that we're the best out there."

Okay, but do you have data to back this up? I witnessed a mature enterprise SaaS company in Los Angeles introduce massive price increases based on their past reputation. However, the competition had caught up over the years and their tech was falling behind (and customers started to notice).

And here comes a 50 percent price hike. Yeah, their churn rate went through the roof and the ability to cross sell or upsell went right down the toilet. Price to value should always be in context and supported by data, qualitative or quantitative.

Look, I know it's not easy to figure out which new features should drive a price increase or package change. **FIGURE 2.1** is a guideline for SaaSletes like yourself to quickly decide what to do with new features and product updates. We'll cover this topic more in depth in later tracks.

These aren't hard-and-fast rules. You should make these decisions in the context of the business, the competitor offerings, and of course, the customer needs. For example, if the competition includes advanced reports in all their packages, it makes it harder for you to charge beyond for the equivalent. As another example, if the customer problem you address evolves into a new job to be done (based on the JTBD framework by Anthony W. Ulwick, which describes the mechanisms that cause a consumer to adopt an innovation), it makes sense to consider charging for solving the new pain.

So, there you have it. Three of the worst pricing mistakes I've seen in action. But don't get me wrong, there are tons of pricing mistakes you could make outside the big three I mentioned thus far. Let me share a few more examples, with visuals, from real SaaS companies that also got it dead wrong.

FIGURE 2.1: HOW TO CHARGE FOR NEW FEATURES

ALWAYS INCLUDED IN THE BASE SUBSCRIPTION
↳ **DOES NOT JUSTIFY A HIGHER PRICE**

- Product defect fixes
- Clean up UX for existing screens
- Enhancements to existing workflows that solve the same use case or problem
- Improvements to performance or API response speed
- Improvements to login, help, search
- Standard security updates

INCLUDE IN THE SUBSCRIPTION
↳ **MAY JUSTIFY A HIGHER PRICE OR PREMIUM PLAN**

- Enhancements to admin functions, permissions, and roles
- Substantial updates to existing integrations
- Expanded mobile functionality
- Improved advanced security and privacy, SSO

BEST NOT TO INCLUDE
↳ **CONSIDER CHARGING SEPARATELY OR OFFERING IN PREMIUM PLAN**

- New modules or workflows that solve a new use case
- New integrations
- New automations or rules
- Higher volume thresholds

GRAY AREA
↳ **IT REALLY DEPENDS ON CONTEXT**

- Expanded statuses, lists, enumerations
- Enhancements to dashboards, reports, and analytics

TALES FROM THE CRYPT

For the love of kale, do not make the same mistakes as these guys. I masked some of the examples and visuals, but they know who they are.

Let's start with the following pricing page screenshot in **FIGURE 2.2**. This model is trying to cover all the bases, but in doing so they make it

PRICING TIP

Highlight three to five of your most compelling value drivers and give the customer an option to go deeper into details.

hard for the buyer to decide which package is best for them. Research has shown the human working memory limit to be around three to five items at the same time. This pricing page has so many check marks to evaluate I'd be madder than a mosquito in a mannequin factory!

FIGURE 2.2: EXAMPLE OF PRICING WITH TOO MANY OPTIONS

CALL US! 555-867-5309	ID Opps $209/mo Billed annually Call for quarterly pricing	Covert Opps $309/mo Billed annually Call for quarterly pricing	
CHECK OUT OUR SMALL BUSINESS PLAN	**GET 14 DAY TRIAL**	**CONTACT SALES**	**CONTACT SALES**
Surveys for Desktop Web	✓	✓	✓
NEW! Surveys for Mobile Web	✓	✓	✓
Responses	Up to 1200/mo	Up to 5500/mo	5500+/mo
Domains	3	5	5+
FEATURES			
Essential Features *	✓	✓	✓
Exit Surveys	✓	✓	✓
Google Analytics	✓	✓	✓
Branding Removal **	✓	✓	✓
Custom Look & Feel	✓	✓	✓
Add **YOUR** Branding	✓	✓	✓
Optimizely Integration	✓	✓	✓
Target Regularly	✓	✓	✓

This next pricing model in **FIGURE 2.3** attempts to keep things simple, but they are leaving money on the table with their lack of differentiation. (I'll cover why this is important to growth and enterprise value in **TRACK 3: WITH MY MIND ON MY MONEY**).

I call this a three musketeers' model: "All for one, and one price for all." The problem here is the lack of options and flexibility to fuel expansion revenue. Put another way, it limits the revenue potential from cross selling or upselling beyond the number of contacts.

Not only does this boost your land motion (winning more business), but it enables the expand motion (upselling and cross selling your existing customers). You need both motions to survive and thrive in the SaaS space.

FIGURE 2.3: EXAMPLE OF PRICING WITH ONE PLAN

YOUR MONTHLY PRICE	Contacts	Selected
$99	Up to 2,500 contacts	☐
■ Up to 10,000 contacts	Up to 5,000 contacts	☐
■ Unlimited emails each month	**Up to 10,000 contacts**	☑
■ Price based on annual agreement	Up to 25,000 contacts	☐
	Up to 50,000 contacts	☐
	Up to 75,000 contacts	☐
	Up to 90,000 contacts	☐
	Up to 100,000 contacts	☐
	Up to 150,000 contacts	☐
BIG LIST? COOL! GET A CUSTOM QUOTE		

PRICING TIP

Offer a few packages, metrics, or add-ons to capture different values from different segments.

GRANDFATHER CLOCKS

Grandfathering is about keeping existing customers on your old pricing plans. And yes, I'm talking about the old pricing or plans you produced back when you had less value and less rigor around pricing.

Grandfathering is often used as a retention tool. We all know some customers may not accept new prices or packages. Many SaaS leaders view grandfathering as a way to reward loyalty, while others use it to kick the can down the road. There are various schools of thought on the topic, but here are the main ways to be successful with grandfathering:

- **PERMANENT GRANDFATHERING.** In this practice, you guarantee to existing customers that the price will never increase for the same product for the lifetime of the account. If the product drastically improves or changes, you can keep the account on the old product or offer a discounted rate for the upgrade. In this scenario, there is no clock. This path complicates support and yields to low-profit customers, but you are hoping that at some point they will see the value of the new plans and upgrade.
- **GRANDFATHER DISCOUNT.** Similar to grandfathering, grandfather discounts reduce the price for a certain period of time that will expire (there is a clock). You want to make the discount exceptionally clear on the customer's invoice or billing statement to condition them that the discount will go away after the next renewal, or in six to 12 months. Customers are more likely to accept a price increase when they feel like they've received a reward for being loyal before the change. A discount could be 25, 50, or 100 percent depending on how much you want to reward the loyalty of your base. This is my recommended approach because it balances loyalty with your growth goals.
- **CADENCE PRICE INCREASES.** More common in the enterprise space, these are price increases that happen 1-2 times per year and condition customers to get in early or sign longer-term contracts to take advantage of the current price. Keep in mind you need to consistently keep track of pricing and customer

research with this method, and of course, you'll need to justify the changes in price with changes in value.

A useful technique applied to cadence price increases is something called the Rule of X, where X is simply the percentage increase in price plus the number of years in the contract term. For example, a two-year contract will include an 8-percent increase in price, but a five-year contract will include only a 5-percent increase in price. This technique directly addresses the tradeoff between getting more price or getting more commitment from existing customers.

Working with hundreds of B2B SaaS companies, I've seen the best results with the grandfather discount, simply because you're balancing impact to ARR and impact to attrition. Keep in mind, the longer you wait to change your prices, the harder it will be to communicate why the change is happening. And if there is no time expiration, or clock, to discounts, it is harder to lock in the revenue growth and solidify the new value anchor for your product.

PRICING TIP

No discount clock, then no revenue lock.

When it comes to pricing, do what it takes to avoid copying others and committing the same pricing mistakes I've shared in this track. If you stay away from these growth killers, you are already halfway down the path to capturing more value. Can I get a fist bump?

Now that we've walked through some of the worst pricing mistakes in B2B SaaS, I want us to home in on the single-biggest focus when it comes to monetizing your subscription software business, and that focus is ... drum roll, please ... Growth!

Yes, growth, and not a mythical profit optimization point on some curve from economics class. Check out the next track to find out more.

WITH MY MIND ON MY MONEY

IT'S ALL ABOUT ENTERPRISE VALUE

ALMOST 30 YEARS AGO SNOOP DOGG TOOK HIGH FRUCTOSE CORN SYRUP AND CHEAP LIQUOR AND MADE THE TRACK "GIN AND JUICE" OFF HIS DEBUT ALBUM *DOGGYSTYLE*.

The song was a recipe for success, with the track opening to the sound of liquor being poured into glasses dictating the start of a great party.

And even as he laid back with friends to unwind, the song's hook sent a clear message that Snoop was all business, with a constant focus on how he will grow his fortune.

And with his mind on his money, Snoop's laser-focus on building enterprise value has made him one of the richest hip-hop artists in history, topping $150 million and growing.

You can model his approach in your pricing game. Armed with an ability to build up your pricing knowledge and knowing how to avoid the biggest mistakes along the way, you're in a great position to move faster and focus your energy on getting results.

So, my message takeaway for this track is: Price to grow.

Most pricing purists, business scholars, and marketing publications will tell you the only way to price to value is to identify the price that maximizes profit.

Sounds great in theory, but it's not what is needed in the fast-paced, winner-take-all B2B tech world we live in today.

Let me explain. Your teams build tangible value sprint after sprint and story after story. With blood, sweat, and tears behind every new release to production, you are plowing more value into your products and services.

What are you supposed to do with all that value?

Share it with the world. But of course, keep some for yourself. And keep just enough to sustain and grow a business model.

That's where pricing comes into play.

I love how Patrick Campbell, CEO and founder of ProfitWell, explained the definition of pricing in this beautifully simple one-liner: "Pricing is the exchange rate on the value you are creating."

Exchanging your value for money is the bottom line. And how much value to give or share will determine how fast you grow. And how fast you grow will shape your economics in a fixed-cost, dynamic, traction-centric environment. At the center of any successful pricing strategy is growth.

And not just any "ho hum" single-digit growth year over year. Nope, we are talking about the mind-boggling-crazy-market-cap type of growth you hear about on TechCrunch! To show you what I'm talking about, take a look at **FIGURE 3.1** listing the top public B2B SaaS companies by market capitalization. These companies had incredible growth rates leading up to their IPO. The growth rate is what fueled the market cap, not profit margin. (We'll cover the Rule of 40 later in this track, which considers growth rate and margins).

Of course, many of these companies had a clear path to profitability and healthy balance sheets.

So, what do I mean by growth? What is growth and what does it look like? I'm glad you mentioned that.

VALUE TO GROWTH

When I say "growth," I mean growing your value as a company, also known as enterprise value, or EV.

As a leader, you should focus on growing the influencing metrics that impact your EV the most. The "North Star metric" you want to move up might be recurring revenue, gross margin, new logo bookings, new users, market share, net profits, net dollar retention, whatever. You can grow more than one metric, but just not all of them at once. (We'll talk about focusing on the right metrics in **TRACK 8: NUTHIN' BUT A "G" THANG.**)

Think about it this way. You want to improve the metric that has the strongest impact on growth depending on your SaaS company's phase, market dynamics, and product maturity. The real metrics you're after are the ones that function as leading inputs into your enterprise value. North

FIGURE 3.1: MARKET CAPITALIZATION OF B2B COMPANIES AS OF JANUARY 2022

RANK	COMPANY	MARKET CAP
1	Adobe, Inc. (ADBE)	$237.9B
2	Salesforce.com, Inc. (CRM)	$215.4B
3	Intuit, Inc. (INTU)	$149.7B
4	Shopify, Inc. (SHOP)	$110.4B
5	ServiceNow, Inc. (NOW)	$101.0B
6	Snowflake, Inc. (SNOW)	$82.0B
7	Atlassian Corporation Plc (TEAM)	$71.5B
8	Workday, Inc. (WDAY)	$61.4B
9	Block, Inc. (SQ)	$54.5B
10	Zoom Video Communications, Inc. (ZM)	$44.0B
11	Datadog, Inc. (DDOG)	$39.2B
12	CrowdStrike Holdings, Inc. (CRWD)	$37.8B
13	Twilio, Inc. (TWLO)	$34.3B
14	Veeva Systems, Inc. (VEEV)	$34.1B
15	Zscaler, Inc. (ZS)	$33.9B
16	Unity Software, Inc. (U)	$31.2B
17	Okta, Inc. (OKTA)	$29.3B
18	Cloudflare, Inc. (NET)	$28.5B
19	MongoDB, Inc. (MDB)	$25.1B
20	DocuSign, Inc. (DOCU)	$23.0B

Star metrics like Net New ARR and Net Dollar Retention tie directly into your EV.

I'm not discounting the value of having a smart sales strategy or excellent operational execution, but if your pricing strategy does not support your North Star metric, you'll have a lot of selling and buying friction that will prevent you from scaling, and hence, slow down your growth. That's not good.

PRICING TIP

Your pricing strategy should support moving the North Star metric in the right direction.

Look, we are not talking about growth hacking at all costs. No one wants to end up like MoviePass, Pets.com, or WeWork (that IPO debacle was ugly!).

To get deeper into growth, let's get into the fundamentals of unit economics. The beauty of subscription software is that you can continue growing without increasing the rate of new logos. The compounding nature of the revenue stream can catapult your EV into the stratosphere, but only if you play your cards right.

The age-old best practice for healthy SaaS unit economics is the 3-to-1 ratio. This ratio compares the customer lifetime value (CLTV), which measures the money you make from a customer before churning against the customer acquisition cost (CAC), which is how much you spend to acquire customers. The lifetime value should be at least three times your cost to acquire them. If these metrics are new to you, check out **FIGURE 3.2** for the basic formulas on how to calculate them.

FIGURE 3.2: CLTV AND CAC BASIC DEFINITIONS

Customer Lifetime Value (CLTV)

(GM X ARPA) / GROSS CHURN RATE

Customer Acquisition Cost (CAC)

(TOTAL SALES + TOTAL MARKETING) / # NEW CUSTOMERS ACQUIRED

Be sure to use the 3:1 ratio as a floor metric, not as a goal. In fact, I've read recent articles pushing 4:1 as the new benchmark ratio for CLTV:CAC. The bar keeps getting higher in SaaS, which means SaaSletes like you need to exhaust every tactic in your toolkit to get ahead.

So, let's connect the dots. Deploying the right pricing strategy and model can increase your CLTV and reduce your CAC, hence improving your most-sacred North Star metrics, accelerating your growth, and finally, boosting your enterprise value.

The real play in B2B SaaS is to build momentum, placing you in a strong position to monetize and increase enterprise value. With the right pricing in place, you can position and capture value until you reach the top! And by top, I mean the New-York-Yankee-World-Series-winning champagne popping that comes from getting a handsome 25X exit multiple. That's somebody valuing your company at 25 times your annual revenue, which means you are getting pizz-aid!

What's that? You want to dig into how 25X multiples are figured out? Well, let me explain.

MONEY TO MULTIPLES

Let's face it. Winning in SaaS is all about the growth engine, and how pricing can support it. It's obvious that no software leader wants to shrink or reduce revenue as a goal. But when it comes to growth, the bigger and more important question is not how much, but how.

Take a moment and ask yourself, "How will I grow my subscription business next year?"

Go ahead, I'll wait.

Back so soon?

For example, 40 percent year-over-year growth in recurring revenue sounds great, but exactly where will it come from?

If you're like most SaaS entrepreneurs, your mind goes straight to how many new logos or new markets you want to conquer. The race for more market share and a larger client list is always top of mind. The "land" part of the growth equation gets a lot of attention, and for good reason. It's flippin' hard!

But for those of you who have done this exercise before, you may have evolved your thinking to go beyond just winning new customers and include the "expand" motion to grow what your customers pay you over time. A clear and consistent upsell and cross sell for existing clients is the rocket fuel behind the most successful SaaS companies in the last decade. Take a look at the list below in **FIGURE 3.3** highlighting net retention rates of top SaaS companies. The trend is evident and undeniable. More net retention highly correlates with more enterprise value.

FIGURE 3.3: EV VS. NET RETENTION RATES FOR SAAS BUSINESSES

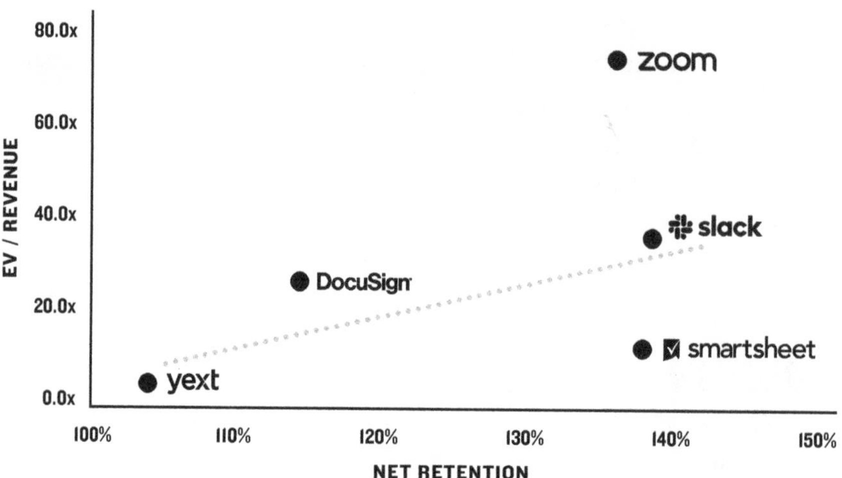

I am confident that these SaaS companies, most notably Zoom and Slack, pay special attention to pricing as a growth lever. They have a process and discipline how they monetize their values, which is something you will have as well as we walk down this path together. Just stay with me.

High net retention de-risks the sales motion and reduces CAC, resulting in less friction to landing new business. And the beauty of the subscription model produces a compounding effect that creates a steeper slope of change, hence driving up the multiples higher and higher.

Fist pump! Yes!

The concept makes a lot of sense. If you price in such a way that expansion of usage and revenue is baked in, your sales economics will have a better mix of low-risk and low-cost revenue (cross and upsell) compared to high-risk and high-cost revenue (new logos), and it's all perched on top of a solid foundation of little-to-no churn. It's a beautiful thing.

If you are looking for a BHAG (big hairy audacious goal) to shoot for to drive your B2B SaaS company value, aim for reaching and beating 40 percent ARR growth and 130 percent Net Dollar Retention. This puts you in the area of crazy 20+ times multiples for valuation.

Let's take a deeper look into the world of technology investing, or more specifically, the world of venture capital and private equity-backed SaaS companies, to understand why growth is not only the name of the game, but the deciding factor in their investment thesis.

THE INVESTMENT THESIS

The dirty little secret is that growth leads to more value creation than profits, so investors weigh it more in their decision-making process. But why?

Turning to the public sector again for a second, you can see the maniacal focus on growth over profits in **FIGURE 3.4**, where most of the B2B SaaS companies with soaring enterprise values post losses. These are significant losses; we are seeing the type of losses that make you say "Daaang!"

FIGURE 3.4: PUBLIC VENTURE-BACKED SAAS COMPANIES

COMPANY	REVENUE	PROFIT / (LOSS)	VALUATION
Airbnb	$3.6B	($1.05B)	$111B
Snowflake	$489M	($423M)	$86B
Palantir	$1B	($1.18B)	$76B
DoorDash	$2.21B	(283M)	$63B
Affirm	$335M	($114M)	$24B
GoodRx	$510M	$19.9M	$20.6B
Amwell	$230M	($197M)	$10B
Lemonade	$97M	($121M)	$9.1B
BigCommerce	$120M	($33M)	$6.4B
Asana	$202M	($175M)	$5.8B

So yes, nine out of 10 of these companies are posting losses in the mega millions.

You may ask, "So Marcos, do profits matter at all?"

Yes, profits matter—just not out of the gate. To get to profits in a subscription relationship revenue model and a fixed-cost structure, growth matters first. Profits only come after you figure out how to grow your business.

Here is why growth matters so much in the venture-backing community. It's because growth means potential, and potential is what investors are looking for to drive up exit multiples. PE and venture capital firms specialize in identifying, creating, and capturing that potential.

PRICING TIP

For me, PE doesn't stand for Private Equity, it stands for "Potential Equity."

To break it down further, the potential we are talking about is money, tenderly known as cold, hard cash, cheddar, cream, bread, paper, loot, green, skrilla. I can go on. But money comes from customers who in various ways receive and perceive value.

And the art of capturing your fair share of that value from customers is called pricing, or using the fancy and more encompassing umbrella term, monetization.

So here comes my logical argument. Investors care a lot about pricing because it directly relates to how much value you can create and capture as part of achieving your potential. In PE speak, this is called the "investment thesis."

I've been through two exits and evaluated hundreds of B2B tech companies as part of due diligence and value creation planning. I've seen how software companies focus on the positive in their pitch decks, and when pressed, squeamishly sweep their financial, operational, or personnel issues under the rug. But the deeper you can go into their pricing strategy and model, the more truth you can uncover on the economics of the business and their growth potential.

To better prepare you for the investment route, I added **FIGURE 3.5** to give you a sense of what the private equity or VC investment process looks like. It's a generic flow, but you get the idea.

FIGURE 3.5: INVESTMENT TIMELINE

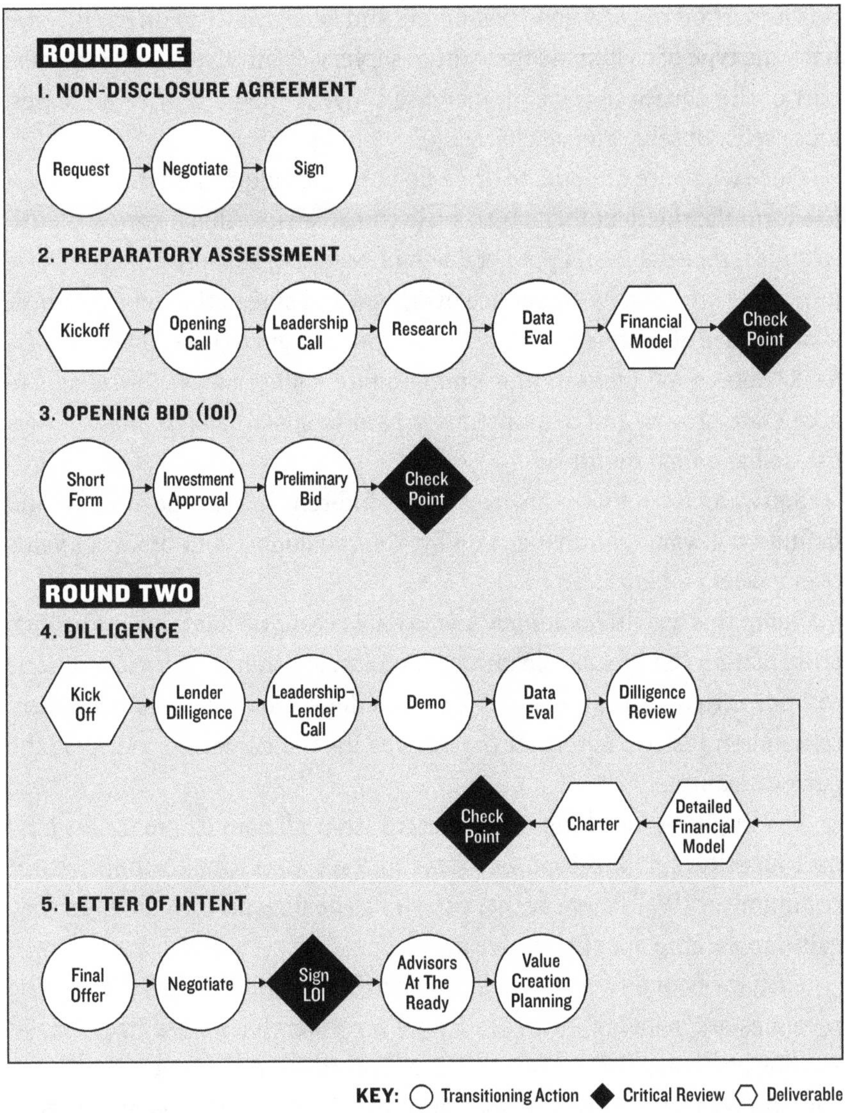

Let me break down the investor mindset even further.

Investors believe growth is not about one decision or one change. It's about a series of decisions and changes over time, driven by talented people, good habits, and solid frameworks for getting things done.

At the most cellular level, the fundamental formula for revenue in any business is Price x Volume. We start here.

The initial focus is always on the volume side of the equation, where it is important to grow good customers and keep away bad ones. Once we have the type of customers we want to serve, we shift the focus to the next part of the equation, price, to increase it over time with price increases, cross sells, upsells, and deal sizes.

Once we figure out how to drive up both the volume and price sides of the formula, the next focus is to scale the business. This means we want to build a repeatable and predictable motion that gets more efficient as we grow the company. As we reduce overhead and spread the fixed cost over a larger base of customers, we get to a profit margin to meet or exceed the SaaS "Rule of 40" (growth rate + margin rate = 40 or more). The idea is to accelerate growth and demonstrate a path to sustainable profits that we can sell at a high multiple.

Software as a Service businesses are different in that the amount and definition of value can change rapidly. You can double your product's value over a weekend hackathon.

Bump this up with extremely low variable costs, no hard inventory, high gross margins and malleable unit economics, and you have the conditions to price for growth rather than for immediate profit maximization. And remember, it's the potential that drives up the valuation, not just the current reality.

You might be thinking, "OK, Marcos, that all sounds great. But how do I position my B2B SaaS business to look attractive to the investor community?" Well, there are certain things deal teams look at when they value an asset to acquire or invest.

First, investor deal teams look for recurring revenue models. If recurring revenues are below 60 percent of total revenue, that's a red flag. A solid starting percentage of revenue that is recurring is typically over 75 percent. The firm wants to help companies push that figure to 90 percent or higher as part of the investment thesis.

Deal teams also look at high growth rates in recurring or predictable transaction revenues; 25 percent or more year-over-year is the minimum. They prefer to see 50 percent and higher growth rates to spark an interest.

They look for signals of strong revenue retention. In the B2B space, gross dollar retention of 90 percent per annum is good, while 95 percent is preferred. A gross dollar retention across the business of 80 percent or below is a red flag. Note that the business can have pockets of smaller clients with lower retention, but it cannot be a substantial part of the overall revenue.

For B2C, micro-SMB, or smaller deal sizes under 10K a year, churn is more commonly measured than retention. Deal teams view gross dollar churn at around 10 percent per year as good, 15 percent to 20 percent is not great but okay, and 25 percent plus is red flag territory.

And if you've been paying attention, then it should not surprise you that deal teams also look for high-net dollar retention or at least a path to high-net dollar retention through what they call "whitespace penetration," which is super attractive because it is considered low-hanging fruit from a growth perspective.

Here's what that means. To capture the "whitespace" opportunity in your business, you need to fulfill the unmet needs of existing customers with new value that extends from current value. The good news is that you are far more likely to win a sale with an existing customer than you are with a new prospect.

PRICING TIP

According to Invespcro.com, the probability of selling to an existing customer is 60–70 percent, while the probability of selling to a new prospect is 5–20 percent. Existing customers are 50 percent more likely to try new products and spend 31 percent more when compared to new customers.

INVESTOR "WHITESPACE"

Why do I add quotes around the term "whitespace," you wonder? Because the unmet needs and target market can be defined differently based on the company, investor, or deal team. I tend to think of "whitespace" as the potential expansion opportunities within the customer base. It keeps it simple for me.

Next, deal teams look at talent. What does talent have to do with pricing? Pricing is iterative and requires strong research, analysis, good communication, and consistency. Great talent means your ability to execute pricing well is higher.

There are strong, talented teams out there ready and willing to craft and execute a pricing strategy, but some don't know exactly how to go about it. Given a framework and some good data, they can run and learn fast as part of the value creation journey.

Operations and process problems are not going to scare investors away. In most cases, process shortcomings are viewed as opportunities to build scale. That being said, having some good processes in place shows investors you can adopt best practices and get better.

And getting better means creating more value.

And more value means more potential to capture.

Now that you know why growth is the name of the game in B2B SaaS, we'll now take a look at staying grounded in reality when it comes to your growth aspirations. The key is to monetize real value under real circumstances, something we will talk more about in **TRACK II: CASH RULES EVERYTHING**. If you find yourself pricing for value that is not proven or even exists yet, then your monetization plan could use a little TLC.

DON'T GO CHASING WATERFALLS

WHY YOU SHOULD PRICE FOR REALITY

T-BOZ, LEFT EYE, AND CHILLI FORMED THE FAMED FEMALE GROUP TLC.

Their smash hit "Waterfalls" was considered one of their biggest successes on the charts. With deep life meaning laced over every lyric, "Waterfalls" reminded us to avoid chasing waterfalls, or in more direct terms, negative habits and reckless behavior. The song sends a powerful and sobering message.

We now know the true goal of pricing to value in SaaS is increasing your enterprise value with an attractive growth story built on value delivered to customers. This takes hard work and patience, but not everyone is willing to make the sacrifice and resort to shortcuts or unsustainable tactics to get results.

That's the point of this track, to remind you to keep it real. Pricing is a powerful tool at your disposal that must be used with integrity and grounded by the real problems your business will solve for real customers to create real value.

In tech, there are countless articles and podcasts telling us to be bolder, take risks, try new things, fail fast and break everything. In this track, we'll cover why it's valuable to take your time when making decisions about pricing. Moving quickly to put new learnings into action is a good thing for a naturally iterative process like pricing. But moving too fast can lead you down the wrong path and next thing you know, you find yourself veering into the dark side of pricing.

Wait, what? There's a dark side to pricing?

Yup.

THE DARK SIDE OF PRICING

I've just spent the previous three tracks telling you about the valuable, powerful, and positive impacts of good pricing. So, what's this talk about the dark side?

As I warned you in **TRACK 2**, there's a lot of misinformation about pricing in SaaS today. If you create a pricing strategy and model with reckless abandon, you can kill growth and kill your business.

But don't worry. It doesn't take much to see the light and get back on the right track. You just need to stay focused on aligning to your current reality by pricing based on your provable value, actual position in the market, and data-driven willingness to pay from your customers.

Some companies get excited about a new pricing model they've derived during some offsite retreat, admiring the innovation and creativity behind the strategy. The new model is considered a "breakthrough" that will "change everything!" In their haste and exuberance, they drop everything to roll it out as quickly as possible.

With no data, no customer feedback, and no analysis, there's nothing to ground the new model in reality. Only after an abrupt pimp slap from a drop in sales or customer tweet uproar do they realize they've entered the dark side of pricing.

Don't let this be you. If you are not careful, rushing out a new pricing scheme without validation is a risky bet that could drive your business off a cliff, and cars can't fly (although I suspect Elon Musk is working on that).

The task is twice as hard when you're rolling out a new pricing model that does not accurately reflect your real value. The majority of B2B SaaS companies out there are undervaluing and, therefore, underpricing for their products.

Occasionally I see companies that are either stuck in the past of the glory days when they had an early mover advantage or are disillusioned

PRICING TIP

B2B buyers are not as price sensitive as many may imagine, so don't hesitate to charge for your value.

about how much better their product is versus the competition. They have what's called a **BLOATED PRICING MODEL** that is overpriced and not aligned to value. Reality check: Other SaaS companies can code, too.

Other companies opt to copy someone else's model that has proven out in the marketplace. Most go after copying one of the members of what I call the "S club" in B2B SaaS. These are six of the most wildly successful B2B SaaS companies that have amassed incredible value, hence seeding many entrepreneurial dreams in making it big in the subscription software space; and their names all happen to start with the letter "s", go figure. Check out the list in **FIGURE 4.1**.

FIGURE 4.1: THE "S" CLUB IN B2B SAAS

PRICING MODELS		
COMPANY		**MODEL**
salesforce	Salesforce	Per User
servicenow	ServiceNow	Per User Per Module
shopify	Shopify	Percent of Payments # of Stores
slack	Slack	Per Active User
snowflake	Snowflake	Transaction Based
Square	Square	Percent of Payments

Whether it is holding on to the market of the past or not acknowledging how you really stack up against the competition, avoid slipping into the dark side of pricing and keep it real by pursuing a proven total addressable market (TAM) with ideal customers that need your product badly, obvious differences in your product that make it more valuable compared to alternatives, and a sustainable business model to open a path to growth and profitability.

Here are some tips to keep in mind to make sure your pricing is based on reality and that you are not chasing waterfalls.

DON'T BELIEVE THE HYPE

First, it's important to be mindful of the information you take in, both from outside sources and from within your own business. The following are questions and answers to help challenge your pricing model and strategy. The point is to pressure test the assumptions you are making, either consciously or subconsciously, when setting your value and pricing architecture. Here we go!

Is your product and/or services value based on reality or hype? It's based on reality if:

- Your product Net Promoter Score (NPS) score is high, for example, 50 and above.
- You consistently deliver high-quality releases with low defects.
- You can measure your positive differentiators versus the competition.
- You continue to take market share from the competition.
- You've been able to raise prices with little pushback and manageable attrition.
- Industry analysts such as Gartner or Forrester rank your product as a top solution in your category.

Is your new pricing model even achievable in the real world? It is if:

- You can change packages and price levels with low to minimal development effort.
- You're able to capture all the key data elements of your pricing such as list price, effective price, win rate, and lost reasons.
- You are in a good position timing-wise to update the sales compensation plan or introduce new incentives (like spiffs).

- You have automated event triggers to route policy and pricing exceptions for review and approval.
- You are able to update your pricing page on your website with low development effort.
- You're able to transition your customer base to the new pricing with low to minimal attrition.
- You're able to train your sales and or customer success teams on the new pricing within a reasonable amount of effort and time.

Do you remember the subscription movie service MoviePass? They came up with a subscription model for watching movies in theaters similar to a gym membership, relying on high-volume signups but limited usage in order to be profitable. The value in the subscription was in having access to watch movies in theaters for a fixed price that was lower than the traditional pay-as-you-go model. Sounds good on paper, right?

But their pricing model changed like the weather with 11 pricing changes in two years, going from two movies a month for $20 to a drastic, and ultimately fatal, shift to offering unlimited movies for $10 and losing money on every new signup to tune of about $40 million a month. Ouch!

In moving to a flat $10-a-month fee for unlimited movies, MoviePass was chasing a waterfall. They hoped and prayed that the irresistible value of unlimited movies would attract enough people and somehow fix their poor economics and open up new value drivers between the powerful media giants and plentiful movie fans around the world.

Pricing will never save a bad business model, poor execution, or controversial tactics, especially with the magnitude witnessed publicly during the comical MoviePass fiasco. However, they poured fuel on the fire and sealed their fate with a one-dimensional pricing model that was not based on data and assumed every signup wanted the same value. With unlimited access for an absurdly cheap price, they handcuffed their ability to differentiate between customers, such as occasional family movie goers and front-of-the-line film enthusiasts who never miss a premier. Their one-size-fits-all pricing model brought in a ton of subscribers but closed off any paths to expand customers or align the right value with the right buyers. They priced based on a dream that they could amass a large-enough paying subscriber base to muscle their way into the middle of the movie distribution ecosystem and profit on both ends from a cut of the ticket and concession sales to selling consumer data back to Hollywood. The big lesson here is to always price based on reality—not a fantasy that lost over $100 million. Will we ever see a MoviePass sequel subscription service based on actual customer data and tangible value to the filmmaking ecosystem? Only time will tell, but I'll have my popcorn and soda pop ready if we do.

PRICING TIP

Stick to charging for the value you can prove with real customer feedback and understanding the operational constraints to capture value over time.

This marks the end of **PART ONE: REWIND**, let's recap what you learned so far:

- Build up your pricing muscle with a virtuous cycle of learning and doing.
- Move faster by avoiding the fatal mistakes others make when pricing their products.
- Price to grow your business value; everything else is secondary.
- Price for real value, to real customers, within your real limitations.

The point of **REWIND** is to use what I learned in the past to set the stage for your pricing in the future.

Now you're ready to take on **PART TWO: PLAY**. In this section of the book, the goal is to show you step by step how to move from guesswork to framework.

Excited? Yeah, me too.

Now hit the *Play* button.

PART TWO: PLAY

Knowing the path is not enough to build pricing skills; you must walk the path. Now you need a framework to GPS your way toward the best pricing model that achieves your growth goals. The next eight tracks lay out the steps you should follow to find the right pricing model and get better at monetizing your value over time.

YOU WILL LEARN	TRACK
HOW TO TELL IF YOUR PRICING IS WORKING	5, 6, 7
HOW TO TALK TO CUSTOMERS ABOUT PRICING	8, 9
HOW TO PACKAGE AND PRICE TO CAPTURE VALUE	10, 11
HOW TO MAKE PRICING REPEATABLE AND SCALABLE	12

KILLING ME SOFTLY

IS YOUR PRICING MODEL SOFTLY KILLING GROWTH?

THE SCORE, RELEASED IN 1996 BY THE FUGEES, IS ONE OF MY FAVORITE ALBUMS OF ANY MUSIC GENRE, PERIOD.

The multi-platinum selling album was full of ear candy, including the chart-topping single, "Killing Me Softly." It's hard not to reminisce over this song without closing your eyes and embracing how Lauryn Hill, with pitch-perfect emotion and lyrical dexterity, covered the famous chorus sung by the legendary Roberta Flack. Just, wow!

"Killing Me Softly" professes about a slow, subtle type of emotional pain that is rooted in the deep connections between words and feelings. It's stealthy and imperceptible. One moment you are grooving to the melody, and before you know it, you're emotionally breaking down, tears and all!

For the SaaSlete who may not be meeting growth expectations but can't pinpoint what is holding them back, it might be something slow, subtle, and hard to detect as you listen to the alarms that warn you growth is in jeopardy. For example, you could be missing the quarterly number, losing the big RFP (request for proposals) to a competitor, or dropping your overall market share. There could be something else that is less obvious pulling you back. Something stealthy, imperceptible, and not well understood.

Yes, I'm talking about pricing (one time!).

Your pricing model could be killing your growth, and you won't even know it. You'll think the slowdown is due to product feature gaps, or it's because your last marketing campaign flopped, or it's the new sales rep who can't seem to close.

Nope! Chances are your pricing model is the culprit behind the sluggish growth. But to know for sure, you have to notice the right signals.

PRICING IS ABOUT SIGNALS

The hard truth is that pricing is hard. I know—we covered that already. But it's not only hard to execute, it's also challenging to know if your pricing model is even working. You need to know how to look for the right signals and how to separate them from the other noise you encounter in everyday SaaS life.

So, what do I mean by signals? A *signal* is a measure or metric that might mean your pricing or packaging is leading your business away from your growth objectives and towards unintended consequences.

Say what?

In other words, you might be either leaving money on the table or losing deals you should win.

Whether it's the metric you charge for, the package you bundle, or the price level you set, a bad signal could mean there's something off in how much value you are exchanging with your customer.

How do you notice these signals before it's too late?

I'm glad you asked.

First, let's dive into some of the common mistakes that lead to bad signals in the first place. These pricing-related mistakes will surely slow down your traction if you do not address them early and often.

CONVERSION KILLERS

In an ideal world, we want to convert a prospect to a customer, a customer to a growing customer, and a growing customer to a staying customer. To explain the concept of pricing signals, let's focus on pricing-related conversion challenges in your acquisition motion.

PACKAGING

When it comes to converting prospects to customers, the first area to explore is your packaging line up or lack thereof. More often than not, the packages you're selling were not carefully crafted with data insights or tested before going live. This can lead to a lot of confusion around the package value, its messaging, its positioning, and the overall fit with the buyer.

The trick is to evaluate your packaging with both a horizontal and vertical lens.

By *horizontal lens*, I mean you should look at the overall lineup of plans and critique the leaps from one package to another. Ask yourself: Does the progression of value align with the different target audiences? Did I test if there is a logical progression from one plan to the next? Is there a point where the customer outgrows the current plan and is ready to move to the next one?

PRICING TIP

The best packaging line ups result in customers buying more or upgrading between two and nine months after the first purchase.

The *vertical lens* helps you understand if the value driving features and services included squarely fit the target audience. Avoid the mistake of many B2B SaaS companies in packing too much value into a single package in a misguided attempt to boost willingness to pay.

It doesn't work that way, and it will have the opposite effect.

Do you believe you are addressing the right target buyer with these packages? If so, do you have proof?

And no, anecdotes won't be enough. We have to keep it real. Do you have real proof from a real customer in the form of a real output such as saved hours, reduced FTE, or increase in conversion rate? You know, something you can poke at with a stick?

Look at each package and ask yourself:

- Are the value drivers clear, and do they directly address the problem our customers are trying to solve?
- Are there other use cases that are incompletely or disjointly solved in this plan?

Buyers don't want more value; they want the right value.

Let's cap off this lesson with an example. **FIGURE 5.1** is an example of looking at your plan mix and pointing out potential pitfalls that could lead to signals that your pricing and packaging are off point.

FIGURE 5.1: EXAMPLE OF PACKAGING TEARDOWN

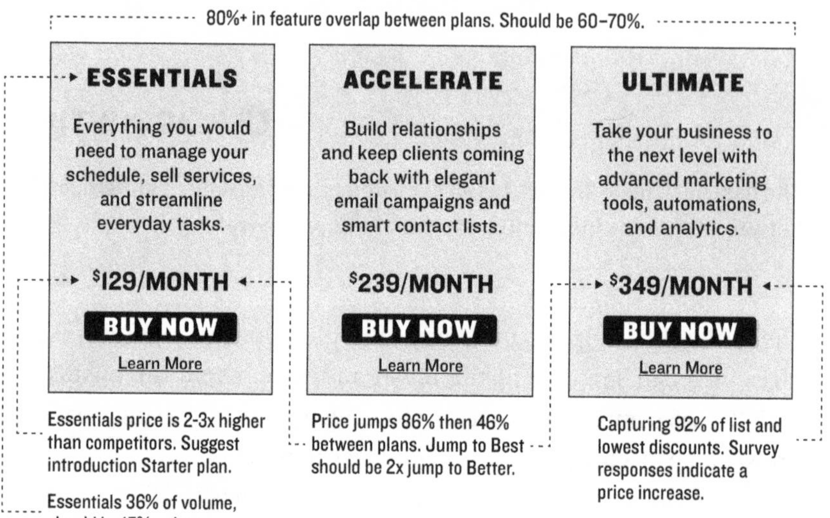

The big takeaway here is that it's imperative to take a step back and evaluate your packages and prices to make sure you're offering the right value to the right buyer for the right exchange rate. *Capisce?* We will cover how to get and analyze the data to help spot signals more effectively next in **TRACK 6: CHECK YO SELF**. We'll also take a deeper dive into packaging do's and don'ts in **TRACK 10: THE CHOICE IS YOURS**.

PRESENTATION

Once you convince yourself that the packages and line up are in good shape, next look at how you should present the packages to the market. While most B2C SaaS companies have a pricing page, in the world of B2B, companies are split on the topic with about half keeping their pricing close to the vest and the other half displaying their pricing publicly on their website. Like most business decisions, there are pros and cons to both paths. For the sake of example, let's assume you display your packages (with or without prices) for this next point I want to make.

PRICING TIP

Effective pricing pages build confident buyers. Design your pricing page with the right amounts of information and guidance.

To keep things simple, spoon-feed the buyer by presenting enough information so they are confident your product will solve their problem within their budget.

Chances are your buyer is checking out your website in between meetings or phone calls and only has three minutes to understand your product. In that window, you need to guide prospects to do the behavior you want. This is known as a "call to action" or CTA. For those who skipped Marketing 101, the CTA is a command that is implanted in the page to invoke an intended action. Without one, your buyer could wander aimlessly and become distracted, unmotivated, and discouraged.

FIGURE 5.2 illustrates the balance you need to strike when displaying your pricing and packaging in a neat and structured manner to build confidence in buying your product.

FIGURE 5.2: INFORMATION VS. ACTION MATRIX

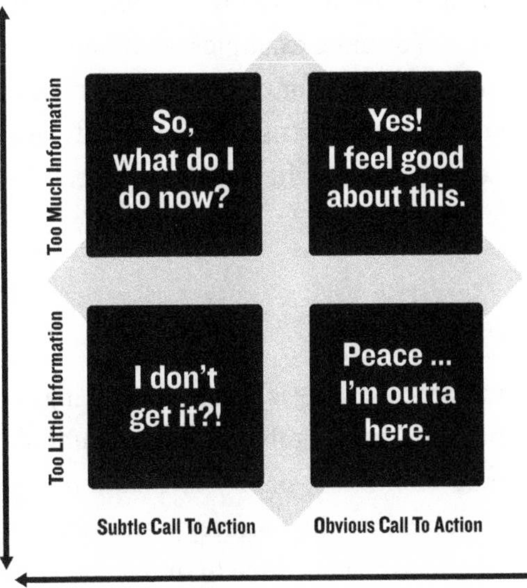

If you don't strike a good balance between information and action, your prospective customers will run into problems. Here are a few common problems that keep people from buying:

1. **Your customers don't understand the context.** The copy on your page, the names of your plans, the feature descriptions, whatever. Customers need clear, consistent, bite-size information on what your product does, who it is for, and what will happen if they use it.
2. **Your customers are stressed and overwhelmed.** Too much information can raise more questions than answers, leading your customers down the path of decision fatigue or paralysis by analysis. Look, more detail is not always the answer when it comes to being clear. Ruthlessly cut text and make your packages easy to scan and understand.
3. **Customers need to be guided.** Some customers hoard information and never make a buying decision. Others flip back and forth incessantly. Giving your customers some clear action and sense of urgency will help your conversion in any buying cycle. Limit your CTAs, plan options, and purchase window to apply a little positive pressure.

FIGURE 5.3 is an example of a pricing page with too little context and too much information. For more examples, visit neilpatel.com. Big shout out to Neil Patel and Brad Smith for the great posts on this topic. Spot on!

Now that we recognize bad signals, what are good signals to capture on your radar? In order to see the right signals, you need sharp vision—like 20/20 vision.

GETTING 20/20 VISION

Another useful truth about pricing is that many pricing problems actually are symptoms of other business problems hidden behind it. For example, those problems may look like a poorly articulated growth strategy, a flawed or poorly executed product strategy, and most commonly, poor understanding of product-market-price fit and customer needs.

FIGURE 5.3: PRICING PAGE WITH TOO MUCH INFORMATION

Plans fit for all team sizes. Try it for 30 days free!

FREE TRIAL STARTS HERE

ESSENTIAL	TEAM	PROFESSIONAL	ENTERPRISE
Minimal setup with all the fundamentals	Improve collaboration for your growing team	Improve and customize performance globally	Ultimate control and flexibility that scales
$11.99 Per agent per month*	$33.99 Per agent per month*	$63.99 Per agent per month*	$113.99 Per agent per month*
*Billed annually or $15.99 month-to-month	*Billed annually or $39.99 month-to-month	*Billed annually or $73.99 month-to-month	*Billed annually or $139.99 month-to-month
• Unlimited email addresses • Twitter channels • Facebook channels • Basic knowledge base • Mobile KSD • Web Widget • Macros Agent	Essential and... • Branding help center • Customer portal • Business rules • Performance dashboards • Public apps marketplace	Team and... • Community forums • Multilingual content • SLAs & business hours • CSAT surveys • Insights analytics • Custom private apps	Professional and... • Custom agent roles • Multi-brand support • Ticket forms • Multiple schedules • Hourly insights analytics • Success Launch program • Admin controls & auditing
TRY NOW BUY NOW	TRY NOW BUY NOW	TRY NOW BUY NOW	TRY NOW BUY NOW

START YOUR FREE TRIAL

Let's put those aside for a moment and stay on the topic of pricing-related signals.

Linking back to the previous section, a poorly constructed packaging and pricing line up and can lead to the following signals:

- **SIGNAL 1:** Too many customers are buying, and staying, in your entry-level plan. Metric to track: percentage of active customers in each plan after six months.
- **SIGNAL 2:** No one buys or sells a specific plan, but rather, sales regularly sell something that is customized for each deal. Metric to track: percentage of opportunity wins with a custom SKU/order outside your standard.
- **SIGNAL 3:** Very few customers upgrade or buy more. Metric to track: percentage of revenue generated from selling more to your existing customers.

We are only scratching the surface here in terms of how many signals to watch to keep your pricing model from killing you softly. Some signals deserve more attention than others, and sometimes, you might notice conflicting signals.

Man, I wish there were a framework around pricing-related signals to use as reference.

Oh, wait! Today is still your lucky day because I created one.

I like to call this framework **20/20 VISION**, and the idea is simple enough. Take a look at **FIGURE 5.4**. Here, I lay out a set of questions that reference a metric threshold of 20. If you answer "yes" to any of the following questions, that is a signal that your pricing model might be wack, out of whack, or both!

FIGURE 5.4: THE 20/20 VISION FRAMEWORK

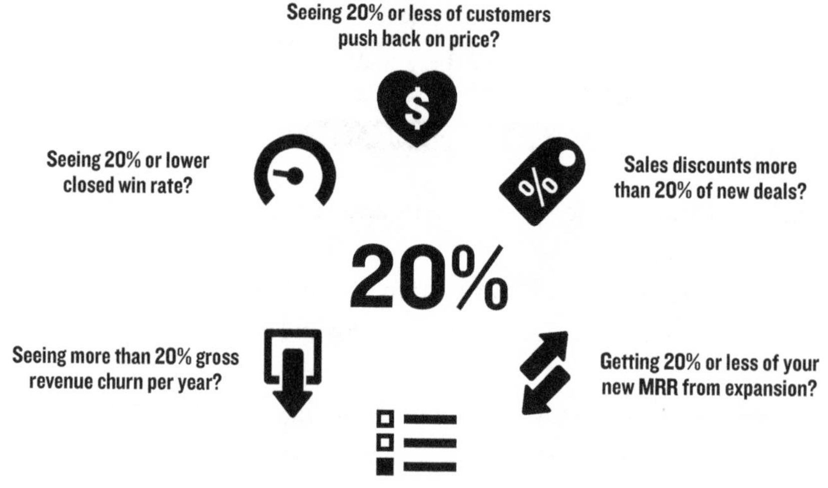
Seeing 20% or less of customers push back on price?
Seeing 20% or lower closed win rate?
Sales discounts more than 20% of new deals?
20%
Seeing more than 20% gross revenue churn per year?
Getting 20% or less of your new MRR from expansion?
Seeing more than 20% of your customers in your low/entry level plan?

The 20/20 Vision framework is a great place to start building up your radar. But for the ambitious, I've also listed in **FIGURE 5.5** the top pricing-related metrics to track in addition to the 20/20 Vision questions. And because I'm "cool like dat," I added a root cause, too. Daaaamn!

There are no shortages of signals to track in the world of SaaS. But it is even more important to look at these signals in combinations versus just in isolation. For example, if your close win rate (percent of qualified opportunities you end up winning) is declining *and* your discount rate is rising over the same time period, you should consider this a major red flag that warrants an investigation into your pricing.

FIGURE 5.5: PRICING SIGNALS WITH POTENTIAL ROOT CAUSES

WINNING MORE THAN 50% OF OPPORTUNITIES

- Misaligned sales incentives
- Excessive discounting
- Under-priced

LARGE VARIANCES IN PRICE FOR SIMILAR DEALS IN SIMILAR CUSTOMERS

- Wrong pricing metric
- Unclear segmentation

ROAD MAP IS HIJACKED BY CUSTOMER COMMITMENTS

- Stale packaging
- No value framing
- Unclear segmentation

ABILITY TO CROSS SELL AND UPSELL IS LIMITED OR NON-EXISTENT

- Wrong pricing metric
- Stale packaging

GROWTH HAS SLOWED DOWN OR IS STAGNANT AT UNDER 5% PER YEAR

- Stale packaging
- Underpriced

COMPETITORS ARE STEALING MARKET SHARE

- Stale packaging
- Poor positioning
- Overpriced

CUSTOMER USAGE DOES NOT CORRELATE WITH WHAT THEY PAY

- Wrong pricing metric
- Excessive discounting
- Unclear segmentation

GROSS UNIT CHURN IS HIGH

- Stale packaging
- Unclear segementation

UNIT ECONOMIES ARE TRENDING DOWN

- Wrong pricing metric
- Misaligned sales incentives

SALES TEAM IS EITHER HITTING QUOTA TOO FREQUENTLY OR NOT FREQUENTLY ENOUGH

- Under / overpriced
- Misaligned sales incentives

INTERLUDE

Hold up! How is a SaaSlete supposed to watch all of this and still run a business? Let me give you an example of how one busy SaaS founder started his journey into picking up the right pricing signals.

I had the chance to sit down with the CEO of Doctible, a fast-growing B2B SaaS company based in San Diego, to dig into how he checked for pricing signals in real life.

Ajit Viswanathan, CEO of Doctible, and I go way back. We worked together as part of a product management team for several years. Our career paths led us both into the B2B SaaS space, albeit entirely different paths. Ajit was awesome enough to walk me through his experience in noticing pricing signals for the first time in his young SaaS company. The excerpt picks up after we exchange our pleasantries.

MARCOS: *How did you produce your pricing model when you launched the product?*

AJIT: We had no idea of product-market fit, and we did not want pricing to be a barrier to buy. We were after usage adoption. We had no idea if the price was right, our goal was to first understand the pain. Then once we learn more, we'll figure out later how to monetize the value of solving that pain.

We were built for speed, kept the price low, maybe too low, for the first two to three years. We were so afraid to touch it the first two years thinking we were going to mess up and stunt growth, the last thing we wanted was to handcuff sales; we were worried.

We noticed that customers never pushed back on our price in the sales cycle. After two years, we tested a 60-percent price increase. We took care of sales from a compensation perspective, committed to a month of rolling it out to new deals only to measure the impact. Before we launched, we decided to measure what the breakeven would be for this price increase to work. In other words, how many sales can we afford to lose?

Our big "a-ha" moment was when we were surprised that price was never a big issue for the customer, and so we were leaving money on the table!

MARCOS: *That's awesome. Where did take things from there to notice more pricing signals?*

AJIT: So we focused on it from a new sales and existing base, started increasing existing customers who were more upmarket, and we saw a very low impact on churn.

Turns out, we cared more about pricing than our customers.

MARCOS: *So what happened as a result of increasing the price?*

AJIT: We did it again, and again. Now, our ARPU is 4X from where we started. We also moved to big contracts and that was also a scary thing. We thought it would slow down sales. But in the end, it really didn't.

Most founders don't factor in true COGS (cost of goods sold), like customer success and onboarding. Most just benchmark against competitors with no science behind the adoption. A big struggle we had is once you raise prices, you wonder how high you can go. We had no idea how high we can charge. At what point are we charging enough?

MARCOS: *What's a bad piece of advice when it comes to pricing in B2B SaaS?*

AJIT: I do not agree with CPI adjustments in SaaS contracts, it's good for mid and enterprise deals, but not good for SMB-type customers. Even explaining it to small business owners is not worth the 3 percent.

MARCOS: *How about sharing some good advice for founders looking to take on pricing?*

AJIT: Check and test on your customer base, take 100 customers, tell them the price is going up by 25 or 50 percent and track what happens. We tested all our price increases this way, and it has been working for us for three years. We also send transparent emails about the price increase and in the background track the results like crazy.

I think more understandable and predictable is the best way to go for pricing. Without that, it causes lots of friction in the sales process.

MARCOS: *So who owns pricing today?*

AJIT: I still own the pricing. I drive pricing changes and experimentation.

MARCOS: *What's next in terms of monetization?*

AJIT: Well, we are running into SKU issues which have become very diverse due to the price experimentation. Next step for us is getting to SKU standardization with not so many variations. We want to produce a quote that is clean, easy to read, and adds no confusion.

A quick and easy rule of thumb to remember is the 2x2 Rule for changing pricing. The rule, like most, is more of a guideline than a hard rule, but it helps to keep it in mind. The 2x2 Rule states you must update your pricing model at least once every two years. and no more than once every two quarters.

The 2x2 Rule is based on experience, not science. Technology is changing rapidly, and B2B SaaS companies are releasing new value-added updates more frequently than before. In two years' time, I'm pretty sure your R&D squads have created enough value for customers to feel the difference, and with most contracts expiring within two years, a pricing change is justified.

The point of the 2x2 Rule is to keep from waiting too long before capturing new value, and on the flip side, avoid overreacting to a new change in the pricing model. Upon rolling out a new change, be sure to allow time for sales to get used to selling the new packages/prices and give customers a chance to react and provide feedback. After two quarterly sales cycles, your sales team should have their new sales pitch and positioning down, and you would have collected enough data to make an informed decision.

In the next track, we're going to talk about is how to analyze and baseline your pricing performance with qualitative and quantitative analysis. To truly find and understand the right pricing signals and improve your monetization, you have to grind out the data.

So come on and chickity check yo self.

CHECK YO SELF

MEASURE YOUR PRICING—EVEN WITH BAD DATA

"CHECK YO SELF" WAS THE THIRD SINGLE FROM ICE CUBE'S ALBUM, THE PREDATOR, FEATURING DAS EFX, THAT DROPPED INTO OUR EARS IN 1993.

The jam was a reminder to check your motives and actions to stay out of the heat. According to the urban dictionary, "check yo self" means to reevaluate your behavior, especially if you realize your current course of action is likely to lead to a troublesome situation.

Sampling from the famous hip-hop bedrock "The Message" by Grandmaster Flash, the message behind this hard-hitting beat is something all SaaSletes in B2B, small and large, should take to heart, and literally.

In the previous track, we covered pricing signals that are easy to see with a few metrics and measures. But to really understand your monetization, you need to run a baseline analysis to diagnose your pricing performance and understand exactly where things are working well and where things need to improve.

This goes beyond the pricing model itself. You might need to improve how you execute pricing, how your sales compensation model works, how you plug value leakage, or how messaging and positioning communicate value on your pricing page.

All those factors matter and are areas you should monitor closely.

In this track, we'll explore how to get the most critical data you need to inform pricing decisions with a solid baseline analysis.

PRICING TIP

Check your pricing before it wrecks your growth!

PRICING TIP

You have to think of pricing as a living and breathing system, not just a number.

FOLLOW THE BASELINE

Copernicus is believed to have said, "To know that we know what we know, and to know that we do not know what we do not know, that is true knowledge."

Come again, Copernicus?

In plain English, be acutely aware of what you can and should measure.

As you read this book, you are probably wondering about the pricing signals in your SaaS business right now. (We talked about those in the previous track, FYI.) In order to know if something is off, you have to measure, and once you measure, you can improve.

Not all data is worth analyzing, and it's not easy to know which information to track and which to ignore.

The point of a *baseline analysis* is to measure and gain an understanding of the current pricing model's ability to capture value. You want to compile your data and learn to uncover hypotheses that inform the next pricing and packaging design, and sometimes, uncover quick hit opportunities to boost monetization immediately.

A word of caution before diving in deeper: Don't boil the ocean! It's tempting to grab every piece of data you can get your hands on, but that will lead to a drawn-out and painful exercise rather than an actionable plan. You'll end up with more questions, leading to more data gathering and an endless cycle of data mining that leads to no real output.

In my experience, it's better to take a "crawl, walk, run" approach to baselining your pricing. Start somewhere and build up with steady, repeatable progress with small wins.

To anchor a pricing baseline analysis, you will need a mental model to help you look for the right data.

And eureka, we have one! The idea is to collect enough data to inform how your current pricing is performing in terms of acquiring new business,

PRICING TIP

Gathering data to understand what is working and not working in how your pricing model captures value. From there, you can plan what to do about it.

expanding into whitespace, and keeping the customers you have.

In **FIGURE 6.1**, I provide a breakdown of a baseline analysis plan that you can use to get started. Thank me later.

FIGURE 6.1: PRICING BASELINE ANALYSIS PLAN

Pricing Baseline Analysis Plan

CURRENT STATE: Show that we understand the client's business; validate we have the correct picture

RETENTION: Understand how price / value impact stickiness in terms of velocity and volume of churn across our base

EXPANSION: Understand how the packaging, pricing metric, and price levels impact cross and upsell motions in terms of expansion frequency and revenue

ACQUISITION: Understand how the pricing, packaging, and controls impact acquisition efficiency and velocity in terms of conversions, deal size, and volume

SURVEY: Understand internal stakeholder and customer sentiment to inform value, packaging, and pricing for new model

COMPETITOR: Understand competitive position and landscape to inform packages and price levels

BENCHMARKS: Compare measures against SaaS benchmarks to illuminate areas of opportunity

FINDINGS: Consolidate insights to support and inform what the new pricing and packaging should do

You can adapt the baseline analysis plan to fit your unique business circumstances, but the eight steps I laid out will apply to most B2B SaaS businesses. Each step represents an important lens for how to evaluate your pricing performance, but it is also important to step back and look at the intersections and relationships, for example, how the competition might make it harder to acquire and expand new customers. The investment in a good baseline analysis always pays off.

But where should you start? I'm glad you asked.

HOW TO 4C THE FUTURE

The baseline analysis plan in **FIGURE 6.1** outlines the key steps, but I also produced a method to organize pricing data into four categories. I call it 4C which stands for **Context**, **Capture**, **Customer**, and **Competitors**. You can see what that looks like in **FIGURE 6.2**.

FIGURE 6.2: CAPTURE, CONTEXT, COMPETITORS, AND CUSTOMERS

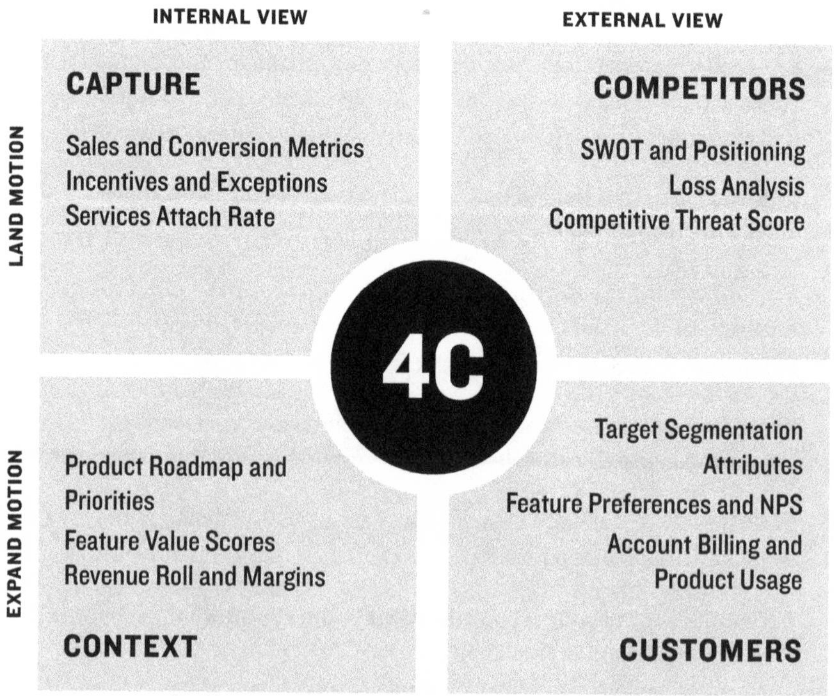

INTERNAL VIEW
EXTERNAL VIEW
LAND MOTION
CAPTURE
Sales and Conversion Metrics
Incentives and Exceptions
Services Attach Rate
COMPETITORS
SWOT and Positioning
Loss Analysis
Competitive Threat Score
4C
EXPAND MOTION
Product Roadmap and Priorities
Feature Value Scores
Revenue Roll and Margins
CONTEXT
Target Segmentation Attributes
Feature Preferences and NPS
Account Billing and Product Usage
CUSTOMERS

Let's step through these data categories together.

CAPTURE refers to your ability to capture value. This is known as your "land motion" and how you win new business.

- Gather data on your ability to convert prospects into paying customers. Where are they coming from and what do they buy?
- See how sales compensation incentives and quota targets align with your pricing model. Are you encouraging bigger deals, faster closing rates, longer terms, and the right product mix?
- Take a deep look at your professional services attach rates, from onboarding to full-scale implementation, to see how services play a role in winning deals.

CONTEXT refers to context around value, such as your SaaS product's growth plan, your brand reputation, and your ability to scale and grow your business.

- Identify and stack up your top product priorities on the roadmap. How do these changes help to achieve your growth goals?
- Measure to understand which features drive value and which ones don't (or at least not yet) to help in defining better packages.
- Get very familiar with financials at a more granular level, such as revenue roll, churn cohort analytics, margin types, sales, product cost envelopes (e.g., CAC), and market share movement.

COMPETITORS refers to understanding and knowing your value positioning versus the competition.

- Go beyond knowing who they are and dig deeper into how they sell, what they charge for, how they grow, and where they differentiate against you.
- Ask yourself this question. How do we position our product to focus on the positive differentiation that frames our unique value when compared to a competitor?
- Understand negative differentiation and how to overcome value shortfalls compared to other options. Negative differentiation happens in areas where your product or service adds cost or effort

compared to the competition such as heavier training, longer sales cycle time, or high-switching cost.

- Include the most common alternative that many customers consider: status quo, do nothing, or do it in house. Make sure that you are able to discourage these alternatives by quantifying the cost of these three paths.

And for one extra point on competitors, it is fine to be aware of all competitors aiming to eat your lunch, but it is best to focus on your top three to five threats rather than a laundry list of companies.

CUSTOMERS refers to how deeply you understand your customers (who they are and what they want).

- Gather metrics on how you segment customers starting with the buyer journey; understand feature preferences and satisfaction using your SaaS product.
- Break down your customer base into groups of profiles to uncover differences in value and willingness to pay.
- Combine these data points to shed light on how well you are serving your customers based on what they value, which in turn infers how that value relates to customer willingness to pay, also known as the holy grail of pricing!

Now that we've covered the four categories of 4C, you have a structure to go about collecting the bits of information you need to start an insightful and impactful baseline analysis. Let's briefly talk about how you actually do a pricing baseline, step by step.

A pricing baseline analysis should take anywhere from two to four weeks depending on how much data you pull and research you can collect.

PRICING TIP

You don't watch competitors to copy or define your strategy. You watch to understand your position in the value landscape.

A good pricing baseline should have an analysis plan that includes both quantitative and qualitative inputs. And just like any project, in order to be set up for success, you also need to start by listing the sequence of steps to produce a schedule, then you manage the schedule. Piece of cake!

To give you a shortcut, take a look at the baseline analysis data inventory in **FIGURE 6.3**.

FIGURE 6.3: PRICING BASELINE ANALYSIS DATA INVENTORY

DATA CATEGORIES	PURPOSE
Opportunity Data	Customer acquisition performance
Customer Account Data	Expansion and retention performance
Product Usage Data	Feature performance for packaging
Current Pricing Sheet	Baseline to work from
Recent Contract with Pricing	Examples of current pricing
Financial (P&L, Rev Roll)	Profitability and efficiency benchmarks
Growth Strategy and Plan	Strategy and execution alignment
Value Proposition and Communication	Value clarity and measurability
Buyers Personas and Segmentation	Buyer journey and value segmentation
Competitive Landscape	Competitive position and price anchors
Go-To-Market Model	GTM motion and incentive alignment

Let's walk through this process together. We'll start with the quantitative analysis so you can listen to what the numbers have to say about your pricing strategy.

When it comes to good pricing analysis, let the numbers do the talking.

DATA ANALYSIS 101

As you start collecting your data, don't be discouraged if you find lots of holes or missing information. That's a major benefit of doing this exercise. You see, it helps to understand what pricing information you can trust to make good pricing decisions and what information you need to go out and improve. It's cathartic in a weird way, like cleaning out that old closet.

To start pulling together the quantitative data, set up a query to pull the following two data sets:

- Last two years or more of won and lost sales opportunities from your CRM with fields to understand details behind each transaction.
- Most recent list of customer accounts, both active and churned, with fields to understand details behind each customer's demographics, revenues, costs, and product usage volumes. This might need to come from different data sources and joined in a single table. This is the harder of the two sets to collect, to be honest.

If you are nagged by legacy systems or data living in different sources, my advice is not to worry about it. We all need to start somewhere. Collect what you have and build up from there. Once you have all the fields you can get your hands on and a chance to review them, be objective in carving out the data points you deem usable, and which go into the junk pile.

For the junk pile data you omitted, I suggest you craft a plan on how to remedy the data issues going forward and not lament on sins of the past. No B2B SaaS company has perfect data, there's usually ways to improve the depth and breadth of transaction and customer data.

Okay, now that you have data in hand, let's get started with the data analysis. See **FIGURE 6.4** for a guide on how to attack the data analysis, one step at a time.

PRICING TIP

It's better to work with a small data set that is accurate versus a large data set that is questionable.

FIGURE 6.4: PRICING DATA ANALYSIS STEP-BY-STEP GUIDE

Pricing Data Analysis Step-By-Step Guide

1. Organize your data and populate a data scorecard, score data provided, review outstanding questions. Repeat as necessary until you have a complete data set. Add recommendations to improve areas where data quality is low. Remember, you never stop improving your data.
2. Summarize the data inputs to quantify what elements are considered in creating the analysis. A good practice is to call out how you manipulated the data (outliers omitted, data ranges, and calculations). This is so people understand any inherent biases or sample limitations.
3. Calculate basic business metrics such as revenue, accounts, users, churn, mix by segment. This level sets the analysis to provide the big picture.

Next, the goal is to understand how the current pricing is impacting the ability to capture new business, expand customers, and keep customers. To keep things simple, I like to look at the data using the **VET** analysis: Variability, Effectiveness, and Time.

4. **VARIABILITY:** Using the sales opportunity and account data, Look for price/volume imbalances across five basic dimensions: package type, segments type, sale type, customer size, and order size. Start with basics like total bookings, revenues, and sales cycle time.
5. **EFFECTIVENESS:** Calculate the following price performance metrics: Win rate, discount rate, discount frequency, Contract term, CAC, and churn versus benchmarks across the five basic dimensions listed in Step 4.
6. **TIME:** Look for monthly, quarterly, and annual trends on basic pricing measures: ARR, ARPU/A, discount rate, discount frequency, churn, volume mix, license revenue mix between software vs. professional services.

PRICING TIP

It is easier to focus a pricing baseline analysis on a single product than expand to other products once you have a chance to work out the kinks with the first one.

The key learning here is that you're always trying to understand and manage the natural tradeoff relationship between price and volume. The way you do this is by looking for and investigating signals within the pricing data during your baseline. See **FIGURE 6.5** to see an examples of pricing analysis in action:

FIGURE 6.5: EXAMPLE OF PRICE VOLUME ANALYSIS

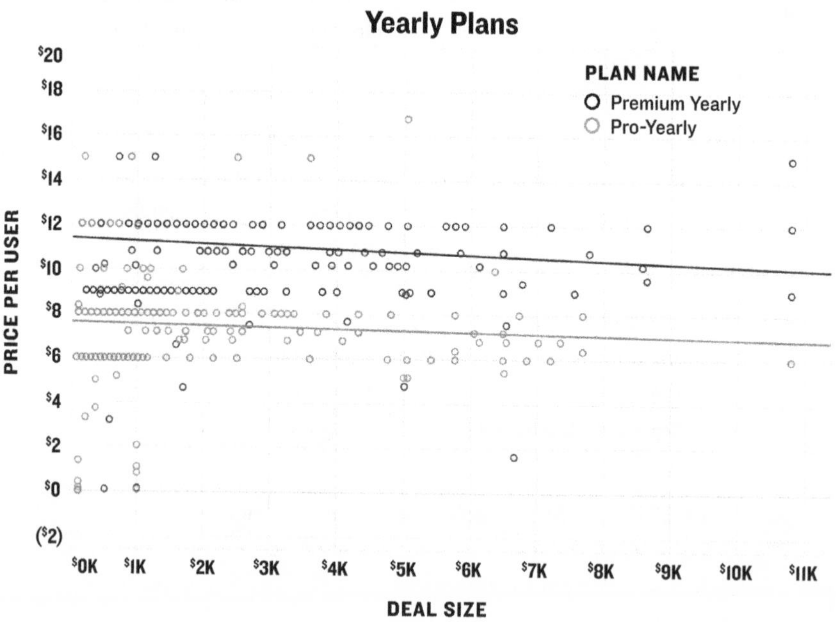

In this example, there were three packages priced at $12, $8, and $6 per user per month for yearly plans. You notice very different prices per user for deal sizes under $1,000. You also see different levels of price variation between the three packages, potentially telling you that you might need a clear discounting matrix with a floor to prevent low LTV (lifetime value) deals.

FIGURE 6.6 shows a set of other findings that are common after doing a good pricing analysis.

FIGURE 6.6: EXAMPLES OF DIAGNOSTIC FINDINGS

FINDING: One dimensional price offer and communication

ACTIONS:
- Understand how price / value impact stickiness in terms of velocity and volume of churn across base
- Introduce core set of add-ons to promote proactive versus reactive cross-sell, upsell
- Publish using pricing page best practices

HYPOTHESIS: Focused plans, clearer communication, and set options will improve win rates across competitive front

FINDING: Opportunity to extend contract terms

ACTIONS:
- Move to multi-annual terms and higher ACV
- Default contract at 3 years, price premium for shorter terms (1 year minimum)

HYPOTHESIS: Larger deals, longer terms will help keep retention high and churn low as you grow

FINDING: Random discounting for new and existing

ACTIONS:
- Introduce quarterly sales plans and bonuses
- Add accelerators to sales comp plans
- Introduce pre-defined services or feature trade-offs

HYPOTHESIS: Longer plans, trade-offs, and incentives will reduce the reliance on discounting

FINDING: Opportunity to expand price metric to capture users

ACTIONS:
- Introduce and test hybrid user/device metrics
- Merge into one device type across plans
- Must clearly define user types—power user vs. device users

HYPOTHESIS: Addressing two growth dimensions will increase expansion ARR

THE VOICES OF VALUE

Let's move on to the qualitative side of things.

As long as software involves humans selling to other humans, you need to understand sentiment and perceptions to get a true 360-degree view of how your pricing is performing. Having hard data is great, but data alone can raise more questions about pricing than provide answers. The best way to bring balance to your pricing baseline is by collecting qualitative data using time-proven tools like surveys and interviews.

The idea behind the surveys and interviews is to get an understanding of how people think about value and their sentiments around the exchange rate they are paying to get that value.

There is a strong psychological component in pricing. For example, you may hear a customer during a sales process make comments like, "I don't know why, but it just feels expensive," or, "The product is way too cheap; there must be a catch." Human emotions, past experiences, mood, rationale, and bias all play roles in everyday buying decisions, and hence, pricing decisions.

The quickest way to gather some perspective on pricing and packaging is to first launch an internal survey (followed by a customer survey, which we'll cover shortly). By "internal," I mean talking to folks within your organization. To get the best results, focus on your team members with exposure to the product, pricing model, and customers. More often than not, this tends to be employees in sales, product management, marketing, professional services, customer success, operations, and technical support.

This is a quick and easy way to get insight on your pricing, so why not send one out today? Here's how:

- Go to your survey tool of choice. If you don't have one, open a free account with one of the hundreds of free survey tools out there. I've used SurveyMonkey, SurveyGizmo, and Qualtrics before.
- Aim to collect 30 or more responses across a good mix of departments in your business.

PRICING TIP

Many say that pricing is both art and science. I say pricing is really art informed by science.

- Draft the survey by using similar questions to those in **FIGURE 6.8**.
- Test the survey on yourself. Bonus points if you can test it with someone else.
- Send a Slack or email to the survey audience to boost responses.
- Send the survey out. I like sending on Tuesday, then a reminder on Wednesday, then close the survey Friday.

And bam! You have the beginnings of pricing feedback in just under a week. How hard was that?

The next area of qualitative research is exploring the competitive landscape. There are services out there that will monitor your competitors for a pretty penny, but I've always favored good old-fashioned hustle and grind to get reliable competitive information. Here's how:

- Set up a Google alert, visit their web pages, pay attention to them at conferences, and talk to their former customers. The key is to focus your attention on your competitor's value perception, packages, prices, and ease of doing business.
- Look for strengths and weaknesses of their go-to market motion. How do they position themselves against you? How do you position yourself against them?
- Summarize this data in a table and highlight your main threat to keep on your radar. Check out the sample table in **FIGURE 6.7** to see what competitive pricing intelligence looks like.

Believe me. When it comes to your competitor's pricing, your customers are paying attention. And moreover, they're comparing you to their value, package, price, and message.

FIGURE 6.7: EXAMPLES OF COMPETITIVE PRICING INTELLIGENCE

PRICING MODEL

MEETINGS
- Monthly: $37.50 user/month, Annually: $25 user/month
- Concierge: $200/month (scheduling), $350/month (scheduling and live calls)

EVENTS
- Monthly: $750/month (3 minimum), $60 user/month, Annually: $750/month, $40 user/month
- $500 event platform fee

CUSTOMER VALUE
- Easily manage multiple calendars
- Accept online bookings through the app
- User-friendly and intuitive
- App allows prospects to easily reschedule meetings
- Helpful in reducing missed appointments
- Intelligent booking assistant
- Real-time lead routing
- Sales development representative hand-off solution

NEGATIVE FEEDBACK
- "Occasionally glitches"
- "Delays in notifications"
- "Inability to control or limit user access, like when staff shouldn't be able to modify existing settings."

G Suite

PRICING MODEL
- Basic: $6 user/month, Business: $12 user/month, Enterprise: $25 user/month
- Free Trial: 14 days

CUSTOMER VALUE
- Google Calendars
- Google Mail
- Google Chrome
- Google Docs
- Google Sheets
- Google Slides

NEGATIVE FEEDBACK
- "Google Sheets needs improvement"
- Customer support can be difficult to reach"

Square

PRICING MODEL
- Card-present: 2.6% + 10¢ per transaction, Online: 2.9% + 30¢ per transaction, Manual key/on-file: 3.5% + 15¢ per transaction
- Free: free plan, 2-5 employees: $50/month, 6-10 employees: $90/month, 10+ employees: quote

CUSTOMER VALUE

SQUARE APPOINTMENTS
- Payment processing
- Appointment setting
- Free online booking website
- Easily schedule appointments at any time
- Calendar management with automated appointment reminders
- Integrates with other Square products (POS, inventory, loyalty, gift cards, ecommerce, payroll)

NEGATIVE FEEDBACK
- "Customization options not robust"
- "Platform is glitchy"
- "Reviewers also wished that it would allow booking recurring appointments in a month."

PRICING TIP

Don't enter a sales negotiation or update your pricing page without understanding the playing field you're in.

To give yourself a leg up on collecting competitive pricing information, take a look at the sources below:

- Websites and Wayback Machine (to view history of changes)
- Software Review Sites (ex. G2, Capterra, Gartner)
- Competitive Intelligences Tools/Services (Klue, Crayon, CI Radar)
- LinkedIn and SlideShare Posts
- Sales Win/Loss Interviews (especially the losses)
- Sales Team and Success Team Interviews
- And yes, customers are full of useful competitive intelligence

Saving the best for last, we have customer feedback as the most critical part of your qualitative research, and frankly, your entire pricing baseline.

Now let's be honest, you're not talking to your customer as much as you should. And I'm not talking about feature-level feedback on your beta or bugs reported to customer support. I'm talking about real conversations about what the product is worth to them.

A value conversation with a customer is different from a sales or demo call. The value conversation centers around what value means to the customer. How do they get it, and how much are they getting? On the flip side, what is not valuable to them at all? What parts of your solution simply do not make sense for them?

And most importantly, be able to identify the "why" behind these answers.

We'll unpack the value conversations and how to use this information to better understand, segment, package for, and price your customers in **TRACK 9: MY PEOPLES COME FIRST**. For the purpose of this section and completing the baseline, consider sending customers a short survey that looks like the example in **FIGURE 6.8.**

Once you have completed the survey, the idea is to summarize your findings and overlay your learnings with:

- What you learned in the data analysis section
- What you observed across your competitors
- What you heard from your peers

FIGURE 6.8: EXAMPLE OF CUSTOMER SURVEY QUESTIONS

Product Market Value Fit

- How disappointed would you be if you could no longer use PRODUCT? [Very, Somewhat, Not]
- What types of users do you think will most benefit from PRODUCT?
- How is the main benefit you receive from PRODUCT?
- How can we improve PRODUCT for you?

Value Preferences

- In terms of PRODUCT'S value, which of the following is most important? Least Important? [List top 5 features and services]

Exploratory Willingness to Pay

- At what point would you think PRODUCT is a bargain—a great value for the money?
- At what price would you being to think PRODUCT is getting expensive, but still might consider buying?
- At what price would you begin to think PRODUCT is way too expensive to even consider—a ridiculous price for the value?
- At what price would you begin to think PRODUCT is so cheap that you would question the quality and likely not buy it?
- How likely are you to buy PRODUCT at a price between the price ranges you gave? [Very Likely, Likely, Unsure, Unlikely, Very Unlikely]

Now you have a strong basis to see any signals of bad pricing, but you can also uncover opportunities to make your pricing and packaging more effective. A 1-percent change in your prices can lead to 11 percent of operating profit according to a Harvard study. It's the most powerful value creation lever you can pull!

"Ok, but what if my data sucks?" you ask.

Let's pile it on: What if you don't have enough customers to survey? What if your opportunity data has more holes than Swiss cheese? What if your competitors play their cards close to their chest?

I find it interesting that B2B software companies have some of the worst data hygiene habits. Old legacy stacks, poor systems, moving too fast. There are lots of reasons. I'm not here to judge. I was once like you.

I suggest leaning more on customer surveys, interviews, internal sentiment, and competitor intelligence as you improve your opportunity and account data.

"That's it?" you wonder.

Of course not. If you know me by now, you probably think that I have a framework for everything. To help you get started with baselining your pricing performance, I have a quick and intuitive method I like to call "5-4-3-2-1."

GET STARTED IN 5-4-3-2-1

What if the qualitative data is scarce? Get used to collecting as much information as possible with every deal. This will help you detect patterns within smaller data sets.

Data is everywhere, but it's not going to fall in your lap. If you don't have it today, you have two options: capture it or create it. Use the tools I gave you in this section and start today!

In 20 years of pricing experience, I learned that it's always best to get started somewhere, anywhere. So, if you are like most B2B SaaS companies and have no idea where to start a pricing baseline, follow the 5-4-3-2-1 approach in **FIGURE 6.9** and build up from there.

FIGURE 6.9: THE 5-4-3-2-1 FRAMEWORK

- **5 CUSTOMERS:** Choose five customers with the deepest experience using your product. Choose different sizes and types to expand your point of view.
- **4 INTERVIEWS:** Select four top-quota-earning and experienced sales reps or BDRs / SDRs; different channels help to broaden your perspective.
- **3 COMPETITORS:** Research your top three competitors: one priced below, priced above, and priced similar to your product.
- **2 YEARS OF SALES DATA:** Gather two years of sales transactions to notice a few quick trends (hint: collect both wins and losses).
- **1 YEAR OF PRODUCT ROADMAP:** Review one year of product roadmap from the last six months and next six months, to identify value delivered and value on the way. This will help you define your value story.

There you have it. An approach you can start with right now. To help motivate you, you can download a bonus cheat sheet for 5-4-3-2-1 for free at www.pricingio.com. Use it to organize your game plan and get started.

So why stop now? We just walked through how to run a pricing baseline analysis, so take a stab at it with the exercise in the **PLAYBACK**.

Yes, I mean right now. We'll be here when you get back.

PLAYBACK EXERCISE

Based on the pricing data elements we talked about in this track, take an inventory of your data to see what you have available. Give yourself a baseline score of I (poor), 3 (okay), and 5 (awesome) for each area of data.

To get a head start, use **FIGURE 6.3** and the data scorecard cheat sheet you can download from my website. Once you complete the task, you will use this scorecard as a baseline to start understanding and improving your pricing data. Think of it as a "Foundation Fact Pack."

INTERLUDE

Dr. Dwight Porter is a renowned economist and pricing strategy expert who's worked with Google, 3M, DoubleClick, and Abacus. With over 40 years of experience, he is the "go-to" for large companies and private equity firms around the world. He's a great person, a genuine friend, and ultra-sharp when it comes to pricing data and analysis. I had the pleasure of catching up with him to pick his brain on the ins and outs of pricing analysis.

MARCOS: *Hey Dwight, it's always fun to chat with you. Let's dig in. Most companies don't have a good handle on their pricing data. Give me your thoughts on what software companies should do to better understand their price-volume equation.*

DWIGHT: That's a super-good question. You're absolutely right. The challenge is that you have to have enough data. They either don't have it or don't have it structured in a way that is useful. So, I approach the problem a different way. I do a value assessment by using a variety of techniques to produce a hypothesis whether they think they are underpriced or not.

At some point the exercise convinces them they are potentially underpricing, and we engage in some price testing to produce some data that either validates their assumptions or not.

CONTINUED →

MARCOS: *Not only do they have a hard time with capturing the right data set, but the other problem is that they don't understand how to measure or quantify their value. What do you think is an effective way to figure out your value?*

DWIGHT: I am a total fan of price value mapping. And I do it two different ways. First, I do it qualitatively allowing a group to use collective judgement about themselves versus their competitors and what the differences are; and the second thing I encourage them to do is a quantitative version of that by moving the opinion toward some level of quantification and/or gathering some primary research data that validates some of the assumptions they're making around relative value.

The second tool I like is the one in *The Strategy and Tactics of Pricing: A Guide to Growing More Profitably* by Thomas T. Nagle, John E. Hogan, and Joseph Zale, Economic Value Estimation (EVE). This teaches the underlying engineering approach which focuses on how much money am I saving you or how much improvement does my product make if it's demonstrably better for the customer.

I take the price value map and the EVE and combine with a third tool of my own, which is all about taking value and telling the story. And then from the story, try to tell which elements can be measured or quantified into a real ROI outcome. Then I combine all that into a proposition that if you can see the value, then the next step is to teach your sales team value-based selling and how to communicate that value in a meaningful and repeatable way.

MARCOS: *So methodical! Why do you think they fall down when trying to collect data and measure value?*

DWIGHT: I think the fall down is because they don't treat it vigorously. They don't take it through four methodical steps: **First step:** Brainstorm and think broadly about the value you produce for your customers. **Second step:** Make sure you know the distinction between absolute and relative value; this is where the price value mapping comes in. **Third step:** Quantify the things you brainstormed, and work hard to see what the various ways are you could impute the value, for example, does the customer actually measure the value you think is important? **Fourth step:** Pull all that together in a combined story that says here is the stuff that is numerically valid and there is the part that isn't, train on it, and put it in front of customers. One other pitfall is using sales teams' anecdotal descriptions of customer responses and letting that overwhelm what the data says. This is one of the most repeated mistakes I see my clients make. They let the sales team stories dominate the value discussion instead of data.

MARCOS: *I've seen that, too, and that is all too common. What's another pricing data mistake SaaSletes should avoid?*

DWIGHT: Another mistake I see is they use the concept of ASP (Average Sold Price), or in general, that an average is something meaningful in terms of what is actually happening to price. I'm way more interested in price dispersion, and does it teach you anything about segmentation and how they respond differently to prices. Your dispersion may not be a function of price sensitivity but a function of the sales team actively discovering price without guidance.

MARCOS: *I couldn't agree more. OK, I have a speed round of pricing questions that were popular topics from my coaching sessions. Are you ready?*

DWIGHT: Let's do it.

MARCOS: *What's the biggest pricing misconception that you run into?*

DWIGHT: I think it's that pricing is fairly easy and doesn't require any time or expertise to get right.

MARCOS: *I've run into a few of those as well. The second question is what is your favorite statistic that demonstrates the power of pricing?*

DWIGHT: Too many people think that better pricing is always higher pricing, and there are situations where higher pricing can make things worse given the competitive situation or business strategy. There have been plenty of times where I've made clients tons of money by lowering their prices.

MARCOS: *I agree, it's more about calibrating your prices to offer the right price, to the right buyer, for the right value. The last question is what pricing model do you admire?*

DWIGHT: Based on my experience with them Medtronic does a phenomenal job of pricing. They are a hugely value-based pricing discipline, there are a lot of people involved, they are multi-functional in how they approach it, they understand the implementation issues, and they do a great job around economic modeling and analysis.

Whoever is in charge of pricing should also be in charge of improving your pricing intelligence. Make sure that this person is not only reviewing your existing pricing model effectiveness but also reviewing and improving the data in which you make pricing decisions.

There is an excellent opportunity every time you change pricing and see how the internal and external forces respond. This response rate will be an important input into your pricing, which we will cover more in **TRACK II: CASH RULES EVERYTHING.**

Now that you are armed with signals and data, it's time to put these newfound assets to work. To help you monetize value, you need to follow a five-part framework to keep you from getting stuck and knocked back.

Said another way, you need to get five on it.

I GOT 5 ON IT

MOVE FROM GUESSWORK TO FRAMEWORK IN FIVE PHASES

THE OAKLAND DUO LUNIZ RELEASED "I GOT 5 ON IT" IN 1995.

It comes from an underrated school of hip-hop that discusses low-stakes and even trivial problems with high-level musicality. The "5" refers to a five-dollar contribution toward the purchase of a guilty pleasure, marijuana. I'm not an herbalist, enthusiast, or anything of that sort. But what stood out to me about this 90s masterpiece (ranked 13th best-selling single that year) is how the song was made. It was a combination of artists who all committed to a common goal over a juxtaposition of a complex beat and not-so-complex subject matter, a beat that controversially hailed from the hit song "Why You Treat Me So Bad," by Club Nouveau in 1986.

The remix version took the song further into hip-hop fandom, inviting five guest artists to share their perspective of the ceremony. If I had to sum things up about this song, it was all about being inclusive as you pass the subject matter from one to the next (after paying your $5, of course).

A good framework should be inclusive, but also set boundaries to guide your thinking with enough flexibility to explore possibilities.

When I think of some of the more timeless and classic business frameworks out there, like Porter's Five Forces, SWOT, the BCG Matrix, or the Ansoff Matrix, they do a good job of being all inclusive to help us think through the implications of a strategy. That's what being strategic is about.

So far in Part Two, we stepped through how to tune your radar to look for signals around your pricing and took a step further with how to collect data to build a solid baseline analysis to confidently craft your pricing strategy.

But beware. Pricing is a politically charged, data-intensive, and naturally intricate subject matter that demands structure. If you choose to wing it, you are inviting a host of profit poltergeists and growth ghouls that will haunt your SaaS business into oblivion. How about that for an analogy?

Yeah, way too much. But you get my point.

Let's continue our journey by taking the eye-opening insights from pricing signals and a baseline analysis and apply some structure to take action. We'll use what I call the 5Q framework to figure out how to change your packaging and pricing, but first, a little background to accelerate your uptake.

THE 5Q FRAMEWORK

"So how much should we charge for our SaaS product, Marcos?"

That's the first question I get whenever I enter the room at any B2B tech company. However, the truth is that's a really hard question to answer, even for me.

But before we try to answer that, you should really understand who is buying your product and their willingness to pay. That's where the 5Q (i.e., five question) Framework comes into play. 5Q is a ladder methodology where each question and answer builds on the previous one (think about the puff-puff-pass motion the Luniz were referencing). This sequence makes it easier to define a well-connected pricing strategy and model.

Using this framework will help you understand how your business is going to grow and how you are augmenting your product value in order to achieve that growth.

Do you see where I'm going?

Once you know why you are pricing, who you are pricing for, and what your offer is, then the question around how much to charge becomes easier to answer.

PRICING TIP

To figure out how much you should charge, you first need to understand what you're charging for.

The last part of the 5Q Framework is solving for which elements of your pricing strategy are working or not working in order to refine the model. It becomes a virtuous cycle from there. So, the five Qs (questions) are:

- Why are you pricing?
- Who are you pricing for?
- What is your offer?
- How much should you charge?
- What elements are or are not working?

By approaching the pricing problem in a structured order, you end up thinking about pricing beyond a number on a webpage. Instead, you think about it in terms of offering the right value to the right buyer for the right price in order to influence the behavior you need to grow your SaaS business.

Now hold up. Wait a minute!

If the rest of this book is going to make sense to you, then you need to truly absorb that last point and feel where I'm coming from.

In my experience, pricing changes have the most profound impact when they're rolled out in harmony with other business changes in the organization. For example, making changes to your pricing page, your messaging, your sales compensation model, and your pricing all at once can yield a more powerful impactful versus changing pricing alone.

I use the 5Q Framework every day with my clients and it's the most effective way to structure the pricing problem. This approach blends strategy and tactical work to arrive at a thoughtful, balanced, and repeatable pricing model that will catapult your ARR growth rate.

Pricing is a skill, a discipline, and just like any skill or discipline it has to be practiced, and with practice comes improvement. In other words, never consider pricing to be a one-and-done exercise.

Pricing is the product of the product. And like any product, it has its own life cycle that demands research, innovation, and good execution.

This framework, shown in **FIGURE 7.1**, applies to software companies of all shapes and sizes, but it is especially powerful for B2B SaaS companies that target SMB, mid-market, and enterprise customers.

FIGURE 7.1: THE 5Q FRAMEWORK MATRIX

1. WHY	2. WHO	3. WHAT	4. HOW	5. WHICH
Growth Strategy	Buyer Journey	Offer Mix	Monetization Model	North Star KPIs
Product Strategy	Willingness to Pay	Feature Performance	Go to Market Motion	Data Discipline
Value Path	Value Segmentation	Value Drivers	Value Metrics	Value Management

5Q assumes three things about your business that must be true to get the most out of the framework:

- First, it assumes that your business or product is growth-oriented. This means that you are trying to grow at scale. If you want to be a steady-eddy or lifestyle business, that's fine, but the framework will be less impactful.
- Second, it also assumes that you are product-led. In this sense, I mean that you derive value from a product or service, or combination of both. If you do not sell a tangible product, then this framework will not pack the punch you are hoping for.
- And third, it assumes that you are value-focused. This means that you want to price to value and capture value as it evolves. If your idea of pricing is cost-plus, copy-cat, or name your price, then this framework will add very little.

Now that we laid down the three tenets of the 5Q pricing framework, let's step through the five phases one by one.

PRICING TIP

Pricing is much more than finding the dots—it's about connecting the dots.

WHY ▪ Why are you pricing in the first place?

This phase is about connecting growth strategy with product strategy and value proposition. First, you should understand how your SaaS business will grow and how that growth is connected to your product roadmap as you execute your product strategy. Then connect the dots further by asking yourself how the growth and product improvements impact the value proposition over time.

To be successful in capturing value, it is critical to understand how the pricing model supports this connected growth story.

Let me throw out an example for you:

Say your growth strategy in part depends on moving down market and capturing smaller-sized businesses. For more color, let's assume you need 20 percent of new recurring revenue to come from SMB and micro-SMB sized clients.

With SMB-driven growth in our focus, we turn to the product strategy to understand how your investment in R & D is going to help serve smaller clients. Let's assume you prioritize building more self-service capabilities and better telemetry as part of your product roadmap.

Booyah! You've just made a connection from growth to product! We will get deeper into pricing for growth in **TRACK 8: NUTHIN' BUT A "G" THANG.**

Now let's move on to the value proposition.

As you fulfill your roadmap and expand your product's self-service abilities, your value proposition starts to change due to the speed in which new clients get up and running in your product, as well as how they seamlessly change workflows and expand their usage. Your value proposition has expanded with more flexibility and agility.

Are you starting to see how this stuff is relevant to pricing yet? Good!

WHO ▪ Who are you pricing for?

You must have a good understanding of customer needs, behaviors, and value in order to create meaningful segmentation that identifies differences in buying behavior and value perceptions.

These differences are important in order to design the pricing and packages and align them to each segment. This is one of the hardest areas of pricing, and to be real, most companies overlook this part and underinvest in getting closer to the customer and the problems their product solves.

SaaS companies that have cracked the code with pricing really understand and get deep into the customer problems, how they're solving them differently than alternatives, and how customers feel about the solution that drives their willingness to pay.

It begins with mapping out the buyer journey. This means detailing how customers find your product, decide they need it, and buy it. There are plenty of templates online if you google "buyer journey map," but many product usage and customer success software tools include journey mapping tools built-in. For example, pendo.io, ChurnZero, and Totango are all popular and worth exploring. With so many options, I suggest evaluating three to four tools, do a short "bake off" between the top two for a week, and just pick one.

Next, you'll need to get a good grasp of pricing sensitivity and the customer's general willingness to pay. There are several techniques that are commonly used to collect data from customers and prospects, such as Van Westendorp (a market technique for determining acceptable consumer prices) surveys. Since customers are notoriously bad at pinpointing and communicating what they are willing to pay, you have to triangulate. I go deeper into this topic in **TRACK 9: MY PEOPLES COME FIRST**.

Once you have the journey mapped and a sense for willingness to pay, it is time to connect the dots and inform value-based segments.

WHAT ▪ What value should you price?

Now that the Why and Who are clear, you need to structure an offer mix that presents the right value for the right buyer. You do this by knowing which features and services drive value for which targets. From here, it gets easier to decide which value drivers should be add-ons versus which ones should be included in the offer.

"But how do I do that?" you inquire.

Well, you have to understand usage patterns, willingness to pay, and importance of the workflow. Ask yourself:

- Is the offer mix informed by feature performance and reflective of the biggest value drivers?
- Are there transactions that grow over time as users get more value?
- Are packages designed for natural upgrades as customers increase maturity, usage, and growth?

Good packaging can lead to bigger deal sizes, stickier customers, and reduces selling and buying friction. That's a major win for your monetization! We will get deeper into packaging techniques in **TRACK 10: THE CHOICE IS YOURS.**

There are misconceptions about bundles and who they really benefit. Bundles solve a customer problem more completely compared to standalone solutions. Bundles also make the evaluation process easier, and they help avoid the paradox of choice to speed up buying decisions.

HOW ▪ How much should you price?

Now we get to scratch the itch in your mind. How much should you charge for your value? You want to monetize based on value and charge for a value metric that grows with usage. You need a model that can be effectively sold by your go-to-market (GTM) team that controls for value leakage. Yes, it's all so obvious, right?

Not even close! Choosing the right monetization path requires a ton of context and clarity. This is why in the 5Q framework we don't decide on the monetization model until we are first clear on the Why, Who, and What.

You can have different pricing models for different markets if needed. Subscription is the most popular model for SaaS companies, but subscription doesn't fit every business.

To illustrate, let's say your customer's usage is sporadic and tough to predict. A subscription pricing model could lead to imbalances in price to value. Customers could pay too much money for little usage, which might result in churn. Or they can pay far less than they should during peak usage, which leaves money on the table. In this scenario, it is better to charge based on usage or transaction levels as opposed to the default subscription model.

A hybrid of subscription and usage based is the best way to go. You're able to get the consistency of a recurring revenue model while still capitalizing on usage patterns. It's also still relatively simple to understand and sell.

WHICH ▪ Which part of your pricing model is working?

The point here is to pay close attention to what's working and what's not in order to continuously refine and improve your pricing model. You should have north star metrics to signal and guide your progress; supported by a strong understanding of your data and where it needs to improve, as we discussed back in **TRACK 6**.

You will need solid governance around value management. This means understanding how value is created from end to end. Manage value from product roadmap, to how it is communicated, to positioning versus the competition, to the pricing page and operationalization.

PLAYBACK EXERCISE

Use the 5Q Framework in this track to score your company or product based across all five dimensions of high-growth, value-based pricing in SaaS. Score each element within the phases of Why, Who, What, How, and Which to uncover where you need the most guidance, and therefore, which tracks might help you the most. This scorecard will save you time by focusing on the elements of 5Q that need the most attention.

INTERLUDE

Dan Martell, founder of SaaS Academy, is an award-winning Canadian entrepreneur, investor, and coach to over 600 SaaS founders including clients like ClickFunnels, Proposify, and Carrot. When it comes to SaaS and how to grow, you can't find anyone out there better than Dan.

I had the opportunity to chat with Dan on his views on pricing guesswork and how powerful the pricing lever can be on growth.

MARCOS: *Always great catching up with you, man. My first question is how did you got into pricing and realize it was such a powerful growth lever?*

DAN: I'll give you the short version of a very long story. I reached out to a mentor that taught me about pricing, and specifically, how incredibly powerful payment terms can be. I had a cash flow problem with a business I was running and almost went bankrupt! He taught me the power of payment terms using a pricing matrix - for example, let's say if you want to do this, this, and that, your price is x. So, you can do quarterly billing or net zero wire transfer and get a discount—this fixed our cash flow problem and it transformed the game.

That's when I realized the financial impact pricing can have on my business. That allowed us to continue our growth and fix our cash flow problem.

MARCOS: *That's really cool. Where do you see SaaS companies struggle the most with pricing?*

DAN: SaaS founders are technical purists and are typically scratching their own itch. And what will happen is they'll want to do something different, like give everything away for one price.

It's like when someone has a restaurant or bar. They do something because that is what they'll want as a consumer, but they don't understand the economic impact of that decision. They'll have this evangelical approach to simplified pricing without understanding how powerful it can be as a growth lever. And then having to walk their way back and out of that model years later.

MARCOS: *Totally agree with you! I see oversimplified pricing in the spirit of transparency, and it can severely limit their growth potential.*

DAN: Oh, 100 percent! They'll block themselves out of industries and verticals because their preference to buy, it can harm them on several different dimensions.

MARCOS: *Yeah! What is the best and worst pricing advice you ever heard?*

DAN: Not to pump your ego, but the 2x2 Rule. I love that idea!

MARCOS: *The shelf life of a pricing model is about two years when you think about the pace of innovation and how quickly a SaaS product*

CONTINUED →

updates (I personally like to change it every year), and if you just launched a new pricing model, give it at least two quarters (or two months if you're B2C) and avoid knee-jerk reactions.

DAN: That is honestly one of my favorites. I had a coaching client, and they didn't change pricing for 11 years. And the simple questions you can ask are, "Has your product gotten better in the last 11 years?" and "Where is that reflected in the value capture side of the equation?"

The worst pricing is the one plan—too simple. I can even tell what kind of backend metrics they're going to have based on their packaging and pricing. And I don't think it needs to be complex, it just needs to be right-sized.

MARCOS: *What are some of the biggest success stories you've seen with pricing?*

DAN: I coach over 150 SaaS founders and one of the first things I look to change is pricing. It is that powerful! I had one client double his prices, change up his packaging, and he hit his revenue goal for the quarter in 14 days! And his conversion rate didn't change. I love that story!

MARCOS: *What pricing models do you admire? It could be any, not just software.*

DAN: I'll give you a few on both ends. HubSpot on the enterprise level. They are smart about what to sell, to whom, and how. So that's on the high end. On the low end is Mailchimp, with $1B in revenue and 50 percent. And Algolia, I feel like they've done a great job to serve a very broad market with a technically complex product to a non-technical person. I also love Twilio's product pricing.

We will dive deeper into each of these five core phases of the 5Q framework in the upcoming tracks.

Let's start by getting deeper into the Why to take a closer look at growth strategy from a young G's perspective.

NUTHIN' BUT A "G" THANG

CONNECT THE DOTS BETWEEN GROWTH AND VALUE

I USED TO HUM ALONG TO THIS JAM ON THE WAY TO HIGH SCHOOL.

"Nuthin' But a 'G' Thang," the first chart-topping inhale of Dr. Dre's iconic album, *The Chronic*, hit the radio waves in 1992. I referenced the same duo, Dr. Dre and Snoop Dogg, in **TRACK 3**, inspired by their other hit "Gin and Juice," to reveal the true goal of pricing in SaaS, which is to achieve the highest enterprise value.

I decided to bring the pair back on this track to shed more light on how to connect the dots between growth, pricing, and value.

Now that you are grounded in the 5Q framework, I'm going to guide you through each question phase, starting with the "Why" and gaining clarity on your growth goals. This is the bedrock of the 5Q framework and sets the stage for your pricing strategy and all the pricing decisions that follow. We'll start with the four most common paths to grow, and then move into how to earn your strategy, then break down how to identify value, applying 5Q as we go.

THE FOUR PATHS

We'll start with four common paths to growing your recurring revenue in the Software as a Service game. Building on top of the growth levers we covered in **TRACK 3**, you already know that successful subscription-based businesses pull all three levers of the value capture cycle: acquisition, expansion, and retention.

But acquire whom? Expand what? Retain how?

These questions become easier to answer if you have clarity around which growth strategy you are prioritizing for your business. Take a look at the chart in **FIGURE 8.1**. You notice price points A and B are notably different because they accomplish different goals.

FIGURE 8.1: PRICE POINTS WITH ECONOMIC CURVES

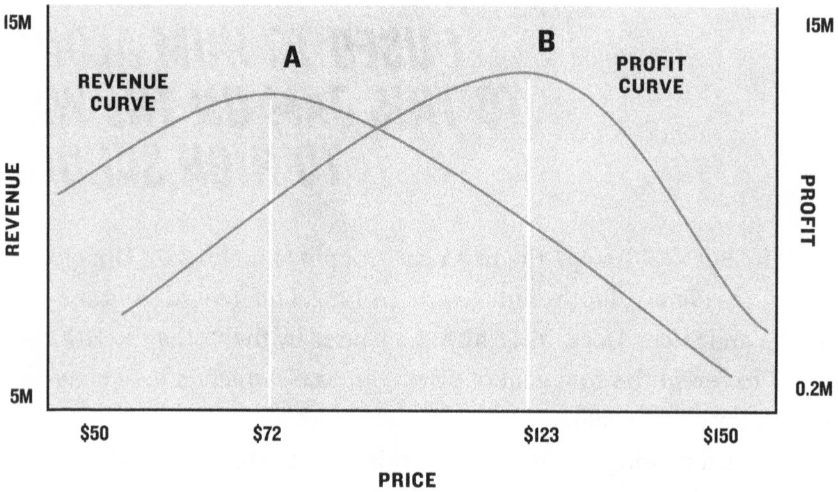

If your goal is to grow your revenue, go with the affordable price point A to attract more customers to buy. But if you want to grow your profit, the higher price point B is a better choice to capture more value from fewer customers. Your growth path directly impacts the pricing strategy, and therefore, you need to be clear on which of the following four growth paths you are taking before deciding the pricing model. There is no magical "one price" that will solve for all of your goals. There is always a tradeoff.

1. CORE GROWTH (same problem, same customer)

Protecting and growing your core business is the lowest-risk strategy and foundational if you want to pursue the other three growth paths. In B2B SaaS, many refer to a related concept, Product-Market Fit (competing in an attractive market with a product that satisfies that market), to measure how well the product is meeting the needs of their target market. From a pricing perspective, it is important to ensure you price your product using a neutral strategy to capture the value you've accumulated over time and build a moat around your core market to keep out competitors.

2. HORIZONTAL GROWTH (same problem, different customer)

Once your core is secure, you can choose to expand your market share by going deeper or wider. With horizontal growth, you are solving the same problem for different groups of customers, in different markets or industries that typically may but sometimes may not share attributes. For example, you completely solved the payroll problem for restaurants, but now you want to expand and solve the same payroll problem for more general retail outlets (different targets but share some of the same attributes). This is also known as expanding your TAM.

From a pricing perspective, the key play is to analyze your pricing metric (the activity or thing that you bill for). In order to see if your pricing model holds up, revisit your packages to remove any industry specific features, and adjust your messaging and positioning around the new set of competitors and customers. Note that this path is higher risk compared to sticking with your core target market, and typically comes after a growth investment round or the $10M ARR milestone, whichever comes first.

3. VERTICAL GROWTH (different problem, same customer)

Similar to horizontal growth, this growth path is also riddled with risk, but it's one of my favorite paths because it combines experience with knowledge and challenges you to go deeper to provide more value. And the more value you create, the more you can capture.

Vertical growth is solving a different problem for the same customer. One common example is providing business management software, then expanding to process payments (versus outsourcing to a third party). The pricing play here is to pay close attention to your packages, particularly what features are included in the base plans, what are add-ons, and what to bundle or unbundle.

4. DIAGONAL GROWTH (different problem, different customer)

Here we have the riskiest growth path of all: expanding to solve a different problem for different customers. More often than not, it has to do with solving a different section of a long, complex supply chain, such as in financial services, telecommunications, or logistics. I see this path later in the B2B SaaS lifecycle, usually when leadership is wrestling with a thesis around untapped market that could significantly increase the TAM.

I also see this phenomenon in trying to serve multiple sides of a marketplace. From a pricing perspective, the play here is to go back to the drawing board, but ensure your pricing is consistent with the tone and overarching structure of your pricing strategy. Salesforce and Atlassian, two examples of having multiple products solving problems for multiple customers, are good examples of diagonal growth strategies executed well.

Now that you know the four paths to growth, what's the next step? The next step is to choose the right pricing strategy to achieve your objectives as you walk down your growth path. But growth doesn't come easy, y'all. You need to work hard for it.

To the contrary, most pricing advice you hear or read today sounds easy and convenient, right? I mean all you have to do to reach success and riches beyond your wildest dreams is to price to value.

Brilliant! Go out there and price to value so you can unleash revenue growth at ludicrous speed! (I know it's hard to read sarcasm, but stay with me.)

The problem is that too many consultants out there have become so "Tony Robbins-ish" about pricing, feeding you platitudes, euphemisms, and cliche after cliche, without telling you how to do it.

So, let's get street for a minute. Pricing to value is freaking hard!

Dramatic pause.

"But why is it so hard?" you wonder.

Because pricing is a means to an end, or in other words, a tool to achieve your growth strategy, which is something that is exceedingly tough to do if you don't have a strategy in the first place, right?

Therefore, start by answering this question first: How do you produce the right pricing strategy for the growth path you've chosen? Well, like I said before, it is not going to fall into your lap. To put it bluntly, you have to E.A.R.N. it.

EARN YOUR PRICING STRATEGY

Admit it.

You didn't have the time, data, or energy to derive an intentional and data-driven pricing strategy linked to your business objectives (hence why you are enjoying this book, right?).

And like we covered in **TRACK 6**, data you need to define your pricing strategy simply doesn't fall out of the sky. You have little chance of freeing up time to gather and crunch the data yourself (You have 1,000 unread emails in your inbox right now, don't you?).

Well, I guess you can hope the pricing model you have today is good enough, except hope is not a good pricing strategy.

As we covered earlier in the book, studies show that SaaS companies spend six hours a year on defining their pricing strategy, despite knowing that pricing is the most powerful growth lever in your arsenal (in fact, four times more than customer acquisition, per OpenView Partners). Based on this, you've spent more time debating over which software requirements make it into the next release.

So what gives?

You now know that the fundamental reason behind the lack of attention to pricing strategy is the lack of data and structure. This is where you get your hands dirty. We'll cover four steps to setting a clear and informed pricing strategy using what we call the EARN approach: Estimate, Align, Reinforce, Navigate, and yes, we gave this acronym a lot of thought.

Here's how it works, step by step:

STEP 1: Estimate your value.

To get started, send a short survey to your prospects, customers, and internal teams to collect ideas on what areas of the product deliver the most value. Choose a subset of responses to schedule 15 minutes interviews to gather more context behind their answers. This data set should serve as a good foundation to start breaking down your value into categories, such as positive vs. negative, or base vs. premium. Here are a few questions to ask yourself as you define your value in this step:

- What ROI is the buyer expecting by investing in our product/service?
- What outcomes do buyers want to improve? How are they measured?
- How does our value change over time or with increased usage?

STEP 2: Align your value, product, and market.

If you thought nailing down your value and differentiation was hard, this next one is not any easier. It's best to do this step with other team members to get a cross-functional perspective of how value aligns with the product's maturity and market dynamics.

This will take a few iterations to get right, but think through the relationship between value, product, and market to formulate an understanding of what you want your pricing to do. Here are a few questions to ask yourself in this step:

- Are customers over-served or underserved in the market today?
- Is our market growing or shrinking and what is our rank today?
- How would competitors react to our pricing?

To help you along, **FIGURE 8.2** includes a common set of pricing strategies in terms of how you base and position your value.

FIGURE 8.2: MOST COMMON PRICING STRATEGIES

BASIS OF VALUE	POSITION OF VALUE
Cost Based Set value based on costs plus a markup/margin	**Penetration** Set your price below value
Competitor Based Set value based on competitor model and price levels	**Neutral** Set your price at value
Value Based Set value based on perceived value delivered and willingness to pay	**Skimming** Set your price above value

STEP 3: Reinforce the strategy by making tradeoffs

Setting a strategic path usually means you need to say yes and no to certain things. For instance, you should not give a deep discount to win deals if your strategy is Skimming. The big tradeoff is topline revenue and market share for profits. Most pricing models are designed to maximize profit; however, we know the realities and pressures to gain market share and top line revenue in SaaS, especially in the venture or private equity backed arena. Ask yourself in this step:

- Why do we win and lose deals today?
- Who is *not* our customer?
- What explicitly will we need to sacrifice to achieve this strategy?

FIGURE 8.3 is a tradeoff matrix we've used with clients to help think through the common tensions in pricing strategy.

FIGURE 8.3: PRICING STRATEGY TRADEOFF MATRIX

PENETRATION Price low in order to:	**SKIMMING** Price high in order to:
Win more + smaller deals`	Win fewer + bigger deals
Drive referral power	Drive brand power
Frequent discounts	Rare discounts
Sample packages	Flexible packages

STEP 4: Declare a North Star

There's an old adage that says you get what you measure. A bigger problem beyond not setting a deliberate pricing strategy is the lack of measurement. When is the time to pivot from penetration to neutral? The moment you set prices, the landscape changes, new information is available, and assumptions have taken a different shape. You may not get it right the first time, and that's okay. Ask yourself in this step:

- Which financial metrics are most important to improve next year?
- What other leading metrics influence our north star?
- What signals should we watch to ensure we picked the right north star?

You're probably wondering how long the EARN approach takes. To give you a classic product manager response, it depends.

No really, it does. It relies on how much data you have and how many people are working on the project. Step one takes the longest, but the remaining steps can be done in less time. If you have the data and make this a focused effort, completing the four steps of EARN should take anywhere from two to four weeks. Aim for version 1.0 and iterate. Do not strive for perfection but strive for done! Learn and improve from there.

I hope the EARN approach will help you spend more than six hours a year on your pricing strategy. I've successfully coached some of the best-run software companies in the world in using this approach, and success is predicated on understanding, measuring, and communicating value.

"But how do we measure value?" you must be wondering.

To answer this question, let's get R.E.A.L. about value for a second.

THE REAL VALUE OF VALUE

Measuring and understanding value takes effort and time; and once you think you've nailed it, something changes like your competitors, your customers, or your product. I don't want to fake the funk about how hard value-based pricing really is in the SaaS world.

The truth is, there will always be a gap between the value received and value perceived, sometimes in your favor, but most of the time, not. This is a notion known as perceived value.

One way to figure out perceived value is to straight-up ask. We'll fully explore talking to customers about value in **TRACK 9: MY PEOPLES COME FIRST**. But to preface, you want to talk to customers about value

PRICING TIP

Customers don't care about what you think your value is. They buy based on their perception of it.

often, such as asking how much the problem is costing them per year, or what the cost would be for an alternative way to solve the problem. It is not a good idea to ask them how much you should charge for something. Because truth be told, most people really don't know.

Here is a quick exercise for you to consider: What is your willingness to pay for a slice of pizza? (New York thin crust style, please.)

Right now, you're recalling all the prices you paid for pizza in the past along with how much you enjoyed the pizza. You'll use this reference data to frame how much is reasonable to pay for a decent slice of pizza. This also factors in all your preferences (cheesy or saucy), your income and budget (baller or broke college student), opportunity cost and alternatives (craving an In-N-Out burger instead), and who knows what else (your keto diet, childhood memories, your first date). So, what does pizza mean to you?

Hmmm, try quantifying that in a spreadsheet.

At some point, your brain will get tired of thinking and eventually land on "Eh, a few bucks makes sense." You'll find $3 to $5 as a 75-percent percentile range of what people will pay for a slice of pizza, but it ranges from $1 to $11, or about 10X for the exact same thing!

Crazy, right?

Well, not really. You'll get 10X differences in value perception all the time due to the indeterminate number of variables in play. And due to all these variables, value can be blurry.

Here is a piece of advice from me on pricing to "blurry value." Or better yet, I call it an anti-guide you might find counter intuitive and even uncomfortable.

My advice is this: don't price to value!

Wait. What?

You read that right. Don't price to value ... at least until you know what the value is and how to measure it. Pricing to blurry value can lead you down the wrong path. You have to be clear about the value you want to charge for.

Try to gain a deeper sense of what people are willing to pay to solve the problem. Rather than calculating your idea of value in an Excel spreadsheet, try to understand how they are anchoring value, what that value means to them, and what evidence you can grab of what people really paid. Find out where in the customer frame of reference you can educate buyers to increase their value perception.

I admit that getting value right is challenging. One challenge is that pricing to value takes a ton of practice and is darn hard to achieve out of the gate. But if you start by casting a net that helps you understand the buyer's frame of reference and desire to solve the problem, you will have a stronger basis to avoid pricing based on blurry value.

The other challenge with value is that it's not static; it's context-dependent and changes over time, especially in technology and software space.

Another challenge is that people don't think of value in the purest form. What I mean is most people compare value to something else. Some of the reference points are for some other anchor.

Remember the pizza example I introduced earlier? It is entirely possible for the value for the same thing with the same person to be different from day-to-day depending on circumstances. My value for ice cold water is different in the winter than it is in the summer. It's the same product, same person, different circumstances, but a different value perception.

"So how the heck am I supposed to price based on something that never stays still?" you're thinking.

This is where the fun begins.

After years and years of working with different tech companies around value, I've produced a simple framework called R.E.A.L. to understand value in a variety of ways. Check it out in **FIGURE 8.4**.

Aw Snap! Let's unpack this, shall we?

FIGURE 8.4: THE REAL VALUE FRAMEWORK

RELATIVITY	ECONOMIC	ANCHOR	LIKELIHOOD
Comparison or ratio between the price for something relative to another amount	Measure of economic cost versus economic benefit—a Return On Investment (ROI)	A direct or indirect pricing reference point to establish a baseline for comparison	The probability of achieving the full or expected value

RELATIVITY

When you think of paying for something often, you think of it relative to something else, usually as a percentage of something else.

Think about how much you spend on your car payment versus your mortgage payment. Or think about one of the most popular ratios from the finance industry, (remember I was a financial analyst once), which is your percentage of your mortgage or car payment to your monthly gross income.

These ratios are very prevalent in B2B companies and how they make decisions. A common scenario is a B2B SaaS buyer who thinks about your price as a percentage of their annual IT or technology budget. For example, if your SaaS product is going to cost them 10 percent of their budget, it could be viewed as expensive, even if the ROI is justified.

Due to these innate ratios, your product value might have an artificial ceiling from the buyer's perspective before they even see your product. This concept is different from the anchoring effect, which we'll talk about in just a moment, but the point with relativity is that you have to take into account the greater context of other expenditures to understand how to frame your value.

ECONOMIC

This is the first thing most SaaSletes think about when they think about value. Ask yourself, is the ROI or the cost-benefit easy to measure? And more importantly, is it proven?

You want to measure the estimated annual return on your product. As a shortcut, Silicon Valley has a rule of thumb to generate 10X to 20X return on investment. That is, you should charge 1/10 to 1/20 of the ROI you can measure and prove.

Thing is, ROI is hard to prove, and therefore, many prospects and customers won't believe them. That's when you go deeper with your research by asking customers who actually experienced the value to give you a hard proof point like labor savings, an increase in sales, whatever they can measure and report with confidence. These proof points go a long way in building confidence behind your ROI.

When asking for ROI from customers, they might give you a proof point you did not expect, which is a great piece of data to inform your pricing model. The deeper you understand how value is generated and perceived by your customer, the easier it would be for you to capture that value based on ROI.

One great technique that allows you to break down value and measure ROI is the Economic Value Estimation method that was brought up in my interview with Dwight Porter at the end of **TRACK 6**. I share an illustration of the technique in **FIGURE 8.5**. You start with the next-best alternative to your product, add all your positive differentiating values, subtract your negative values, and calculate the economic value pool in which to share with your customer.

FIGURE 8.5: ECONOMIC VALUE ESTIMATION

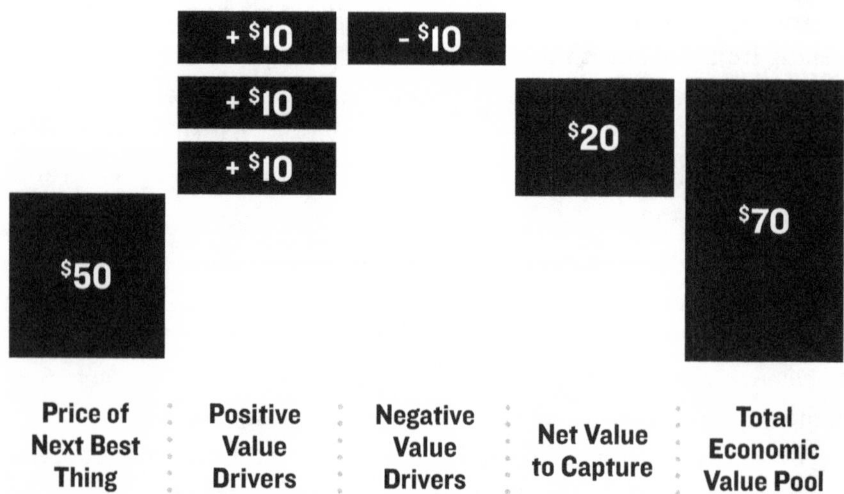

ANCHOR

This is one of the most powerful aspects of pricing to value. Understanding value is understanding how your buyers anchor that value. In other words, you want to understand what they are comparing your SaaS product to when determining if it is cheap, fair, or expensive. And if that comparison apples-to-apples.

The most readily available alternative can be a competitor or could also be something less tangible such as building it in-house or staying in the current status quo. The big lesson here is if you don't understand the anchor, you won't have an opportunity to correct or influence the anchor in order to frame your value the right way.

> **PRICING TIP**
>
> Numerical anchoring is a powerful and inescapable way to frame value.

LIKELIHOOD

This is the most forgotten aspect of value. Software is really a promise of value, not value in and of itself. Just because they bought software does not guarantee they will get the benefit. There is always some work on the customer's end to get set up, complete training, and use it properly over time in order to realize the savings, sales, or risk avoidance they hope to achieve.

So why does likelihood matter? The longer it takes to get to value or the more work on a customer side to experience value, the more it influences their perception of value—by reducing it!

Understanding, defining, measuring, and communicating your value is the underpinning for any successful pricing model. There are no shortcuts

> **PRICING TIP**
>
> Fast value makes fast friends! And the quicker the path is to the value, the more of the value you can capture.

PRICING TIP

Stop guessing and know your value with concrete proof. It is what separates the good SaaS businesses from the great ones out there.

to knowing your value; it just takes hard work and consistency. And yes, it can get frustrating and tedious trying to figure out your value, but it's important if you are serious about capturing your fair share of it.

I'll take it up a notch and say you need to know your value for each target customer segment you want to serve. And trust me, knowing your customers is the key to good pricing. There is no way around it. The better you know your customers, the easier it will be to identify their needs, estimate their willingness to pay, and grow them over time.

So let's dive deeper into knowing your customers. In the next chapter, we are going to take a "dilated" look into how to segment customers by what they W.A.N.T., because when worst comes to worst, your peoples should always come first.

MY PEOPLES COME FIRST

FIND AND LOVE THE RIGHT CUSTOMER

THIS URBAN CATCHPHRASE, A LAID BACK VERSION OF THE LYRIC FROM MOBB DEEP'S HAVOC IN THEIR BANGER "SURVIVAL OF THE FITTEST," GRACED THE AIRWAVES IN 1995.

I love how Dilated Peoples took just one line to an entire new level. And moreover, how an east coast lyric became a west coast anthem, an example that hip-hop isn't about violence, drugs, and womanizing. To me, it's really about unity and harmony among people.

And people, in all their imperfect beauty, are the cause and effect of all technology. They are, and should always be, at the nucleus of every tech product we build and price.

With clarity around your growth goals, product strategy, and value from the previous track, you are now ready to focus on the next question in the 5Q framework. Shifting from understanding the "Why" to identifying the "Who," you must now focus on understanding your most ideal customers and the painful problems they want to solve and are willing to pay for. I will share my method for talking to customers about pricing and segmenting them into meaningful buckets to make it easier to monetize the right value. Nothing happens in business until customers pay you money.

In order to put people at the center, you need a well-defined set of customer profiles with meaningful differences in willingness to pay and value. Ask yourself:

1. Are buyers well-defined and have different CAC or buying behavior?
2. Do buyers show different usage, complexity, or necessity that leads to differences in value?

But where does it all start? It starts by knowing your customers, and more importantly, knowing what they W.A.N.T.

WHATCHA WANT?

In many B2B SaaS businesses, the rule for segmenting customers has always been to break them up into small, medium, and large-sized customers. Rather than taking a fresh and innovative approach to grouping customers, most overlook critical attributes that govern why and what customers buy. In other words, they don't know what customers really want.

Like most things in life, knowing what customers want is easier said than done. While trying to segment customers, we can easily be dragged from the forest down into the trees and deeper into the branches of spreadsheets, feature lists, revenue targets, sales demands, RFPs, and board decks.

And since my calling in life is to make the ambiguous concepts in pricing easier to understand and more approachable, I have a method for how to think about segmenting customers. Let's dive in.

Segmentation is coined as a marketing strategy to target messaging and positioning for advertising and sales leads. And yes, this is true, but it's not the full story.

What many pricing strategists know, but might not tell you, is that segmentation is the key to unlocking true value potential. The punchline is that you need to sell different values to different customers to gain traction and scale. Problem is, this is hard to do with a vanilla and primitive segmentation by size only (e.g., number of employees or revenue size).

Because I know you've been dying for more economic theory, take a look at the chart in **FIGURE 9.1**. If you only charged one price (**P1**), you'll attract a limited audience to create demand-driven volume. However, if you charge different prices (**P2** and **P3**) for different offerings, you will attract different audiences, and hence, higher volumes and more overall profit. This is known in economic theory as moving from "rectangle to triangle." With value-based segmentation, you can capture more business and grow faster by offering different prices for different values to different customers.

FIGURE 9.1: FROM RECTANGLE TO TRIANGLE WITH SEGMENTATION

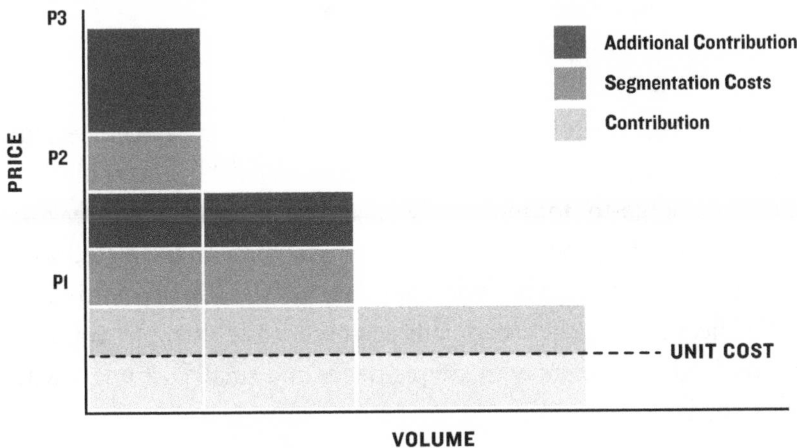

For those who are not too grounded in economic theory (which is most of us), I offer a more intuitive way to think about dimensions for value-based segmentation of customers. Meet the four dimensions of the W.A.N.T. framework, which is to segment your customers by:

1. **Who** they Are
2. How they **Act**
3. What they **Need**
4. How they **Think**

Check out the example in **FIGURE 9.2**. It shows how RideShareCo uses deep knowledge of who their customers are and what they want in different ride hailing options.

FIGURE 9.2: EXAMPLE W.A.N.T. SEGMENTATION BY RIDESHARECO

RideShareCo: Customer Segmentation

Highest WTP	**RideShare Fire**
Value Extra Space	**RideShare Soccer Mom**
Value Speed	**RideShare Whip**
Lowest WTP	**RideShare Bus**

To better understand the W.A.N.T. framework, I'll unpack the four dimensions one by one:

WHO THEY ARE

"Who" refers to the observable persona, company attributes, or characteristics of your customers. Commonly called "firmographics" in SaaS, this is the "go-to" for most early-stage SaaS businesses to break up their customers. The good news is that firmographics are correlated with different buying and usage behavior, but they fall short in accounting for the differences in value between your customers. For example, you may encounter large customers with simple needs and small customers with complex needs.

PRICING TIP

It is okay to start with firmographics, but as soon as you gain more customers and are headed toward product-market fit, you should quickly evolve from this form of segmentation.

In my experience, the disheartening reality is that very few firms evolve their segmentation because the status quo is ingrained with how they report (P&L), how they market (messages), and how they sell (channels). Changing it up can seem like a heroic effort, so why bother?
Guess what? Your pricing segmentation does not need to be the same as your sales, marketing, or customer success segmentation schemes. For pricing, you can break down your target customers into well-informed sub-groups to reveal differences in how they act, what they need, and how they think. You don't need to turn your company upside to improve your customer segmentation, so exhale in a sigh of relief.

HOW THEY ACT

The next step to evolve your customer understanding is to observe and track metrics on how they act. To do this, you need to have a good set of reporting metrics on how customers buy and use your product. The research tips and techniques we covered in **TRACK 6**, will come in handy in this case.

You will be one step closer to identifying what value means for your customer's business. What users do in your software tells you how much complexity they're dealing with, how much help they need from you, and how much money they're willing to spend. You don't need 10,000 customers to start an activity analysis. You can start with as little as 30 customers to detect early patterns.

WHAT THEY NEED

The most elusive but most important factor in segmenting customers is knowing what they need. The answer to this question is critical for not only determining how much to charge, but also, what value to charge for. The best way to figure out what a customer needs is to ask them; there is no other way around it. The rub for most SaaS companies is that customers struggle with articulating what they need. They're more adept in explaining their problem and how it impacts them. It's up to you to tell them what they need in order to solve the problem. That's right, you!

I know that is not a satisfying answer, but the best doctors, mechanics, counselors, accountants, and lawyers out there can figure out the need after listening to the client explain the problem. The key is in the line of questioning to uncover the true needs behind the problem, especially the needs they are willing to pay for in your product. **FIGURE 9.3** offers a set of sample survey questions you can ask customers to unravel their true needs behind the problem to bolster your segmentation.

FIGURE 9.3: QUESTIONS TO UNCOVER CUSTOMER NEEDS

- What does value mean to you?
- What do you measure?
- What does success look like?
- How do you make your customers successful?
- How much do you estimate this problem costs you per year?
- What solutions have you tried to date? Why haven't they worked?
- What other tools do you use to solve the problem?

The list of questions in **FIGURE 9.3** should help to open your line of questioning. We'll cover how to construct a good customer survey in the next section of this track. But for now, let's hit on the last part of the W.A.N.T. framework.

HOW THEY THINK

Saving the best for last, you might be assuming. Actually, I'm saving the most abstract for last: getting into your customer's head to understand what makes them buy, use, or cancel. Getting into their perceptions of value, such as whether they view your solution as a cost center or profit generator, a critical business need or a nice to have extra, a brand-boosting premium product or the thriftiest option available.

Surveys work well to start digging into perceptions, but you must supplement survey responses with deep dive interviews to truly understand your customer's motives, mental framing, and opinions they have about your product.

Truth is, not all B2B SaaS companies have the time and resources to do deep dive customer research. Teams are tied up staying on top of their day-to-day responsibilities, and who has the free time for customer interviews?

No one does. You'll have to make an earnest effort to make the time and invest the resources. You can get up and running with a third party as a boost, then make customer research a central part of your discovery process over time.

The best way to tease out how your customers think about your product is using open-ended, but carefully crafted questions that probe into the why behind their purchase and usage. Whether it's Simon Sinek or Japanese auto manufacturers, getting deep behind the why is the best way to understand how your customers think about value, how your solution fits into their world, and how price factors into their decision making.

PRICING TIP

The closer you get with the customer, the closer you will be to realizing your full potential to deliver and capture value.

The W.A.N.T. framework is a process to capture meaningful data to better understand and distinguish your customers, which will lead you towards a value-based segmentation that will make pricing easier. Each element in W.A.N.T. is additive to the other, and will fully inform your target personas, pricing metric, packages/bundles, and your prices.

"But Marcos, how do we talk to customers about value in the first place? What should we say or not say?"

Okay, let's talk about talking to customers.

HAVING THE TALK

Listen, I know that talking to customers is easier said than done. First, you have to be careful not to mismanage their expectations as most customers have a limited understanding of what it takes to build software. And second, they are focused on their own work and are busy doing their thing, so getting their undivided attention is a challenge. It is fair to say that talking to customers will take effort and planning, but they're also the reason you're in business, right? To keep it real, you need to show love to those who love you.

You might be tempted to straight-up ask customers what they are willing to pay for your product. I strongly advise you to fight this urge for a few reasons:

- Some buyers might not fully understand the use cases and impact of your product; moreover, some users may not understand the cost of your product or alternatives.
- Customers have a narrow context for which to value your product (they might be using 10 percent of the product), so willingness to pay may not represent the value completely.
- And yes, some customers may not be honest with how much they are willing to pay. They have an incentive to pay as little as possible, and they don't want to invite a price increase.

If you simply ask people what they want to pay for your product, you might walk away with bad advice. Your monetization strategy might be based on lies; not the nefarious lies, but the "guesswork with no proof" kind of thing that could send your growth down the toilet.

The better path is to ask people about value, not price. Here are a few quick steps to help you frame a conversation around value with a customer:

- First, start with the basics. Ask about how they use the product today and how it's working for them. Is the product delivering on the value promise for the job they hired it to do?
- Second, what features do they care about and what features do they not care about at all? This is important to understand if your packaging is effective and you're giving them what they want versus what they need.
- Third, you want to get a sense for how they feel about the structure of the pricing model. Is the pricing metric right so they feel good about what they pay compared to how much they use the product? Is billing predictable and easy to understand? Do they feel like they're getting a good bang for the buck overall?

If you want to take it further, **FIGURE 9.4** has a quick-reference customer survey or interview questions to help you structure your conversations with customers.

Virtual high five accepted!

Ask customers about price to get a lie; ask them about value to get the truth.

"But Marcos, what about the difference in talking to users versus buyers?" you ask.

Especially in enterprise software, users and buyers are typically different people, so who should you take the time to talk to?

My bias is towards talking to buyers, but you want a sample of users to really understand how they're extracting value. So, the short answer is both, but be sure to add a filter question to compare answers between buyers and users.

Continuous conversations with customers are a common trait among successful SaaS companies. In fact, health and beauty software leader

FIGURE 9.4: CUSTOMER SURVEY/INTERVIEW QUESTIONS

Screener

- Do you feel knowledgeable enough about the topic to answer some questions?
- How familiar are you with the features, benefits and costs of PRODUCT?
- How often do you use PRODUCT?

Product Usage

- Which COMPANY package do you currently use?
- How often do you use PRODUCT / PACKAGE?

Product Market Fit

- What is the main benefit you receive from using PRODUCT?
- On a scale of 1 to 10, how would you rate PRODUCT overall?
- It's great to hear you are a fan. Which features do you value the most?
- Thanks for your feedback. Our goal is to create the best possible products and services. How can we improve your experience?
- Thanks for your feedback. We value all ideas and suggestions from customers. What is missing or disappointing in your experience with us?

Product Benefits

- The next question asks you which features are important when [situation or job to be done when using our product]
- In the list below, choose which is the most and which is the least important to you when [situation].

Willingness to Pay

- What would be your preferred way to license PRODUCT?
- Which frequency of license payments do you prefer?

CONTINUED →

- Consider the benefits you marked as most important. If all those benefits were bundled together, and the licensing metric (users/volume/fixed rate) and billing cycle were set as you wished ...
- Hypothetically, if PRODUCT were no longer available, what would you do?
- How much time and money do you estimate that would take?
- Which competitors would you consider?
- How would that impact your operations?

Demographics

- Which is your type of organization?
- Which of the following best describes the area or department you work in?
- What is your role in purchasing software solutions for your company?

Anything Else & Thanks

- Is there anything else you would like to tell us?
- We'd like to invite you to participate in a 30 minute follow-up discussion session, exploring further your ideas and opinions. Would you be able to participate?
- Thanks a lot for agreeing to help further.

MindBody deploys a dedicated research team to keep their finger on the pulse of their customer base. Staying well in tune with how customers feel, how they value the product, and areas where you can add more value are critical ingredients to your monetization plan. Try the Playback exercise at the end of this track to get a better sense of what your customers need. I guarantee you'll learn something valuable.

PRICING TIP

As a shortcut, send the customer value survey to the same audience as your Net Promoter Score (NPS) survey to keep things simple.

SECRETS TO SEGMENTATION

Now that you put your "peoples" first by understanding what they W.A.N.T. and listening to learn what value means to them, it is time to figure out how to group them into logical buckets. The art of segmentation is tricky, and you'll find 1000 ways to break up customers into groups. The permutations can be overwhelming.

I'll let you in a little secret...there are only a few key dimensions that really matter in value-based segmentation.

I like to think of **FIGURE 9.5** as a convenient complement to my W.A.N.T. approach. It does a nice job of laying out examples of behaviors, attitudes, and needs to look for in your data, surveys, and interviews. These common dimensions are a great place to gather ideas for what to use for segmentation.

FIGURE 9.5: DIMENSIONS FOR VALUE-BASED SEGMENTATION

Behaviors

- Range or type of products and services bought
- Reasons for style of product use (buying for re-sell)
- How purchase decisions are made
- Attitudes to decisions (level of risk involved)

Attitudes

- Is the product or service critical to the business
- What is the desired relationship / partnership
- Emotional attachment to the industry
- Expertise or knowledge level
- Level of loyalty

Needs & Preferences

- Product specific functionality requirements
- Level / nature of customer support or service
- Commercial terms
- Preferred buying channels

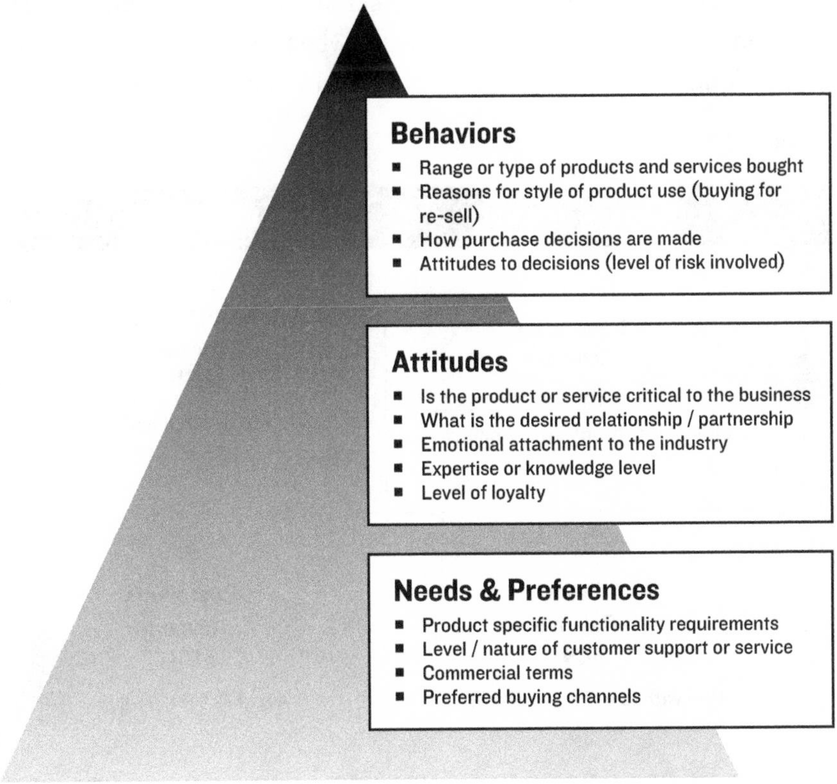

The more information you capture across these three dimensions, behaviors, attitudes, needs/preferences, the easier it will become to segment customers based on value. This in turn makes it easier to build packages to better serve the target customer segment (which is the topic of the next track, **TRACK 10: THE CHOICE IS YOURS**).

A thorough segmentation analysis project, from research to recommendation, could take a few months to complete. But what if you don't have the time or data to do a robust segmentation analysis?

Like I mentioned before, there are only two dimensions in value-based segmentation that you need to focus on the most:

- How much value they want
- How much they are willing to pay for that value

Focusing on these two dimensions will get you 80 percent of the way there in defining your value-based segmentation. I still encourage you to do the more robust segmentation analysis when you're ready, but to move things along, I will share my segmentation shortcut in **FIGURE 9.6.**

FIGURE 9.6: THE SEGMENTATION SHORTCUT

	LOW USAGE INTENSITY	HIGH USAGE INTENSITY
HIGH WTP	**% Customers** **% Revenue** **ACV** Win with add-ons and stickiness	**% Customers** **% Revenue** **ACV** Win with premium offering and services
LOW WTP	**% Customers** **% Revenue** **ACV** Win with low friction offerings	**% Customers** **% Revenue** **ACV** Avoid like the plague

Think about willingness to pay (WTP) as the customer's budget and appetite to spend on software/services. And think about usage intensity as how much they want to use from software/services. Let me explain the four main segments you see in the chart.

Customers with a low willingness to pay and low usage intensity can be served with a simple package and straightforward price that requires little activation energy to get started; the play is to win with low friction, not necessarily with low prices.

Let's move on to customers that exhibit a higher willingness to pay, but low usage intensity with simple needs. This group is appealing but beware as these customers tend to attract a lot of competitors. Because of this, the best play is to offer a package that meets them where they are in their maturity lifecycle, quickly expand as their appetite grows, and sign them up for annual contract terms or longer. Monitor this group closely and look for signs they are ready to take on more of your product.

Customers with a low willingness to pay but demand high usage intensity will find their way into your customer base. To state the obvious, you want to avoid these customers like the plague, or at least minimize these types of customers in your base; say less than 10 percent. For those that make it into your population, the best play is to try to right-size these customers into a lower-priced package or nudge their contract up with add-ons or services to cover their high demands without a full upgrade to the next tier.

Customers that show high willingness to pay along with high usage intensity are a prime group for your most premium package. This package includes most of your features, some add-ons, higher usage limits, and the most hands-on experience in the form of more training, onboarding, and customer support. The play for this group is to roll out the red carpet and give them the attention they deserve.

There you have it. A full breakdown of understanding and measuring what your customers W.A.N.T., a quick hit list of questions to help you set up value conversations, and a shortcut chart for how to segment your audience.

You can thank me by trying out the exercise in the Playback. It will be worth your time, I promise.

PLAYBACK EXERCISE

There is no better time than the present. Write down your friendliest customers. They are the ones in your latest beta testing group or are active members of your VIP Council. These types of customers always show up to your conferences, give you feedback on your releases, and refer you to other customers. You should be able to rattle off a few in short order. Here's the assignment:

- Write down five customer accounts and get their contact info (email at least, phone if you have it).
- Use the customer survey and value questions to craft a short script, run it by a colleague.
- Email the five accounts and ask for time to talk about what value means to them (customers love to tell you how to give them more value, especially if they are happy already).
- Talk to all those customers, record the calls, and write down what you learned. It's that easy to get started.

To put it all in one line, talk to your customers. To succeed with pricing, you need to have a solid understanding of who they are, how they act, what they want, and how they think about your product. Use this information to feed your value-based segmentation, define buyer journeys and triggers to buy, and map out user interaction points within your product throughout their problem life cycle.

INTERLUDE

I can honestly say that one of my most fun interviews was with fellow pricing thought leader, Kyle Poyar. I met Kyle at a SaaS conference and quickly realized we shared similar roles in our respective investment firms and similar points of view on pricing.

Plus, Kyle is an all-around good dude who keeps it real.

Our interview explored a variety of topics around pricing, but I loved his view of customer segmentation. Here is an excerpt from our interview, enjoy!

MARCOS: *Let's jump in. I've spoken to scores of SaaS founders about their biggest pricing challenges. What are you hearing out there as challenges or blind spots for founders when it comes to pricing and segmentation?*

KYLE: I think some SaaS founders have become too product centric. Too many companies don't step back and ask themselves questions like what do we want to be when we grow up, what does our brand stand for, and how do we win in this market as it relates to pricing?

MARCOS: *I completely agree. Some businesses over-index on features A, B, and C. But in reality, you are pricing a specific experience for a specific target audience. Any tips or tricks to help founders segment better and define their target audience, especially if they don't have a rich data set?*

KYLE: Yeah, so the simple version of what I do is take a download of all opportunities for the last year or 18 months, enrich that data with services like Clearbit or offshore resources to help out. Then, get information on where the company is based, their industry, the size of the company, and the seniority of the most senior person you talk to, and I also like to look at use cases, which are different from the other factors.

So, I take that information and the easiest thing to track is to the expected ARR for every 100 of these opportunities you have, which is multiplying the win rate and the deal sizes that you see.

Then what you tend to find are pockets that are four to five times better than everything else. From there you decide which pockets to go deeper on and take a more in-depth approach with and qualitative insights, feedback from the sales team, look at what competitors are doing, talk to the product team on what capabilities are needed to win in that space. To me, this basic analysis will give you a lot of the hypotheses and ideas to lean into.

MARCOS: *I really like the step-by-step you laid out. I've always looked at the opportunity data to find customer pockets where you find buyers that are orders of magnitude more findable, winnable, growable, and "happyable."*

KYLE: There's a mentality, especially in venture-funded software, there's going to be a dominant player and you need to be there as fast

CONTINUED →

as you can—a "winner take all" market that you can dominate but keeps getting debunked. A salesforce might dominate CRM, but there are plenty of successful companies serving niche CRM spaces. It's actually not just one CRM market out there. Think about different plays and how to win in different niches.

MARCOS: *Great advice and I agree, there's a race to be king of the hill, but there are many hills out there. If you go after a niche that you serve really well, you can double-down and dominate that hill, resulting in better product market fit and lower CAC from referrals.*

KYLE: Segmentation plays a huge role there. And when I run a segmentation project, I look for pockets where the company has had success to date: higher win rates, faster deal cycles, bigger deal sizes, better retention, and expansion.

You can focus on these pockets in the market where the company has great traction so far and others are underserved by other players, you can lean into on the product side by building a bigger moat in that space and on the GTM side by giving your BDR (Business Development Rep) outbound team the list of 10,000 best leads and exhaust that segment first, then expand from a position of strength, either by going deeper to provide more value with more product, going more horizontal, or by going upmarket or into verticals with similar leads.

MARCOS: *Solid and smart way to grow! Most clients start segmentation with a small, medium, large, and may not have much data to do a full-blown scientific analysis. Is there a piece of advice to SaaSletes to get better at segmenting target customers?*

KYLE: When I hear things like, "some customers push back on our price" and others find us "really cheap," that usually tells me that there might be a segmentation issue.

MARCOS: *That's a great signal to look out for. Any last thoughts on how segmentation relates to pricing?*

KYLE: To me, a lot of pricing and packaging decisions start with knowing your target customers and quantifying the value (saving time, reducing risk, generating revenue, even if back of the envelope). But, if you can pick a subset of your personas to really price well for, as opposed to theoretically fitting the entire market – this is super foundational and provides insights that allows you to set the right balance in pricing to value.

Now that we talked about knowing your customers inside out, let's keep this train moving from the WHO in the 5Q framework to the WHAT and unpack the topic of crafting packages of specific value for your specific audience.

If the topic of packaging is intimidating, don't fret. We'll break it down with a framework to make it as easy as herding sheep (or should I say black sheep?).

THE CHOICE IS YOURS

PACKAGE THE EXPERIENCE, NOT THE FEATURES

A WOLF IN SHEEP'S CLOTHING WAS ONE HELL OF AN ALBUM.

In fact, it sold well, hitting No. 30 on the Billboard chart. It was easy to be overshadowed in the wave of artists in the Afro-centricity movement, but Black Sheep continued to punch above their weight, making witty music laced with satire, crisp lyrics, and a beat that could ignite an audience.

The duo clearly realized things were changing in hip-hop, so they didn't follow the famed 90's hip-hop collective, Native Tongues', template like the other groups. Nope, Dre and Mr. Lawnge (pronounced "Long") did their own thing on their album, letting assumptions slide off them like Teflon. They made their own decisions about their music. The song "The Choice Is Yours" clearly reflected the vibe and message of the group in a way that empowered anyone who listened to it.

Now it's time for you to make your decisions about what value to package up and offer customers. In this track, we'll build on what we learned to craft the right experience for the right buyer. Armed with a clear focus on how you'll grow and a crisp definition of your target customers, I will teach you how to approach packaging using plenty of meaty examples from successful B2B SaaS companies, as well as techniques to help you avoid copying others and take control of your packaging.

PRICING TIP

Don't follow the pack when it comes to packaging. The choice is yours to decide which value to include for which customers. You are in control.

THE OFFER MIX

Anchoring to the 5Q framework, now that you have a good sense for the WHY behind your pricing strategy, and WHO is buying your product, we can get to the part around WHAT to offer them.

This is known as designing an offer mix.

An *offer mix* is more than a list of software features your customer will have access to in the product. It is a combination of value drivers that will shape the customer's perception and experience around your brand, from discovery, to onboarding and training, to billing and customer support.

PRICING TIP

When designing an offer mix, think about the entire customer experience, not just the feature set.

There are a number of ways to build an offer mix, so how should you go about choosing the technique that is right for you?

First, use the 5Q framework to ground yourself by referring to the insights you've gathered determining the WHY and the WHO. Take a good look at your growth plan and segmentation and ask yourself:

- Where is the growth coming from? Existing or new markets? Price or volume?
- Do I have the right value to serve these segments well? Is there a segment we should stop serving?
- How will customers of tomorrow look compared to our existing customers?
- Do my customers have vastly different budgets, alternatives and use cases?

Answers to these questions will drive purpose and clarity around your target customer segments. This is a critical first step in packaging, as any package without a target will always miss the mark.

In **FIGURE 10.1**, I summarize the most common packaging structures in SaaS today. Use this list to get some ideas and inspiration for your packaging structure.

FIGURE 10.1: COMMON SAAS PACKAGING STRUCTURES

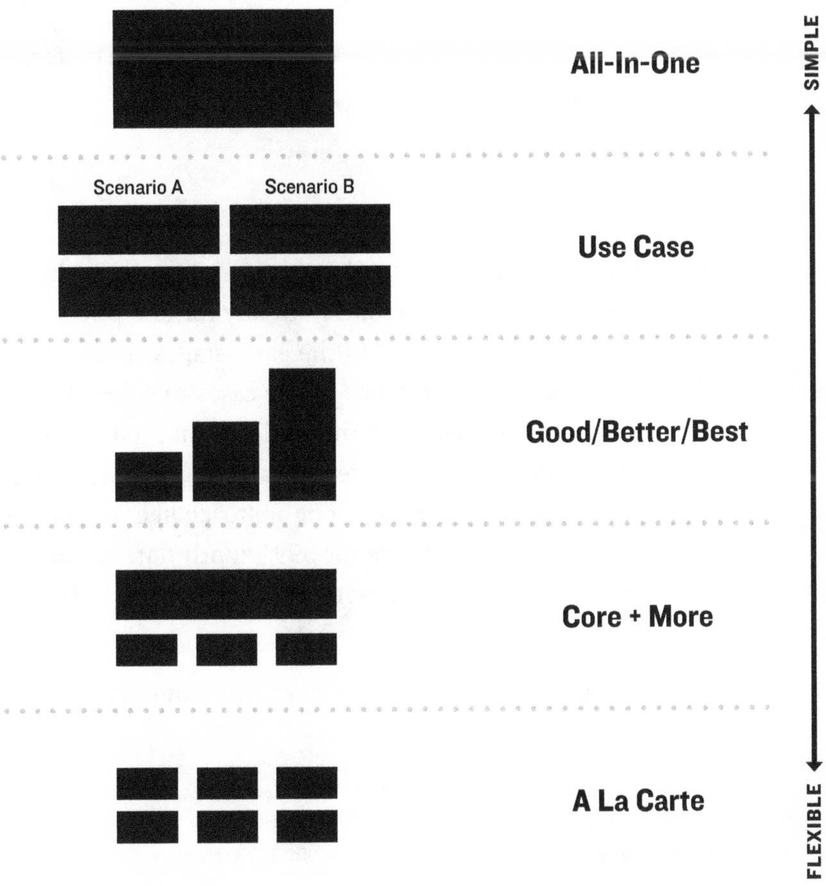

SIMPLE

All-In-One

Scenario A Scenario B

Use Case

Good/Better/Best

Core + More

A La Carte

FLEXIBLE

These five packaging structures cover the spectrum of techniques used by practically all B2B SaaS companies. Ranging from the most flexible way to offer value, the A La Carte menu, all the way to the simplest form of packaging, giving away everything for one price.

There's nothing like real examples to illustrate the different packaging structures out there. Let's look at example structures used by some of the most successful SaaS companies, starting with **FIGURE 10.2**, the All-In-One.

FIGURE 10.2: EXAMPLE OF ALL-IN-ONE PACKAGING STRUCTURE

BUSINESS PLAN
All for one price: $99/MONTH

No value metric for capturing growth. No onboarding or training required or offered.

Includes all features:

- Unlimited projects
- Unlimited users
- Unlimited access to templates
- Unlimited third-party access
- Premium features like advanced admin controls + priority support
- Only limit is file storage space

This structure works for early-stage SaaS businesses with limited features but grow out of this model and add a value metric and tiering once you gain traction.

The **ALL-IN-ONE** packaging structure does a nice job keeping things simple for the audience with only one option to buy for one price. This is a great structure when the product is in the early stages, and you are laser-focused on a specific target audience or use cases to solve. As you gain traction with customers and build out the product, you should expand into one of the tiered structures to offer different value to different buyers. However, if you want to stay using the all-in-one approach like the famous Basecamp project management software for $99/month flat, be sure to optimize your entire operations to generate great economics in lieu of fast growth.

FIGURE 10.3: EXAMPLE USE CASE / USER PERSONA PACKAGING STRUCTURE

Focus is on specific use case to find the right leads to maximize close rate. Value metric is **leads.**

Starts at $80/MONTH and up

- 50 message credits
- Premium filters
- Unlimited searching
- Potential leads
- Company intelligence

Focus is on specific use case to find the right leads to maximize close rate. Value metric is **candidates.**

Starts at $150/MONTH and up

- 50+ message credits
- Premium filters
- Unlimited searching
- Candidate tracking
- Project dashboard, and more...

This structure works well for workflow software that solves specific but different needs and willingness to pay. Be sure to harmonize across plans for consistency and include add-ons and tiers under each plan for expansion revenue.

Go with a **USE CASE/USER PERSONA** packaging structure as seen in **FIGURE 10.3** when you need to cater to different target audiences that do not have much in common and would rarely overlap. In this type of structure, it is important to define the outcome of the use case and how your product achieves this outcome. No SaaS company uses this packaging structure better than LinkedIn. LinkedIn offers specific packages to job seekers, networkers, sales reps, and recruiters to solve for their unique use cases within their platform.

FIGURE 10.4: EXAMPLE OF GOOD BETTER BEST PACKAGING STRUCTURE

STARTER

Focus on quick and easy entry point into the product at $19/**MONTH**. Value metric is **users**.

Base features:

- 5 projects
- 1 workspace
- 1GB storage
- Community support

PRO

Focus on growing customers in the sweet spot at $**49/MONTH+**. Value metric is **users**.

Base + advanced features:

- Unlimited projects
- 5 workspaces
- 100GB storage
- Priority support with chat
- Automations
- Integrations
- Add-on options, like SSO

ENTERPRISE

Focus on large and complex customers looking for custom features and services at $**99/MONTH+**. Value metric is **users**.

Everything in Pro, plus:

- Unlimited projects
- Unlimited workspaces
- Unlimited storage
- Dedicated representatives
- Onboarding + training
- Premium or custom APIs and integrations
- Fancy security & privacy features
- SSO
- Extra control-freak super admin functions
- Needlessly complicated reports and analytics

This structure works well for most software with enough features and service differentiation. Be sure to limit the right usage in the entry plan so that 50% or more grow into your sweet spot plan in the middle.

GOOD BETTER BEST, shown in **FIGURE 10.4**, is used by over 70 percent of SaaS businesses because it works so well. B2B SaaS companies like Slack have taken the most common packaging approach in SaaS, Good Better Best, and made it into a powerful growth lever by sticking to the principles of the 5Q framework. For example, Slack's growth goal was clear from the beginning: Get as many people using the product as quickly as possible. They focused on their target customer of high-tech companies, and finally, built three experiences to serve the right need for the right audience by artfully limiting access to message history, storage capacity, and other features. Slack's packaging is Good Better Best at its best.

FIGURE 10.5: EXAMPLE OF CORE AND MORE PACKAGING STRUCTURE

HR BASE PLATFORM

Every customer starts here no matter what. Value metric is **per employee per month**, starting at $5/**MONTH**

Core features serve as foundation to get up and running. Includes:

- Standard workflows and automations
- Standard integrations
- Standard implementation
- Standard support

PAYROLL SOLUTION	**BENEFITS SOLUTION**	**VENDOR SOLUTION**
Includes payroll integrations and workflow solutions	Includes benefits administration and support	Manage contractors and third parties with TPA
Add $5/**MONTH**	Add $8/**MONTH**	Add $5/**MONTH**

This structure works for more complex platforms with extensive modules. The common foundation builds scale and has standalone value. Add a growth vector by tiering the base plan. Each add-on solution solves a complex use case from end to end.

The **CORE AND MORE PACKAGING STRUCTURE** shown in **FIGURE 10.5** puts a different spin on tiering in order to manage lots of variety in usage. This archetype assumes everyone starts from the same core product but can have very different sets of add-on workflows once they are up and running. And just like LEGO blocks, the Core and More model allows you to bolt on a set of solutions to the base plan. This works well for more complex enterprise applications that suppowrt many different workflows. Zenefits is a great example of selling a core base of HR management with bolt-ons to cover payroll, benefits, and more.

FIGURE 10.6: EXAMPLE OF A LA CARTE PACKAGING STRUCTURE

NETWORK MONITORING VISIBILITY Value metric is **devices and time.**	**SENSITIVE DATA SCANNING** Value metric is **per GB scanned.**	**INCIDENT MANAGEMENT** Value metric is **per user.**
INFRASTRUCTURE VISIBILITY Value is **per hosts per month.**	**LOG MANAGEMENT VISIBILITY** Value metric is **log events.**	**SYNTHETIC MONITORING VISIBILITY** Value metric is **test runs.**

This structure works for highly technical and complex platforms. The choice variety is appealing to technical buyers. Most value metrics are usage-based, and may differ between offerings. Each offering may include tiering and additional features.

FIGURE 10.6 shows the **A LA CARTE** model. Amazon Web Services (AWS) is a pioneer in the A La Carte packaging structure and has grown exponentially by giving their target customers what they really want—flexibility and control. This packaging method works well when there are too many variables to build a standard package. I usually see this technique applied in heavy technical and infrastructure products, such as servers, databases, data processing, and IT monitoring.

UNLOCK YOUR VALUE STATEMENT

These examples should help you think about a few common structures to start with. But features are not the focus point here, they are merely a means to an end. And that end, call it an outcome, impact, whatever, is really what the focus of the offer mix should be. Use this trick to unlock the value statement behind your features:

Ask yourself: What does the customer want to see as a result of using my software? Now, link that answer to what your software does (action verb). Use this action verb in your value statement. See the difference in this example to nudge you in the right direction:

- **These are features:** Gmail or Outlook integration
- **This is a value statement:** I need to access my email without leaving the software.

Here's another one:

- **These are features:** Payment portal integration, automated payment processing
- **This is a value statement:** I need to get paid seamlessly and quickly.

The advantage that value statements have over feature lists is that they force you to focus on the problem you are solving, not the features solving the problem. This shift in point of view makes it easier to bundle and unbundle features that might address the same need or potentially serves a different need for one specific segment. The key to good packaging in SaaS is to give the customer exactly what they want, no more, and no less.

FOCUS ON SERVICES

Like I mentioned in the beginning of this track, an offer mix is more than a list of features. Let's talk about how services play a role in the offer mix. Spoiler alert: for B2B subscription software, it typically plays a major role.

Services come in many different forms: onboarding, implementation, data migration, training, and strategic consulting. Considering the recent explosion in customer success as an expanded functional role in SaaS companies, the line gets blurry between services and support, so for the sake of argument I will lump in support as part of my definition of "services." You can argue against it, but hey, I view services as any way people can help the customer become successful using your software, period.

Many articles advocate for charging your services separate from your software license and keeping a clean line between the two fees. I partially agree with that advice, since one is a recurring value, and the other is

PRICING TIP

Services exist to shorten the path to value for your customer; and by shortening the path to value, you enable more recurring revenue.

a one-time value. You don't want to find yourself in a tangled mess of accounting, billing, and revenue recognition issues (not a core subject of this book, but not a bad topic to read up on).

My thesis is that if you want to craft the best experience for the right customer, you must factor services into the equation. In most cases, this leads to the question:

How much in services, such as onboarding, consulting, or training, should I include in my packages?

The answer: As little as possible to help the customer get from point A (no value) to point B (desired value). Services included as part of a package must be lean and well-defined with a clear scope, limits, period, and resource types.

Including services in your packages does not mean giving them away for free. This is a common mistake many SaaS companies make in a misguided effort to capture more recurring license revenue. Price to have some margin in your services to avoid a major drag on growth.

To show you what I mean, let's compare the three-year impact of two different services pricing strategies on SaaS financials:

- **Company A:** Provides services with an annual value of $1 million with a -20 percent gross margin, resulting in a $200K annual loss. Total losses over the three-year period are $600K.
- **Company B:** Provides the same $1 million annual value of services, but at a +20 percent margin, resulting in a $200K annual gain. Total gain over the three-year period is $600K.

Company A would need to sell $600K more in license fees to break even, while Company B has an extra $600K to invest in R&D, onboarding, or support.

When it comes to premium services like strategic consulting or priority support, consider making these add-ons or selectively added to your more extensive packages. White glove attention and expertise matters a lot to B2B clients with complex needs, and therefore, should be reserved for those who are willing to pay for them.

To offer an example, **FIGURE 10.7** shows you the general idea of how B2B SaaS companies like Mindbody and Jamf include foundational services in all their packages to help customers get up and running:

FIGURE 10.7: EXAMPLE OF SERVICES INCLUDED IN EVERY PACKAGE

With each package, you get:

- 1-on-1 setup and training
- Data migration support
- Unlimited staff logins
- Business education resources
- Live customer support
- Access on any device

What you'll notice in this example is how the business includes training, data migration, and support in the packages as part of the base experience their customers need to be successful. To be more specific, they know that data migration support is a major concern for most, if not all, of their customers, so they included the support right from the get-go.

But there are cases where services vary between customers or can extend beyond implementation. As an example of a different approach, SaaS companies like HubSpot and Marketo position their premium services as an add-on offering that be ongoing, as shown in **FIGURE 10.8**.

Marketo and HubSpot are intuitive and easy-to-use marketing platforms, so what's with the services? They knew they had a segment of their customer base who needed technical and strategic support, but not all of them, which makes this different compared to industry-focused companies like MindBody. In HubSpot's case, they offered customers an option to add services and therefore personalize their experience. They did so in a clever way that increases subscription revenue by charging for a fixed limit of hours per month (use them or lose them). Really smart packaging!

View services as a path to getting more subscription revenue. I recommend including just enough to get started as part of your base

FIGURE 10.8: SERVICES OFFERED AS A SUBSCRIPTION

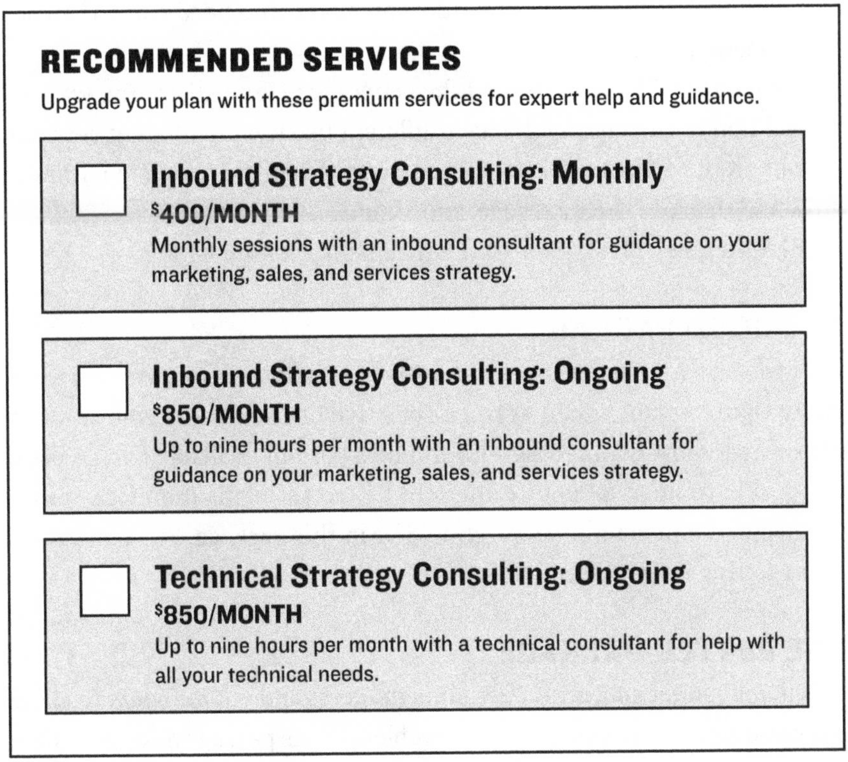

RECOMMENDED SERVICES

Upgrade your plan with these premium services for expert help and guidance.

☐ **Inbound Strategy Consulting: Monthly**
$400/MONTH
Monthly sessions with an inbound consultant for guidance on your marketing, sales, and services strategy.

☐ **Inbound Strategy Consulting: Ongoing**
$850/MONTH
Up to nine hours per month with an inbound consultant for guidance on your marketing, sales, and services strategy.

☐ **Technical Strategy Consulting: Ongoing**
$850/MONTH
Up to nine hours per month with a technical consultant for help with all your technical needs.

packages, and charge more for premium services. It might be less obvious what to include when you serve large customers or enterprise deals, but we'll talk more about that in **TRACK 14: MO MONEY, MO PROBLEMS**.

Armed with a solid foundation on how to build an offer mix, let's jump into the granddaddy of all SaaS packaging techniques, The Good Better Best model. This bad boy gets it's own spotlight because it is the proven leader when it comes to offer mixes.

YOU DOWN WITH GBB?

With over 70 percent of SaaS companies employing it, the runaway most common packaging method is Good Better Best (GBB).

It's an easy and effective way to align value with needs and willingness to pay. I love the way Kyle Poyar of OpenView Partners puts it: "Advanced features ... may be mission-critical for the Enterprise buyer ... but would be a 'bundle killer' for the mom-and-pop buyer who needs only the core functionality."

The idea of GBB is simple, and the benefits are immediate. You want to serve different customers who have different needs with different versions of your product. The trick is to do it in a way that allows them to naturally grow and upgrade their package over time.

Here's a quick breakdown of the mechanics behind GBB:

THE GOOD PACKAGE

This is usually your entry point into the software. In general, it's a lightweight version aimed at price-sensitive or basic users who want to get started. Most features are either limited or not available in this plan; the goal is to upgrade you to the middle, better plan. Therefore, about 15-20 percent of your business should be in this package. You don't want them getting too comfortable.

THE BETTER PACKAGE

This is your sweet spot and offers enough access and entitlements to allow the customer to solve most of their problems. This package also enjoys the psychological benefit of the "Goldilocks Effect," coined by sociologists Beth Bowman Hess and Joan M. Waring in 1978. Simply put, most risk-averse buyers will default to the middle option. You want to get this right as most of your revenue will come from this middle option. Look for 50 percent or more of your business to be in the Better package.

THE BEST PACKAGE

This is your most advanced package aimed at the "enterprise" buyer, which is code for buyers with larger volumes, more complex needs, and are most demanding in terms of services/support. Load up this plan with higher limits, beefy security/privacy, and white-glove services. You'll also need more flexibility around contract and payment terms, as well as offer-scaled pricing for high volumes. Some SaaS businesses make the mistake of trying to position this package as the most popular, however, the reality is that fewer buyers will be looking for this type of complexity and spend commitment. About 30 percent of your business should fall into this package.

Sounds great, right? GBB is all good in theory, but it's deceptively hard to pull off.

For one, you have to know your customers really well for GBB to work. This is why understanding the WHO before designing your packages is an essential prerequisite. There's no easy way to get specific customer information. It comes down to a combination of what activity you see in your customer base (both active and churned) and what you hear in product feedback. If you are still fuzzy around who your customers are and what they want, skip back to **TRACK 9**.

I want to briefly touch on the customers' willingness to pay (WTP) again. GBB simplifies the buyer's journey by showing them exactly what they get in easily digestible chunks. Buying difficulty is inversely related to WTP, so if you decrease buying friction, you increase WTP. Using the GBB model will do just that!

No doubt about it, the Good Better Best approach is the most common in SaaS because it's pretty darn effective. Especially if you serve different segments of the market that grow in maturity, size, and therefore, expand their usage and relationship with your product. They graduate from one plan to the next at certain inflexion points, allowing you to capitalize by giving them more value. That's a beautiful thing, right?

But the sad truth is that many B2B subscription companies do GBB wrong. Yes, even with the plethora of *Medium* articles out there telling what to do and not to do when it comes to GBB. Let me tell you a few mistakes to avoid by giving you my best practice guidelines for GBB in **FIGURE 10.7**. It's called the **Guide of Five**.

My Guide of Five is designed to give you the proper guide rails when designing your Good Better Best packaging. Starting with the differentiators, packages need to stand on their own and exhibit obvious differences in value and experience, so make sure your customer can point out five differences between packages, such as limits, features, services, reporting, and support.

Once you choose your package differentiators, make sure they give customers a reason to move up to a more premium package or buy more

FIGURE 10.9: THE GUIDE OF 5 FOR GBB

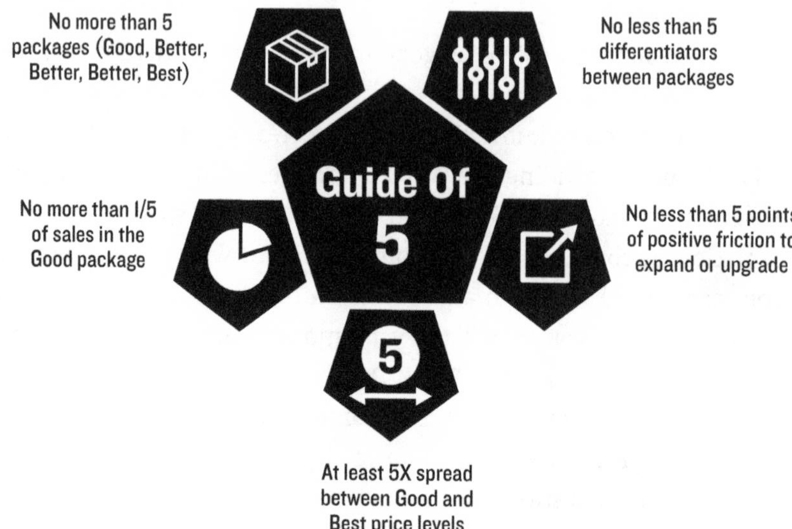
No more than 5 packages (Good, Better, Better, Better, Best)
No less than 5 differentiators between packages
Guide Of 5
No more than 1/5 of sales in the Good package
No less than 5 points of positive friction to expand or upgrade
5
At least 5X spread between Good and Best price levels

as they increase their use of the product. The idea is to introduce five points of what I call "positive friction," which is when a customer runs into a constraint or limit because they're getting more value than the plan allows as opposed to "negative friction," which is when limits in the plan prevent the customer from realizing the intended value. Add five or more reasons for your customer to expand their purchase, such as more data storage, more users, or more collaboration features.

Once you've added obvious differentiators that introduce positive friction points across plans, make sure there is a decent price spread between your lowest and highest plans to address different willingness to pay and budgets. My team at Pricing I/O ran a study with over 200 B2B SaaS companies and uncovered that the average price difference between the lowest and highest plans was about five times in order of magnitude (for example, if the lowest plan was $50, the highest was around $250). This is not a fixed rule, but make sure the price levels of the plans are different enough to capture customers with different budgets.

Now with a healthy band of options to offer your target audience, make sure the lowest option, what I call the entry plan, is not too generous. Offering too much at the lowest price point is a common trap door that many B2B SaaS founders fall into in a misguided attempt to over serve new customers. But the reality is that some customers will not use all the features, and others that do would have access to more value without paying for it. Both scenarios end up with limited expansion opportunities, and hence, limited growth of your SaaS business.

The last step in the Guide of Five is stepping back to make sure you didn't create too many options to choose from. People love options, but too many choices can lead to paralysis by analysis. Make sure that you can address your target audience with under five packages. Three to four is the most common number of packages in SaaS today. If you need more than five to cast a wide net and fully serve your market, then I suggest dividing your packages into two or three themes and show specific packages to specific buyers in each theme. For example, if you serve freelancers and agencies, you can highlight two separate sets of packages to each audience.

ENTER THE MATRIX

Every offer mix you market and sell must have a clear theme behind it. By theme, I mean it has to exist to achieve a business goal (remember the **why** in 5Q). An example of a theme is creating an offer mix that is a lightweight plan designed for quick sales cycles and market penetration. This is a classic theme in B2B SaaS, known as the land and expand motion.

The point is that when we put together packages, we really think through why the package exists and write it down. Here are a few more questions to help you out:

- What is the goal of the package? How does it link to my growth strategy?
- Who are you targeting with the package? Who should not buy this package?
- How do you know if the package is working? What signals tell me the customer has outgrown the package?
- What metric should you see moving as a result of the package? Example, should deal sizes go up?

PRICING TIP

A package without a purpose is pointless. Always assign a theme that links what you sell to how you plan to grow.

Once you have a lineup of package themes that make sense and align with your growth objectives and target segments, now is the time to figure out what value to put in them. This is the most challenging part of creating the offer mix.

A tool that I've always found useful is a feature-value matrix. The concept of a feature-value matrix is that you plot your key value drivers on two dimensions: willingness to pay and importance. These dimensions serve as a proxy for value and help you sort out which value to differentiate along, and which to just include in the offer mix as table stakes in every package or as add-ons.

The willingness to pay dimension is more elusive to capture, but there are ways to start with a "good enough" approximation.

Most SaaSletes won't have $150K burning a hole in their pocket to run a comprehensive pricing research study on the willingness to pay from a sample of thousands of prospects that meet our exact buying criteria.

But if you look into your customer base, you can do a few things to approximate willingness to pay:

- Remember the techniques we covered in **TRACK 6**. Calculate the correlation between feature usage and effective unit price. See if there is a relationship between prices paid and features used. You may not see any correlation between anything if your current pricing model is poorly capturing value. If this is the case, don't look for definitive answers. Instead, use this data to see if your pricing is getting better or worse in capturing value over time.
- Ask customers a price-value related question in a less intimidating way, such as framing it in a way that talks about bang for the buck, with more focus on the bang than the buck.

Try something like this: "On a scale of 1 to 5, how much value do you feel you are getting for the money?"

A low score tells you they feel the price is high, a high score might be a signal that you're too cheap. Try to get at least 100 responses to get insights that are directional, but 300+ responses offer better statistical significance.

- Use the answers from the two proxies to plot your value drivers on the two dimensions of the matrix, willingness to pay vs importance as shown in **FIGURE 10.10**.

FIGURE 10.10: FEATURE VALUE MATRIX

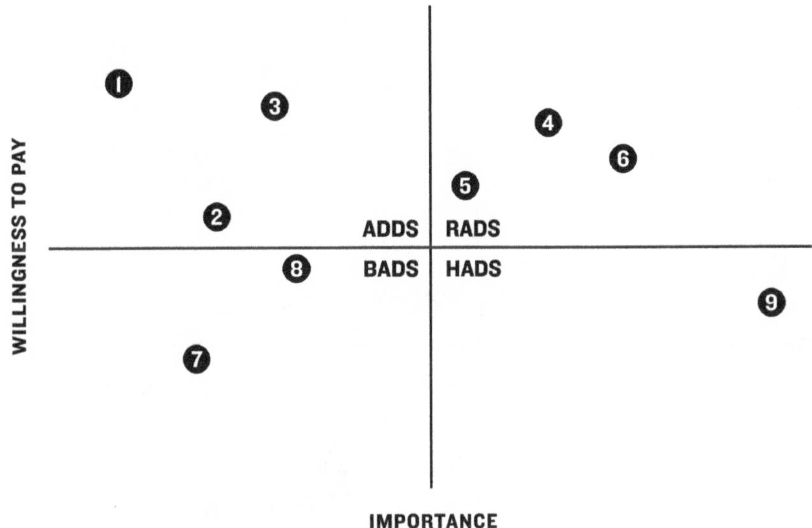

Ok, now we have a cool matrix chart. But what do you do with this?

How about we answer one of the toughest questions in pricing and packaging: Should we include the feature in the package or sell it as an add-on?

Let's get street again and tackle this question head on with how to interpret each quadrant in the Feature Value matrix.

RADS

Upper right quadrant. These are value drivers that rank highest in willingness to pay and highest in importance. This means that any value driver falling in this category should be considered as your "radical" differentiators. Also known as premium value that you can charge more for more access. Use these to layer and differentiate your offer mixes across your audiences.

HADS

Lower right quadrant. These are what are known as table stakes. These should be included in all your plans as the base of your product that everyone should get. To give you an extreme example, the ability to login is a HAD. Think about features or services that would be expected and would render your product useless without them. Over time, what was once considered a RAD can migrate to becoming a HAD as software competition heats up and as consumer preferences rise.

ADDS

Upper left quadrant. The opposing force of the HADS are the ADDS. These are the value drivers that are high value to a smaller audience. Consider these as add-ons in your packaging line up.

"But don't add-ons increase complexity?" you ask.

Not if you set a high bar for add-ons and keep them to a small set of options. I have seen businesses go to the extreme and have 20+ add-ons to choose from. This creates a "nickel and dime" sensation with your clients and could lead to paralysis by analysis for prospective buyers.

If keeping add-ons below six is troublesome, try bunding related add-ons as an "Add-On bundle" to reduce the choices the buyer has to evaluate.

> **PRICING TIP**
>
> Value drivers that apply to specific use cases or carry a variable cost are ideal for add-ons. If less than 20 percent of your audience uses a feature, consider it as an add-on.

BADS

Lower left quadrant. Last but not least, these value drives rank lowest in terms of willingness to pay and importance to your customer base. Some call this area trash land or waste, but the features could also be new to the base or early in its life lifecycle. When it comes to these features, there are three things you can do:

1. Continue to prioritize enhancing them on your roadmap to drive them up and to the right in the RADs quadrant.
2. Carefully focus the feature and messaging to appeal to a smaller audience and charge it as an add-on by moving it to the ADDs quadrant.
3. Admit that it is a low value feature, remove it from your product, and move on.

Now that you know how to build Good Better Best packages effectively, it's important to understand how people build perceptions around your offer mix and how much it is worth to them.

As long as humans are buying software, you should have a grasp on how psychology plays a role in evaluating offer mixes and prices. Most buying decisions are emotional, not rational.

MIND PLAYING TRICKS

There are a myriad of techniques to help customers comprehend the price, frame the value, and get comfortable with a purchase. The goal is to make it easy for your buyer to absorb the right context and avoid confusion, anxiety, or false perceptions. Most purchases are triggered by emotion and rationalized by logic later. That's just how people work.

Let's break down a few psychological techniques that apply to packaging your offer mix. Here, I want to expand on how the human mind evaluates options. For those who want to geek out on the subject of pricing psychology, I highly recommend picking up the book, The Tangled Mind, by Nick Kolenda. His website is also fantastic and full of quality content.

Before you jump into the table and checklist below, I need you to accept some basic truths about how humans act when evaluating something:

- People are not stupid; they're just a product of conditioning and accumulated experiences.
- Perception is not only stronger than reality but also the only reality in their minds.
- People sub-optimize decisions to optimize for low mental effort; it keeps us sane.
- People have an innate desire to stay alive, and therefore, only do things that are perceived as safe, familiar, and require low mental effort.

Now that we have the groundwork established, I summarized some of my favorite packaging psychology in the table in **FIGURE 10.11**.

Use this table as a guide, not as law. You'll notice some of these techniques might contradict each other. Well, human beings are walking contradictions, so some techniques have opposite effects. The way to get the most value out of the list is to really, I mean really, know your customer.

FIGURE 10.11: PACKAGING PSYCHOLOGY

- **Use language that matches perception** (don't use terms like "high" for your low price plan)
- **Reduce package congruence** (elevate one obvious choice, don't make plans exactly proportional price to value)
- **Central gaze cascade bias supports the Goldilocks Effect** (pick plans in the middle)
- **Any high number anchors the buyer** (number of hours, users, days, etc.)
- **Sort high to low to take advantage of anchoring**
- **Place large quantities on the left, lower price items on the right**
- **Call out the most popular or recommended** (follow the herd)
- **Rule of 100** (show savings in dollars if more than $100, show percentage if less than $100)

INTERLUDE

I met Alice Deer, CEO of a scrappy but upcoming bootstrap SaaS business in late 2019. And much like Ajit from Doctible in **TRACK 5**, Alice is a smart, hard-working, SaaSlete looking to take her startup to the next level of growth. For this Interlude, I'm doing a little show-and-tell instead of an interview. Let's take a look at what Alice's team pulled off at GatherContent.

GatherContent is a pure SaaS business that provides a content management platform to freelancers, agencies, and large institutions to streamline collaboration over rich content. Their small but mighty team was hungry for ARR growth and expansion and improving their overall expansion revenue through higher ACV from bigger clients. In other words, they wanted to move upmarket.

They also struggled with packaging for years and were unsure what features to include in each package and how to monetize new innovations in their roadmap. Sound familiar?

They solved the packaging problem head on by embracing 5Q and connecting the Why, Who, and What to produce a Good Better Best line up of tailored packages. The new plans not only gave customers what they were asking for, but the structure allowed for lower friction when upselling to the next tier.

To put things in perspective, check out an early version of their package on their pricing page in **FIGURE 10.12**. You'll notice a few issues that got in the way of growth:

- Items were not a well-understood concept and led to buyer confusion.
- Lack of identity for each plan, leading to more confusion as to which one to pick.
- Unclear linkages between the price jumps and differences in value, further compounding confusion.

And like the quote we saw in **TRACK 5**, "A confused mind always says no."

CONTINUED →

FIGURE 10.12: GATHERCONTENT PRICING PAGE—EARLY VERSION

	Starter $83/mo Start a free trial	Plus $166/mo Start a free trial	Pro $249/mo Start a free trial	Company $333/mo Start a free trial	Need a bigger plan? Get in touch
Items	500	1000	2000	3000	3000+
Active projects	10	25	50	75	75+
Unlimited users	✓	✓	✓	✓	✓
Real-time content editor	✓	✓	✓	✓	✓
Structured templates	✓	✓	✓	✓	✓
Workflow stages	5	10	Unlimited	Unlimited	Unlimited
Custom roles & permissions	Default roles	2 custom roles	✓	✓	✓

Let's fast forward to the good part and talk about how they did it. In short, they solved for three key things:

- First, Alice and the team clarified and aligned on exactly who they are and what they want (and just as importantly, what they don't want). This type of introspection is hard but sets the groundwork for good packaging. It took a few sessions with the team to get real about their secret sauce and value proposition, their pace of innovation vs. the competition, the ideal sales motion, and the economics they needed to build a sustainable business model.

  They decided to go more niche in the space and push upmarket where the problem with managing high stakes and complex content across vast stakeholders was more pronounced. And solving this problem for this group was a more compelling business than being just another player among the maelstrom of SaaS project management providers out there.
- Second, they dug deep into their customer base to uncover differences and similarities to improve segmentation. What they discovered was notable differences in the number of projects, types of roles, active users, and training needs. Once they extracted the data, they got fancy by applying a clustering

algorithm using AI to break up the segments. How about that for taking it up a notch?

- But they didn't stop there! They called dozens of customers to talk to them about value. Yup, after getting fancy, they took it old school by straight up asking customers about what's behind the trends they saw in the data, and what they cared about and not. Even Alice herself rolled up her sleeves and was on the phone. I love that!

Do you see the 5Q framework in motion? Aww yeah!

After several dozen interviews, Alice and team confirmed and better understood their customers' distaste for user-based pricing, confusion over the existing limits, and desire for more hands-on training. Armed with a sharp growth story, clear value-based segmentation, and solid feedback on where customers find value, GatherContent designed a new set of packages offering the right experience to the right audience that met their growth objectives. See the new line up in **FIGURE 10.13**.

FIGURE 10.13: GATHERCONTENT PRICING PAGE—NEW VERSION

Monthly | Annually

Psst! Scale and Transform annual plans come with added benefits! Take a look.

Start	Scale	Transform
For smaller teams getting started with content operations $99/mo Try for free	For teams collaborating on larger volumes of content $299/mo Try for free	For organizations that are expanding content operations across multiple projects $799/mo Try for free
Unlimited users 3 projects 3 components per project **Basic** workflow **Basic** permissions	**Unlimited** users 15 projects 15 components per project **Advanced** workflow **Advanced** permissions	**Unlimited** users 60 projects **Unlimited** components **Advanced** workflow **Advanced** permissions
30 days revision history	1 year revision history	Unlimited revision history
–	Basic sharable links	Advanced sharable links
–	–	Archive projects
–	–	Single sign-on

CONTINUED →

Here's what I love about GatherContent's new packaging:

- All plans have a clearly defined target buyer and user case. Even the package names: Start, Scale, and Transform communicate different points along the value curve.
- They simplified the value metric to only projects, but fenced the plans by history and advanced features, giving them multiple dimensions to encourage upgrades.
- The price levels are easy to consume and reflect the jumps in value from plan to plan.

They put in the work and come out with a data-informed and purpose-driven set of packages that fits their customers and economics. After rolling this out, Alice cited a major boost in expansion revenue, lower sales friction, and higher ACV. I love it when a plan comes together!

You now have the tools to figure out how to craft an offer mix, aim it at the right target customer, and ensure it is adding the right value to the right buyer. And by doing so, you can drive your business closer and closer to your growth goals.

To put these techniques into actions, take a look at the Playback exercise below. Completing this exercise will help cement the learnings, so don't skip it if you want to get the full value of this book. I'm just being real with you!

PLAYBACK EXERCISE

Let's put some of these badass techniques into play. For this playback, I ask you to evaluate your own packaging and score it based on what I call the FITT scorecard. FITT stands for **Fluency**, **Identity**, **Taste**, and **Transition**. You can download the scorecard for free from pricingio.com. When you're done, decide where you need to improve packaging the most based on your score.

Of course, packaging by itself is only part of the monetization strategy. Now we get to the part you've been patiently waiting for: how to charge for your value to capture your fair share. The answer might surprise you, but if there is one lesson that any business has taught us, it's that cash rules.

CASH RULES EVERYTHING

THE ART OF MONETIZING VALUE

THE FIRST THING THAT DRAWS YOU INTO WU TANG CLAN'S 1993 ICONIC MAGNUM OPUS "C.R.E.A.M. (CASH RULES EVERYTHING AROUND ME)" IS THAT PIANO.

RZA chopped up a sample of the 1967 Isaac Hayes-produced track "As Long as I've Got You" by the Charmels. The keys are high and staggered, providing a dark melody that's augmented by looped, moaning vocals by the textured voice of Method Man, adding a touch of longing, as though there's something knowingly out of reach that he still can't help but yearn for. But it's also why a song that was meant to be an indictment of the conditions created by a capitalist economy has become synonymous with capitalist pursuits. In other words, a song about not having money ends up becoming an anthem about making money.

So far in this section of the book, we've covered the first three questions in the 5Q framework to set the stage for the fourth, and, most pressing question in your mind, the How. With these core three pillars in place, it is eminently easier to figure out how to price to value. In this track, I will unpack the most effective models to monetize value in B2B SaaS, including how to connect pricing with sales and how to make sure you charge for the right value to bring in those dolla dolla bills, y'all.

You're in business to make a living by providing value to others, plain and simple. You build solutions to problems, this in turns provides value, and that in turn entitles you to a portion of that value to keep for yourself. This is commerce at the purest level. And yet, so many B2B SaaSletes out there struggle with capturing their fair share of commerce. Their focus is so squarely concentrated in building the right value and accumulating an audience who wants the value that they leave little mental space for how to capture value in the best way to sustain short- and long-term business growth.

With that, let's get into the art and science of monetization.

MODELS THAT MATTER

There's more than one way to capture value. A monetization model adds some structure to what and how you monetize value. This is where the 5Q framework all comes together. The **Why** fuels your pricing strategy. The **Who** focuses your target audience. The **What** defines carefully crafted offer mixes to sell. Now we'll get into the **How** in terms of how to price the value to win in a hyper-competitive market of subscription software.

The goal should be to monetize the right value in the right way. Yes, it's much easier said than done, but charging for the wrong thing in the wrong way is not going to get you far. And frankly speaking, that is exactly what you are trying to avoid by reading this book.

In order to monetize the right value, you need a value-based model and metric that can be effectively sold while controlling for value leakage. Value leakage, to sum it up, is anything in your model that leads to either losing deals you should win or leaving money on the table. For example, over-discounting is a form of value leakage that leads to leaving money on the table. Over-stuffed packages resulting in poor product-market-price fit is another form of value leakage, ending up in lost deals that you should win.

To ensure your plan is connected with how you sell, here are two key questions to ask yourself when thinking through a monetization strategy:

- How does the monetization model factor in usage and influence desired behavior?
- How does pricing align with the sales motion, offer flexibility, and promote positive sales habits?

There are four main categories of monetization models, highlighted in **FIGURE 11.1**. Each has its own pros and cons to weigh before deciding which to employ for your B2B SaaS business model.

FIGURE 11.1: MONETIZATION MODELS

Uber

Consumption Based, Pay-As-You-Go
Pure transactional, pre-load / re-load

Revenue Share, % of Revenue Split
Revenue % payout, bill based on revenue %

Tiered Subscription, Set Price by Tier
Tierd by functionality, hybrid—tiers / transactions
(72% of SaaS today)

Free Offer, Free Entry Price
Free limited by usage, free limited by time

We will step through each of the above four models to set the context.

CONSUMPTION-BASED

A consumption-based model charges customers for what they use, no more, no less. Another widely used term for this type of model is usage-based pricing.

Seems fair, right? Most would agree that it is the fairest monetization model in terms of balancing the price-value equation. In this model, there is no shelf-ware effect that drives the buyer to wonder if they are paying for something they are not using—the number-one reason for pausing before a purchase.

Silicon Valley (and the SaaS industry as a whole) has fallen in love with usage-based pricing. Many frame it up to being the holy grail of value-based pricing. Afterwards, you get value only if you use something, right?

Well, tell that to insurance companies, cybersecurity software, or any other product or service that provides value in giving access to or protection from something sporadic in nature. Consumption based pricing is my favorite form of monetization, but it is far from perfect with its own set of drawbacks.

It's best to use this model when usage is consistent, predictable, and easy to count, and each event has discrete value. This model works particularly well with IT, technical, or infrastructure buyers. Avoid this model if usage is random and can result in sticker-shock bills.

Uber is a fantastic example of consumption-based monetization. It's easy to count the discrete value of a ride. Another famous consumption-based model is Amazon Web Services (AWS). Many of you reading this book are probably running your business on AWS or using something from Amazon's tech stack, and therefore should be familiar with the concept of consumption-based monetization.

REVENUE SHARE

Affectionately known as the "rev share" in software circles, this monetization model gives thanks to the Apple Store for putting it on the map in the SaaS world. The revered 70/30 (Apple keeps 30 percent) split for accessing Apple's audience was one of the best monetization strategies in technology.

Since then, other tech behemoths have made "bazillions" from revenue share models, from Salesforce's Exchange Marketplace, to Etsy, to Shopify's massive ecommerce platform.

This approach is well suited for ecommerce and marketplace applications. The idea is that you are splitting the work, so you should split the money. In the most basic sense, in order to facilitate commerce, you need something to sell and a buyer to buy it. Using the rev share model, the value to monetize is facilitating the exchange of downstream value of users. Think of it as a commission rate, just as you would pay a real estate agent 6 percent for facilitating the buying and selling of a home.

Aside from the obvious chicken-and-egg problem this model inherently wrestles with, this monetization model is also highly susceptible to outside market forces such as economic downturns, and the revenue flow is highly variable and hard to predict.

Lastly, because the rev share rate is so squarely in the center of the model, the relationship between you and your customer tends to be more transactional in nature, leading to higher churn when new competitors arise. In **FIGURE 11.2**, I list a set of popular companies who monetize with revenue share rates along with factors that influence the rate. Just a tip: Rev share rates are also known as "rakes" (from the commissions casinos earn on poker games).

FIGURE 11.2: RATES AND FACTORS FOR POPULAR MARKETPLACES

COMPANY	RATE	COMMENTS
OpenTable	1.9%	Reservation & flat fees
HomeAway	2.5%	Commission
eBay	9.9%	Listing plus commission
AirBnB	11.0%	3% plus 6–12%
Expedia	11.9%	Commission
Amazon Marketplace	12.0%	Range 6 to 15% plus fees and $39.99 subscription
TicketMaster	26.0%	Rate table
Apple	30.0%	Revenue share
ClassPass	35.0%	Commission
Groupon	50.0%	Commission, 90-day payout

Factors

- Audience
- Network Effect
- Alternatives
- Transactions
- Seller Margins
- Volume

Models

- Subscription or Membership Levels
- Commissions or Listing Fees

Goal

- To enable repeat and low friction exchanges at scale

TIERED SUBSCRIPTION

Ah yes, the home that Salesforce built. Well, not really, but Salesforce, and to a lesser degree, Slack, have combined to accumulate approximately $230B of market value running on the tiered subscription monetization model. Wow, that's almost a quarter of a trillion dollars (well on its way to a bazillion).

PRICING TIP

In the tiered pricing model, you are monetizing across a spectrum. Charge customers a fair price for where they are today, and progressively charge more as they move up the spectrum.

Make no mistake. The tiered subscription model is by far the most popular monetization model in SaaS today, B2B or B2C. The concept is to charge different amounts for different tiers of value to capture value at various levels. Genius! SaaS companies did not invent this model. Gym memberships, publications, and cable television have been running on tiered subscriptions forever. And different packages of value have been in front of us for most of our lives, from fast-food menus to the trims of a Honda Accord to the fluid list of Verizon phone plans. Tiers of value are nothing new.

Tiered subscription plans make the most sense when you are trying to capture various segments of buyers that need different capabilities and access; the assumption is that many of these buyers will mature and grow with higher demands over time, hence moving up the proverbial ladder so your business captures more value as a direct result of their growth.

While this form of monetization is the most widely adopted in SaaS, it too has its limitations. For one, the model assumes you know exactly what your buyers need within each tier, an assumption that is heartbreakingly almost always untrue. The other trap is offering too many choices to the buyer, blinding and paralyzing them with a blitzkrieg of options and losing deals you should be winning.

Use the tiered subscription model when you have an offer mix that can be grouped into graduating degrees of value, usually in the form of handling more complexity, more speed, or more volume. A huge benefit of tiered subscription pricing is the ability to tier using different dimensions, making this one of the most malleable forms of monetization.

FREE OFFERS

To free or not to free, that is the question. Oddly enough, free offerings are often considered more of an acquisition strategy than a monetization model. I think the argument is valid. You offer something free as a way to get people to try and buy something.

In the SaaS world, free offers pop up in two common ways: the free trial and the freemium version of a product. Both offer a taste of value to convert users from free to paid, except trials are time bound while freemium, in stark contrast, is a value-bound approach. Both have their difficulties when it comes to monetization models. Let's untangle the two techniques.

The short answer is that you want to use freemium when you can reach enough users and have a product with enough paywalls to convert them to paid users. On the flip side, you want free trials to give untethered value to users for a specified period of time because the accumulated experience is what drives the value.

Straight up, the preferred route in B2B SaaS is to go with free trials, whereas freemiums work better in B2C. I'm not talking in absolute terms. There are plenty of anti-cases and exceptions out there, but I will explain more of my thesis in the next section. Stay with me.

We touched on each of the four main monetization models above to give you a high-level sense for how you can opt to monetize your value. Each method deserves its own dedicated track that I may choose to elaborate in future publications, but for now, you have the Cliffs Notes you need to pick one and move on.

The thing about free is that it's a widely misunderstood concept. The term "free" can mean a lot of different things to different people. In our world of subscription software, free typically means using some of our technology at no cost, but there are strings attached. For example, free access could really mean:

- Pay by giving me your data to sell.
- Pay by helping me attract others to pay.
- Pay to unlock more stuff.
- Pay for something else.
- Pay later when you're hooked.

In the acclaimed book, *Free* by Chris Anderson, the concept of "Free" is deeply researched and explained as a radical idea and pricing model.

PRICING TIP

Choosing not to monetize something is a form of monetization strategy mainly because you are doing this in an effort to monetize something else.

Chris argues that data and technology yearn to be free, so it's best to strategize how to use free to monetize value in creative and evolving ways. He goes on to explore various economic models fueled by Free and argues that Free is really just another versioning scheme, whereby the price of the free version is simply zero, and the other versions are paid, as an example.

Fair enough, and thanks to Chris for proving my point that free is a monetization strategy, in whole or in part. I highly recommend reading Chris's book. It's a short read that opens your mind about how to monetize by using free options. In the meantime, check out **FIGURE 11.3** to see how Calendly used both freemium and free trial options to achieve wild growth.

FIGURE 11.3: FREE TRIAL FROM CALENDLY

Try Calendly free
Sign Up →
After your 14-day trial of our Teams plan, enjoy the Free version of Calendly – forever.
To inquire about our Enterprise plans, click here.

PRICING TIP

It's better for B2B SaaS companies to go with a Free Trial. The conversion rates from free to paid are 14 percent compared to 7 percent for Freemium. The execution risk is lower, and the cost is easier to contain.

Calendly is an online scheduling juggernaut founded by a Nigerian immigrant who focused on his passion and gave up his nights and weekends for over seven years to launch a successful SaaS business. At the core of Calendly's success is an extremely low friction hook to entering the software with a free version that provides quick value and takes only a few clicks to get started. Many users were fine with sticking with the free version, but a healthy amount outgrow the free plan and upgraded to enjoy more benefits. The path to upgrade works so well, it's almost poetic.

Freemium works great for Calendly, but it doesn't mean you'll have the same success. If you are unsure if going with a freemium is right for your business, ask yourself the following questions and count how many times you answer yes:

- Does your service have viral adoption potential?
- Does your service have a huge potential market?
- Do you have a clear and compelling migration path for your users?
- Does the value of your service increase the longer that people use it?
- Do you have the capacity to prevent people from gaming your system?

If you answered "yes" to at least three of the questions, then you may want to consider going down the freemium path. To maximize your chance for freemium success, make sure you take these fundamental four steps:

1. Maximize marketing spend efficiency to generate excitement and virality around the freemium offer.
2. Minimize the cost to serve freemium subscribers.
3. Fence your paid offers from your freemium offers in a way that minimizes cannibalization and creates a compelling free-to-paid migration path.
4. Establish clear, effective calls to action to drive conversion from the freemium pool of users.

And to make sure I steer you in the right direction with freemium, I'll share with you the basic types of freemium options in **FIGURE 11.4**.

FIGURE 11.4: THE BASIC TYPES OF FREEMIUM

TYPE	DESCRIPTION
Time Limited (free trial)	# of days free then user pays
Feature Limited	Basic version is free with a more sophisticated paid version
Seat Limited	# of people can use for free, any number over X has to pay
Customer-Type Limited	Small companies use it for free, big companies have to pay
Storage/Capacity Limited	# GB of storage come free, more than that requires paid version

There is more than one way to offer something for free. Learn these five basic types of freemium to produce a free version of your own, assuming you want to go down this route to attract new customers. If you are unsure where to begin, start with free limited by time (a free trial) and see who signs up. If the user feedback signals customers are not getting enough time to experience value, then with using the information you collected thus far, switch from time limits to a combination of seat, customer-type, capacity, and feature limited freemium. Remember the way to build pricing knowledge from **TRACK 2**, read, put something out there, learn, then rinse and repeat.

GTM TO ATM

Nothing matters until you sell something. If you have a sales-led motion (say versus a product-led one), there is very little a pricing model can accomplish on its own. In fact, the best pricing models tend to make the product easy to sell and easy to buy, two sides of the same coin.

Say you've opted to go down the route of hiring salespeople. Whether they are lead-converting business development representatives (BDRs) or closing account executives (AE), or some hybrid of both, it is critical to properly arm them with tools and training to extract the full potential of your pricing model and monetization strategy.

Your sales team will prove your pricing model right or wrong, whether or not it's really right or wrong.

Think about it this way. Imagine that your pricing model is the long carbon fiber pole, and your sales rep is an Olympic-level pole vaulter. The height and weight of the pole and vaulter need to match in order to produce the best possible mechanics and physics to achieve the right lift. Pole vaulting, like sales, requires thinking, timing, coordination, and skill in order to soar to new heights.

To keep the analogy going, in order for the pole to create lift from force, there needs to be a stop box. This box produces the counter force necessary to drive the athlete up and over the crossbar. This stop box in pricing is your exception management policy including deal discounting, nonstandard terms, and quota requirements.

We all know that sales takes the path of least resistance to make the most money. In fact, it's the practical thing to do. For sales, it's about the deal, the deal after that, and the one after that. All that matters is transaction and volume to hit quota, not value to the customer.

So how do we ensure your go-to-market (GTM) plan is successful and can run with the new pricing model? No shocker here. You need to connect your GTM goals with sales incentives and compensation. Or more specifically, link GTM outcomes with variables in the sales compensation model that motivate behaviors and lead to rewards.

Sales compensation variables include measures like total contract value (TCV), annual contract value (ACV), average contract term length, gross margin, average discount from list price, and others. The trick is to keep the number of variables low, say under five, and look at sales rep quota achievement over time to measure effectiveness.

If more reps are hitting their quota after adopting the new pricing, that is a positive signal that your updated model is making it easier to sell.

To successfully connect the dots between pricing and sales, you need to give sales flexibility to navigate and close business. And to navigate, they need a simple structure and flexible options to encourage behavior that results in them and your company making more money. Here are a few examples of aligning pricing and sales incentives.

- **REAL EXAMPLE 1:** A B2B software analytics company updated their packages to include a competitively priced entry package at $10K/year. But guess what? The sales compensation package did not count any deal under $20K toward the quota, so the new package was dead on arrival. The lesson here is to update quota targets to align with the deal sizes you expect from the new packages and prices.

- **REAL EXAMPLE 2:** A Marcom SaaS company wanted longer-term contracts to improve customer expansion and retention. However, the sales incentive plan did not compensate for long term deals, so the reps kept selling month to month contracts. The company updated compensation with a kicker for longer terms and almost "overnight" reps were closing annual contracts. The lesson here is to add the right variables that drive short- and long-term ARR.

Discounting is a cocaine-laced crutch that helps you win in the short term, but you ultimately lose in terms of attracting and serving the right customer. Recklessly discounting your prices can lead to capturing customers who are less willing to pay and are three times more likely to leave you the first chance they get. Sure, you get to win a sale in the short run, but you end up losing profit and growth momentum in the long run.

So, what's the answer to deter discounting, or at least use it sparingly as a surgical scalpel versus a chainsaw?

Give sales another way to negotiate. The first wave of options should be built into your monetization strategy with different packages and add-ons, but **FIGURE 11.5** is another set of "gives and gets" for sales to lean on while negotiating to close a hard-fought deal.

I list these alternatives to discounting to give sales a fighting chance to close a deal that is just out of reach. One way to protect your subscription revenue from discounting is to give more value to the customer in a way that will enhance their experience for the same price. On the flip side, you may want more than just avoiding a discount on your license fee depending on your stage and market, so I listed a few things you can ask for in exchange for a discount to open a pathway to more revenue.

FIGURE 11.5: SALES NEGOTIATION ALTERNATIVES

Gives	Gets
▪ Extending payment terms ▪ Placing in priority implementation queue ▪ Providing extra users ▪ Additional add-in tools or modules ▪ Offering priority support ▪ Create marketing assets to promote customer ▪ A-Team priority	▪ Payment upfront or accelerated payment terms ▪ Longer term commitment ▪ Guarantee of future business ▪ Serve as a reference / case study ▪ Referrals to other parts of the organization ▪ Press releases

Transitioning from landing to expanding for a minute, customer success (CS) falls under the same sales umbrella with a few nuances.

The theory is that engagement leads to more value, and more value will lead to more purchase. Some call the CS team a softer touch sales function, and that is exactly what it is. However, the incentive structure must reward long term relationships rather than short-term selling. While BDRs and AEs are the hunters, the CSs are the proverbial farmers, and farming takes time and patience.

For the CS function to be successful, your pricing model must have built-in growth triggers that CS is trained to monitor to find signals the customer is ready for more, such as volume limits in each plan, add-on options, storage limits, or support tiers.

Whichever go-to-market path you choose, it needs to be connected with your monetization strategy by aligning the right incentives, supported by the pricing and packaging model.

PRICING TIP

Customer Success should be compensated to grow accounts, not sell to them.

READY, SET, CHARGE!

Choosing a value metric that matters is a critical step in defining your pricing model. In fact, your model is highly dependent on it. So how do you charge for the right thing?

First, value metrics go by many names, but don't be confused. We are talking about the actions or things you charge for in the software, period.

You want a metric that is easy to predict, links value and usage together, and represents a shared benchmark for growth between your business and your customer's business.

Avoid anything that is hard to understand, requiring too many moving parts or criteria, and for the love of God, avoid charging for something that will discourage usage. This is especially important when activating new customers.

So wait. Then why doesn't Netflix charge users by the number of shows or viewing hours? For the same reason Slack doesn't charge you per channel or message. It discourages usage.

Here is a quick five-step process table for figuring out the value metric:

1. List objects and actions you can count.
2. Score them.
3. Survey your three highest scores.
4. Test, test, test.
5. Roll out.

I love David Skok's take on the topic of value metrics. He suggests three dimensions when it comes to charging for software: how many people have access, how many capabilities they could use, and how much of the capabilities they *actually* use. Charging on one dimension is a start (like features or users), two is better, and three is optimal to capture value.

PRICING TIP

Ideal value metrics are easy to understand and grow as customers use the product and get more value from that usage.

In my experience, the most common dimensions are users and features, and the most overlooked is the depth of usage, mainly because it takes time and data to figure out where to place the limits so you don't inadvertently discourage customers from using your product.

Let's look at a few examples of value metrics and compare two website content management systems. Webflow splits their audience into two separate buckets: pay-per-site and pay-per-user. This allows them to define two different metrics for two different sets of needs. Platform.sh, on the other hand, decided to go with one plan and a price calculator because engineers love to calculate stuff. The final price depends on three variables: application, pageviews, and quantity.

In case you are wondering, it is possible to monetize the same audience in different ways. While both solutions offers a way to manage content, Webflow is looking to monetize on all three value metric dimensions: users, features, and depth. Platform.sh, on the other hands, is placing a much stronger emphasis on the usage dimension, which ties well to their messaging that they are an infrastructure that scales with you.

Let's also compare and contrast between two data platform giants. Snowflake goes down the road of pay up front or pay as you go for capacity per second. Mongo gets more granular by charging on cloud providers and CPU power, then on clusters based on a price per hour.

Which one has the better approach, MongoDB or Snowflake? There is no right or wrong answer. They both monetize in a way that's right for them and aligns with their core values. For MongoDB, they care a lot about automation, speed, and being built by and for developers who love a transparent, yet modular approach that lets them build the offer mix they want. Snowflake leans more on being a one-stop single platform to house and unify all data workloads. This led them to a model that scales in a predictable way as customers add more data.

Customer relationship management (CRM) applications are also everywhere, so let's compares two trailblazers in the space. Salesforce sticks with good old users, no frills, no fluff. HubSpot loves the contact idea for marketing but shifts to users for sales and services.

Both Salesforce and HubSpot are hugely successful B2B SaaS companies with very different pricing approaches. As I mentioned earlier in this track, Salesforce is a pioneer of tiered subscription pricing starting down the path in 1999, and with the tremendous value that every sales rep gets from the platform, still makes sense to charge by the user seat. HubSpot, with a respectable $32 billion market cap, on the other hand, is regarded by any in the SaaS world as a pricing innovator with sometimes multiple updates to their pricing model in a year due to their fast-growing product offering. And because HubSpot focuses more on higher-volume sales leads that come inbound, they price based on contacts.

Now let's compare two of the most ubiquitous project management software providers with impressive growth metrics. In 2021, Asana sported a 120 percent NRR (net revenue retention), and Monday's revenue growth is 75 percent year over year. Both charge by the user, but in different ways. Asana goes down the path of charging by the feature dimension while Monday charges for actions, or the usage depth dimension.

Both Asana and Monday enjoy explosive growth benefiting from a well-defined, user-based tiered subscription model. However, Asana pushes their team and task collaboration features more than anything else, and charges more as customers work across initiatives. Monday refers to their product as a work operating system that is flexible enough to handle any action and hence, builds in a metric that charges more for more actions per month.

Data is not easy to monetize. ChurnZero decided to monetize based on the amount of revenue they analyze; it gets more expensive with more money and more complexity. ProfitWell decided to charge by money recovered, a play from the old pay-for-performance playbook, or in other words, commission. You win, I win, we win.

These two fast-growing SaaS companies want to fight and improve the problem of customers churning for other companies and monetize in two different but valid ways. ChurnZero places the accent on tracking and nurturing customer health and tiered their features to correspond price with more benefits in managing customers. ProfitWell decided to keep their pricing based on the one thing that matters in their eyes: reducing the amount of money leaving the business due to churn, and in their case, choosing to price as a percentage of dollars recovered.

I hope the examples in this track have proven useful and hammer home the idea that choosing how to price is just as important as what to price. Briefly, when it comes to picking the value metric:

- Pick something you can count and that grows steadily.
- Make sure it is easy to understand and see.
- Avoid anything that makes the user think about the usage.
- Don't be greedy and stick to a few simple axes.

If you keep these four tips in mind when choosing what to charge, you'll have a far better chance of monetizing the right value, from the right customers, for the right reasons. And at the very least, you will be able to see what works versus what doesn't work and iterate quickly.

AND THE ENVELOPE, PLEASE

Okay, here is where things get even more interesting. How do you produce the prices themselves?

The number one thing I can tell you here is do not base your pricing off one reference point. You need to have a spectrum of price reference points in order to determine what your price should be. This is art informed by science at its best. The spectrum of price points is what I call a **price envelope**. See **FIGURE 11.6** for an example.

Think about it as a range of price levels that you could charge based on collected data or evidence. For instance, you can have price levels suggested from a willingness-to-pay study, historical captured prices in a time series, most relevant competitive prices, and an ROI-based price yielding 10X return to the customer. If all these price references (the science) suggest a range of prices between $100 and $200 per month per user, for example, then you can feel confident about strategically selecting price levels (the art) to achieve your business goals.

This is where the WHY comes in. Maybe your roadmap is aggressive, and value is going to shoot up. If so, price on the high side of the envelope.

For the most effective price envelope, the more granular the better. Create an envelope for each offer mix that is aimed at a target customer segment. The better defined your offer mix and target customer segment (the WHO and the WHAT), the more insightful and useful the price envelope.

Or if you are not 100 percent confident in the data behind the willingness to pay or competitive figure, then perhaps you want to aim in the middle or lower part of the spectrum.

Setting the price points communicates value, positioning, flexibility, simplicity, motivations, and brand. It is not something that is blindly cranked out in a spreadsheet. You need to think about what you want, and the behavior you need in order to get what you want, and finally, the pricing that will influence that behavior.

FIGURE 11.6: EXAMPLE OF A PRICING ENVELOPE

	WEIGHT		INTERNAL			EXTERNAL	
		15%	15%	10%	30%	30%	100%
#	PRICE RANGE	HISTORICAL	INTERNAL	PV	WTP	COMPETITION	WTD AVG
1	High	75	100	90	120	110	104
2	Median	45	50	60	70	50	56
3	Low	33	40	35	45	35	38
4	Floor		20				0
5	Other						0

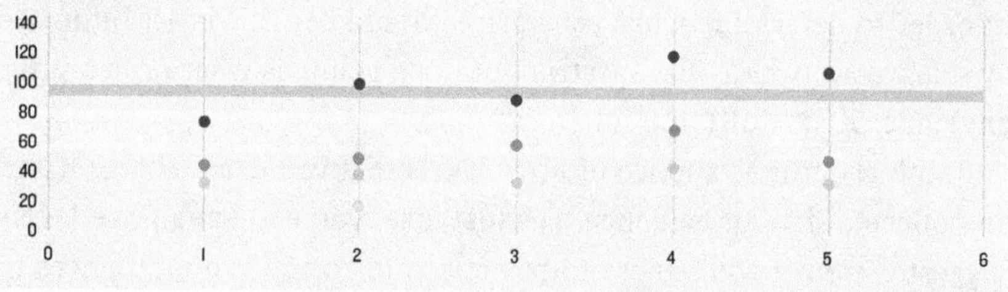

Producing a good pricing envelope takes hard work and good data. Most B2B companies have little bandwidth to dedicate the hard work and lack the data discipline to capture the good data required.

But I have some good news. It is always possible to start somewhere and build up. You have to look at the pricing journey as a climb, not as an elevator. When you are starting on the ground level, you may not have full clarity on your strategy and best-fit customers, your value proposition might be shaky, and your data could have holes in it. Even still, you can produce a coherent plan to monetize your value, and more importantly, get better over time.

There is more than one way to look at the relationship between price and value in order to build your price envelope. **FIGURE 11.7** shows six common ways to approach deriving a relationship construct between price and value, and in some cases with little data at your disposal.

FIGURE 11.7: SIX WAYS TO SET PRICES ★ = My favorites

1. **EVE**
   Calculate alternative and differentiation value pool. **Price at 10 to 40%.**
2. **Fair Value Exchange** ★
   Plot price / value versus competitors. **Price close to FVE line.**
3. **WTP-Based** ★
   Survey customers on willingness to pay thresholds. **Price between mid and high point.**
4. **10/20 Rule**
   Calculate 10X to 20X return based on 3-year ROI. **Price by segment.**
5. **LTV-Based**
   Calculate predicted LTV to CAC ratio. **Price from 5:1 to 10:1.**
6. **Industry Margin**
   Calculate contribution margin delta to industry margin. **Price to industry.**

These six methods are not exhaustive, but they offer a collection of different angles to measure value in order to triangulate a fair price for your product's value. I like to consider them as a series of tools in a toolbox that can be used when the data and context allow for it.

Let's take a quick stroll through these six options to lay some groundwork in building a price envelope.

ECONOMIC VALUE ESTIMATION (EVE)

This technique was popularized by Dr. Thomas Nagle in his book, *The Strategy and Tactics of Pricing*, a foundational read that I mentioned in my opening track. The premise of EVE is based on how much difference in value you deliver vs. the next best alternative to capture a fair share of the difference in price. Based on experience, I suggest capturing around 10 percent of the value difference on the low end if your competition is stiff, and up to 40 percent on the high end if you are the only game in town or have a unique market advantage. In order to use the EVE technique, it is critical that you can measure how the product value is different versus other viable solutions.

FAIR VALUE EXCHANGE (also known as a price-value map)

This option derives prices by comparing your product's price to value among a set of substitute competitors to produce a price based on positioning in a market. Think of it as a version of economic game theory, which simulates interactions between competing players to model behavior in a strategic setting. Once you plot the price and value of your product and each competitor (choose between three and five to keep the exercise manageable), you then run scenarios to price higher or lower depending on your goals. To use Fair Value Exchange, you must compete in a market with high price transparency to collect the competitive price points.

WILLINGNESS TO PAY (WTP)

Discussed in **TRACK 9**, this is a popular option if you have the time and resources. The idea is to give a sample set of respondents some context around your product's value and ask them, in a roundabout way, what they are willing to pay. Two most commonly used survey tools are Van Westendorp and Gabor Granger (aka price laddering). Both have their benefits and drawbacks, but a side bonus is that you learn a lot about what customers or prospects find valuable and not. A WTP survey campaign can cost well into the six figures depending on your target market, which is why not every SaaS business goes down this path, especially startups.

LIFETIME VALUE (LTV)-BASED

This is a useful technique if you have different sales channels (inbound sales, field sales, self-service) and a well-calculated cost to acquire new customers (CAC). The benchmark ratio of lifetime value to acquisition in SaaS that I shared in **TRACK 3** is 3:1. Taking this ratio further, I noticed that high-performing companies who monetize well enjoy an LTV to CAC ratio of 10:1, sometimes higher. For each sales channel, calculate the price that yields 3:1, 5:1, and 10:1 ratios and align with your packages to see if they can provide enough value at those LTV levels. This pricing technique requires a lot of data on customer and sales transactions.

INDUSTRY MARGIN

This is my least favorite and works better when there is a meaningful and measurable cost to deliver the product, such as professional services labor or a variable hardware cost. With so many SaaS companies traded in public markets, it is getting easier to collect financial data on competitors. To use this technique, research the costs, revenue, and margin profiles of any public competitors and calculate a price that yields similar results for your business. This pricing method is more of a math exercise compared to the others, but it can at least help in defining a floor price to ensure you cover your costs and stay in business.

10/20 RULE

And finally, the ROI based 10/20 rule is by far the most common way to set price and is adorned by the pied-piping Silicon Valley bunch that we all know and love. The rule is simple. Price your product such that you give your customer a 10X return on their investment. For example, if your customer gets $1000 a year in value from your product, then price it at $100 per year.

Since the ROI-based approach is the "go-to" for startups with little-to-no customer data, let me take a moment to improve this approach to make it more effective. First, this is famously adopted by startups who have no idea what their value proposition is or their best-fit customers. The problem here is that you don't have proof of the value you are calculating, nor do you understand your customers well enough to attribute this value. If you do have a few customers, some social proof, and an easy-to-understand, almost obvious, way to produce the measurable value, then this technique works pretty well to produce a price that is perceived as "fair" in the general sense.

To modify this approach, I would consider doing the ROI calculation by target segment and take into account the business dynamics. If your product is very sticky, highly differentiated, and with little competition, you can capture more value and offer 5X returns to your customers. On the other side of the tracks, if you're in a highly competitive market and your differentiation is not obvious, then consider pricing to 20X ROI until you've built up enough differentiation and steam in your value train.

To give you a general price range by B2B market segment size, see the chart below in **FIGURE 11.8**. This is an order-of-magnitude type of range, so don't set your prices to these ranges. Rather, think about how your prices and packages fit within these categories. Are you selling $25K deals to SMB clients? If so, you might consider a lower-priced option to capture more business.

Using these general ranges based on target segment size services as a sanity check for your prices. You will know something is off if your product for small to medium businesses (SMB) is priced above $100K a year.

FIGURE 11.8: COMMON ANNUAL PRICE POINTS IN SAAS

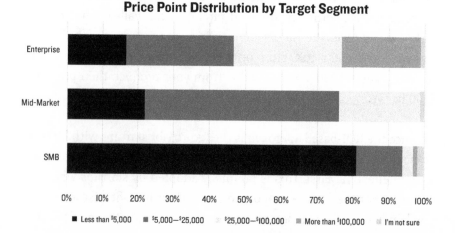

By now you've chosen your price levels, or at least where you want to position your plans within the price envelope. But how should you display the number? In the world of pricing, looks matter.

In **TRACK 10**, we went over a few psychology techniques to ease the cognitive load of someone evaluating your packages or bundles. Now let's cover some techniques to help reduce any mental gymnastics with reading the prices themselves, and while you are at it, make the pricing seem or "feel" more appealing.

When the price "feels" right, there's no rationale going on; that's human emotion taking over. The comfort sensation waltzes in when your mind can swiftly satisfy its built-in urges to check boxes.

For instance, if your mind sees the numbers 6 and 2, the brain (again, because of years of conditioning) wants to add them to 8 or multiply them to 12. Same with reading the number $1210 and $1,210. The first one is two syllables to read (twelve ten) and the other is 7 (one thousand, two hundred, ten).

Another word of caution before applying every technique here. Be very cautious of what behavior you are trying to induce from your target audience. For example, don't think, "I want someone to buy my stuff." Rather, think, "I want someone to buy the middle plan in less than three clicks with no sales intervention." This is a better way to apply pricing psychology. Here are some top pricing tips supported by psychology research:

- Remove currency symbols to make the price feel lighter or make them smaller or ghosted.
- Remove commas and decimals to reduce auditory magnitude.
- Break prices down to smaller denominations to reduce the pain of paying for smaller customers.
- Add distance between original and sale price.
- Odd numbers are associated with competence and even numbers are associated with warmth.
- If selling to a rational buyer, be more precise. If you are selling to an emotional buyer, be more rounded in prices.
- Charm prices do not have as dramatic of an effect in software, but in general, 9s signal a bargain.

Use these seven tips to ensure you frame the value properly to your audience and reduce buying confusion or hesitation. Applying these practices to your prices will help in making the price "feel" right and will hopefully lead them to pull out the credit card or sign that contract.

Simplifying the pricing structure will help smooth the sales process, increase the stickiness of the customers, and may give a long-term competitive moat. Getting pricing right is as important, if not more, as it is to getting the product right. Pricing separates a self-funded firm from an investor-dependent firm. The startups that are able to get their pricing strategy at the center stage early on will end up surviving this new age of value investing.

But not all software is the same or creates the same type of value. Most SaaS providers fall into one of four key categories. In **FIGURE 11.9**, I make a few suggestions on how to approach monetization for each SaaS category.

FIGURE 11.9: SAAS CATEGORIES AND MONETIZATION

Back Office

Has a natural cap on value, need to differentiate beyond labor savings

Sales Enablement

WTP and value capture higher with apps that make money

Collaboration & Workflow

Takes a while to get the full benefit, but race to capture users to create stickiness

Development Tools & Infrastructure

Normally a very price-sensitive audience, DIY is more common competitor, must prove value over time, short time to value, and allow scale and bulletproof support

PLAYBACK EXERCISE

To really ingrain the benefits of a price envelope, you'll need to put one together from scratch. Take the pricing data you've collected in previous tracks and construct a draft pricing envelope. What is your price envelope range?

INTERLUDE

When DocuSign introduced their electronic-signature technology, they knew they wanted to get the service out into the marketplace as quickly as possible, so they launched with the freemium model strategy. DocuSign's initial freemium version gave users everything they needed to use the service; so much so, in fact, that initial users didn't have much incentive to upgrade to the paid version!

So, DocuSign reworked their strategy and started offering a "free trial" version (with a 14-day termination deadline) for users who came in through paid search-related marketing. DocuSign realized these were the people who needed the product the most and therefore would be the most likely to upgrade when the trial was over.

This shift in strategy proved to be a winner, and free trials are now DocuSign's biggest revenue source. They have generated millions of new accounts, and DocuSign apportions part of its marketing efforts (emails, etc.) with a goal of converting those free users to happy and loyal paid subscribers.

The lesson here is that offering something for free is only part of the overall monetization and go to market strategy, in fact, going free sits right at the heart of their intersection.

This track is the most important in the book, so I wanted to spend the time to step through all the tools and techniques you will need to demystify price setting and successfully craft a coherent pricing strategy. If you just read this track and said to yourself, *Damn, this is super helpful,* then I've done my job!

But I would be lying to you if I said your work is done after setting the price.

Nope.

The work is just beginning. In the next track, you'll need to get back to business basics with good process, data, and management discipline—cuz I'll never come whack on an old school track.

THIS IS HOW WE DO IT

BUILD UP YOUR PRICING MUSCLE

ARTISTS IN THE '90S WERE CHANGING THE MUSICAL LANDSCAPE ...

... and Montell Jordan's debut album was a perfect encapsulation of R&B in the '90s, which I view as the softer side of hip-hop music.

The song "This Is How We Do It" stayed at #1 on the Billboard charts for seven consecutive weeks and remains the definitive song by one of the greatest R&B artists of the '90s. This track about going to a club was a team effort. There are nine credited songwriters, including Jordan. The song is a loud and proud proclamation of how they do things based on their culture, preferences, and resources. If you want this new pricing muscle to get stronger, you need to declare, emphatically, how *you* do it with your company's philosophy and approach to monetization.

PART TWO: PLAY is about helping you walk the walk by sharing my proven techniques, tricks, and playbooks on how to capture value in SaaS and monetize at scale with the 5Q framework. So far, we've covered the first four questions of 5Q to build a model that connects growth and pricing, and now it's time to round out the playlist with the most overlooked question: Which? As in: Which part of your pricing is working or not working?

In order to answer this question, you need to officially establish your process around how your company measures and improves pricing. Some of the most successful companies I work with have a well-defined and well-funded pricing system in place. And when I ask, "How do you capture value?" my favorite answer that puts a smile on my face is, "This is how we do it. Let us show you."

In this final track of **PART TWO: PLAY**, my goal is to share the best practices in setting up an effective pricing system in your business that allows you to get your growth on and get better at pricing over time.

We'll start things out with how to start things out.

WHO'S ON FIRST?

Most business leaders wonder who in the company should own pricing. I like to focus on how to own pricing, instead.

It's tempting to say "So and So" will run point and own all things pricing, or something similar. That is not a bad place to start, but more ideally, you need a pricing system that will outlast "So and So" and help build a repeatable system.

> **PRICING TIP**
>
> Building a pricing function is a lot like building muscle. You need form and repetition.

So, what does a pricing system look like? I like to boil it down to what I call the three Cs: **Centralize**, **Cadence**, **Connection**. Let me elaborate on each briefly.

CENTRALIZE

House all pricing-related material online and make it easy to access. Avoid using a random Excel spreadsheet off someone's laptop. At least use something everyone can access on the cloud, like G-Suite, Office 365, Confluence, SharePoint, or anything along those lines.

Start with a basic folder structure and turn on notifications to keep the site active. This is a fundamental step to establishing your pricing function because you need a source of truth.

CADENCE

Schedule regular pricing reviews and integrate pricing as a dedicated topic in business updates and management meetings. Hold pricing committees at least quarterly but start out monthly for the first quarter to work out all the kinks. Meet more frequently if information is changing or if there are lots of moving parts, such as when you're releasing new features or when you're entering a new market. In order to make this new cadence stick, remember to build a rhythm that goes with your culture.

CONNECTION

Connect your pricing discipline across functions like product management (roadmaps), sales/GTM (compensation, value selling), marketing (messaging, competitive position), and finance (forecasts, margins). If you establish a centralized source of truth and a cadence that goes with your culture, connecting the dots becomes far easier.

Start a pricing artifact matrix that calls out each pricing artifact and the responsible function. This keeps transparency high to avoid one of the top killers of establishing a pricing function: solo heroic efforts done in a vacuum. Bind your company's connective tissue to make it natural for the business as a whole to think about pricing, not just one person.

That's great, but who is best to put in charge of pricing?

I encourage you to look at a post by James Wood at Insight Partners summing up the question of which department should own pricing for the company (see **FIGURE 12.1**). I've seen the most success when pricing is under a strong and mature product management team, but I've also seen monetization thrive under a marketing team as well.

Each department ownership of pricing comes with their unique pros and cons. I mentioned that product management and marketing tend to perform best with pricing given their proximity to the customer and product value. On the other end, I find that sales ownership of pricing leads to problematic conflicts of interest given their natural objective to operate at a transactional level.

If you've reached the "scale up" stages of your business and are not sure how to split up the responsibilities behind good pricing habits,

You don't need a superhero; you need a system.

FIGURE 12.1: PRICING OWNERSHIP BY DEPARTMENT

OWNER	BENEFITS	RISKS
Finance	Deal desk discount control	Decision making can become clouded by cost and/or margin
Product Management	Influence on product strategy and roadmap	Decision making can be driven by product priorities rather than customer value
Sales	Deal desk ops and enablement driven by sales collaboration	Reporting to sales leadership can make it harder to enforce control over discounting practices
Marketing	Insight into segmentation and customer feedback helps with pricing differentiation	Influence on sales and product strategy questionable
Business Ops	Center of cross-functional relationships across the business	Little influence on product and sales/discounting

check out pricingio.com for a special gift just for you, a pricing roles and responsibilities matrix to give you a head start. You're welcome.

See **FIGURE 12.2** to see how the functions in your SaaS business that have a role to play. If I had to give one piece of advice, it would be to not approach pricing in a vacuum. Be open and transparent about the value you capture and why.

If you are the leader or founder, it is your job to be fluid and consistent on what value you're trying to capture, how you're trying to do that, and how that ties into your growth plan. You are the beacon everyone's going to look to. You and your story need to be consistent so everyone will follow you to the promised land.

A superhero will save the day! But a good system will pave the way.

FIGURE 12.2: THE PRICING WORKING TEAM

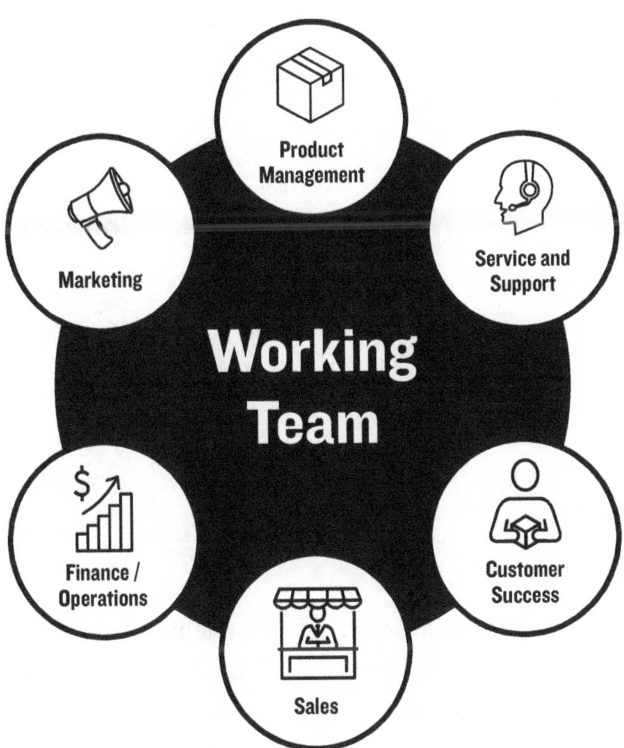

Building a pricing function is a lot like building muscle. You need form and repetition. If you follow the simple 3C model I laid out, you will hit the ground running and be a step ahead of the pack.

THE NORTH REMEMBERS

I am not at all referring to noble, naive dire wolves or treacherous, incestuous lions, or mentally unstable, larger-than-life dragons.

No, I am talking about establishing a North Star to measure against and drive towards with your pricing strategy. The way you price your software and services should lead you toward a goal that you benchmark, research, measure, talk and debate about, and celebrate as a milestone.

So, the questions to ask yourself are: What are we trying to measure? What is our North Star?

FIGURE 12.3 is a common set of North Star measures and KPIs that SaaS companies look at when they roll out new pricing.

FIGURE 12.3: COMMON NORTH STAR KPIS

Product NPS	**Average Deal Size**	**Average Contract Length**
LTV / CAC	**Closed Win Rate**	**Average Renewal Uplift**
ARPU / ARPA	**Discount Rate**	**Net Dollar Retention**

The point here is that you should have a deliberate target that you're after with the pricing model. If you see the results coming in below target, then it's up to you to adjust and refine the model.

If I had to give you most common North Star KPIs that I've seen in over 20 years, it comes down to these three:

- **Annual Recurring Revenue (ARR).** I've seen total ARR, new ARR, and year-over-year ARR growth rate as common North Stars. For example, best-in class-companies with high EV and exit multiples shoot for 40-percent topline growth rates.
- **Net Dollar Retention (NDR)** or **Net Revenue Retention (NRR).** This metric neatly captures your pricing effectiveness on all three dimensions: acquisition, expansion, and retention. The best of the best aim to achieve 130 percent and up.
- **Lifetime or Customer Lifetime Value (LTV or CLTV).** The heart and lifeblood of a good SaaS business needs a growing LTV, and one that is at least three times the cost to acquire customers. It is common for SaaS companies to achieve 9X LTV: CAC rations after optimizing their monetization strategy and execution.

As you make pricing and packaging decisions, you need to ask if these changes will get you closer to the North Star. This is a great way to resolve debates quickly and get everyone on the same page and agenda.

IN DATA WE TRUST

Make no mistake, better data makes it easier to identify your North Star and know if you are getting closer or further. You should constantly be striving to improve your data intelligence in order to improve your pricing decisions.

To me, data discipline is a living and breathing skill that never rests. The way you ran the willingness-to-pay survey yielded less-than-ideal results, and you're going to have to modify the questions or modify your target.

For example, the data set collected from sales opportunities were not actually reflecting true capture prices. Or maybe your competitive intelligence is stale or limited. Or you accidentally introduced bias in how you phrased the last round of customer survey questions. There will always be room for improvement in the quantity and quality of pricing intelligence. It is a part of value-based pricing that can't stop and won't stop.

But let's tackle this one step at a time. First, always audit your data sources and look for the areas of improvement that matter the most. Don't try to improve in too many directions at once. You can use a data scorecard to track this. **FIGURE 12.4** shows an example of what a data scorecard looks like.

Pricing data comes from having good discipline in your operations and systems, much of which we covered in **TRACK 6**. To help make it easier to remember where data comes from, I like to think of three main sources: Talks, Transactions, and Tests.

TALKS

If I haven't drilled this point hard enough in this book so far, then I'm not doing a good job. You have to talk to your customers and stakeholders to stay ahead in pricing. This is the best way to put data into context, find relationships and patterns that matter, and make sense of it all.

FIGURE 12.4: EXAMPLE OF DATA SCORECARD

DATA CATEGORIES	SCORE	COMMENTS
Sales Opportunities Data		Richer win/loss details, deal structure
Customer Account Data		Formal churn reasons and types
Financial Summary Data		ARR roll / P&L not provided
Growth Strategy and Plan		Aligned strategy, growth, roadmap
Value Proposition and Communication		Ongoing, expand proof points
Buyer Personas and Segmentation		Must breakdown by usage, use cases
Go-to-Market Model		Discount matrix and comp accelerators
Governance and Controls		Pricing exception management unclear
Employee Feedback		Survey not completed; 3 deep dives
Customer Feedback		Run semi-annually to increase N
Competitive Landscape		Run competitive study semi-annually
Product and Feature Data		Track deeper usage and feature preference

So how do you get thoughts into bite-sized data elements you can analyze and monitor? The answer shouldn't surprise you if you read **TRACKS 5** and **6**, so say it with me: "surveys and interviews!"

You get better data by asking better questions, going deeper behind an answer and by filtering the data in new ways that uncover insights. Adding new filters, such as demographics, is the easiest way to improve your qualitative data, so take advantage of it early and often.

In opaque industries or large ticket enterprise deals, competitive intelligence is hard to come by. You'll need to rely on talking to customers and colleagues to understand what you might be up against in a sale. The unseen benefit in opaque industries is that people tend to stay in that industry forever and hop from company to company. There's a good chance that someone on your team worked at a competitor or that a customer has used another competitor in the past.

TRANSACTIONS

As I said earlier, nothing happens until you sell something, or at least try to sell something. The key to improving your transaction data is extending the fields you capture during the lifecycle of an opportunity, a customer, and the product. I know this doesn't happen overnight but getting more granular data will aid your team in detecting patterns that could lead your pricing strategy down a better path.

For example, an enterprise SaaS company decided to add a field to capture which competitors were in the deal, known or assumed. This led to an insight that revealed a specific competitor was erratically discounting to win deals, which helped the company reframe how they positioned themselves when that specific competitor was in the mix.

TESTS

Moving forward in your data discipline also means moving from capturing data to creating data. Testing, whether in a controlled environment pilot or A/B rapid prototyping, is a must. You need to structure the test to capture the data you want to analyze. Sounds logical, and it is, but it is not easy.

From a new pricing page design to a new services bundle, implementing the right data capture mechanisms before you evaluate will save you a ton of wasted time and effort while maximizing the investment of every test you do.

THE VALUE TRAIN

You need a good governance structure in order to get better at pricing. There's no way around it. For change to drive action, you have to own it. For action to drive results, you have to measure. Like anything else, a

PRICING TIP

The best way to unify your team behind pricing is actually not to rally behind pricing but rally behind value.

solid pricing function needs proper resources and attention. Half-stepping your way through pricing will leave you and your team frustrated and ineffective.

This is the quintessential sequence of business growth: to create value then share it with those who need it and are willing to pay for it, and finally capture a fair share of that value.

A pricing committee is a perfect way to keep everybody aligned and keep pricing front and center. You want to have seen your representation in these pricing committee meetings. Again, pricing decisions impact 100 percent of your revenue. **FIGURE 12.5** shows a common structure or model to use as well as a sample agenda to reference.

FIGURE 12.5: MANAGING PRICING AT SCALE

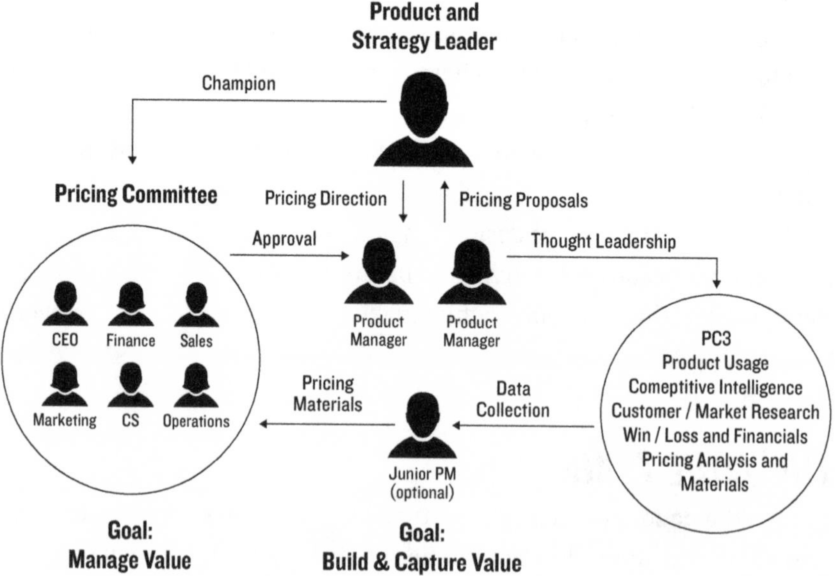

Here is a quick way to get your pricing committee off the ground:

- Hold a cross-functional brainstorm session to decide content and cadence.
- Design as a quarterly meeting but start the first quarter monthly to refine content.
- Start with basic content (metrics and informational readily available) and build up.
- Send a short survey after the meetings to measure effectiveness.
- Document and store all meeting notes and actions in a centralized, accessible tool.

The point of these meetings is not to review a bunch of transactional pricing exceptions. It is really to get a good sense for how the pricing is performing, what initiatives are in flight today, and to get approval for the next course of action. **FIGURE 12.6** is a sample of agenda topics to discuss during the meeting.

FIGURE 12.6: SAMPLE PRICING COMMITTEE AGENDA

TOPIC	SUGGESTED CONTENT	TIME
Pricing Performance/ Metrics	ARR to plan, Conversion rate, ARPA, Expansion MRR, Churn by cohort and reason, LTV/CAC, Margin	30 min.
Voice of Customer	Top deal objections, win/loss report, NPS, value survey	20 min.
Competition	Competitive price/package changes, promotions	20 min.
What's Working/ Not Working	Top wins/renewals, YoY up trends, deep dive topics, top losses, YoY down trends	30 min.
Value Initiatives	Active/future pricing campaigns/ roadmap monetization	20 min.

PLAYBACK EXERCISE

Like any new skill, it takes practice to work out the kinks and get good at it. Try not to over-engineer or complicate things out of the gate. Start with what you have and what you know and build up from there. Here is a checklist of next steps to get started:

1. Decide monetization strategy ownership.
2. Choose a lead; fits well under product management, marketing, and founder roles.
3. Assess pricing maturity and data quality.
4. Use 5Q to quickly rate strengths/opportunities (but keep it simple).
5. Start small but start something.

As your value train leaves the station, you need to manage pricing based on what is most important for the lifecycle of your SaaS product. Sounds rational, right? A new application in the early stages needs a more rapid iteration and testing, but a platform in mature stages needs stronger analysis on transactions and deeper looks at usage trends.

Think about placing the emphasis on your monetization improvements that matter most based on your product's lifecycle, as shown in **FIGURE 12.7**, and the impact of your efforts will be even greater.

FIGURE 12.7: PRICING ACROSS THE PRODUCT LIFECYCLE

As your SaaS product and customers change throughout the four-phased spectrum of the product lifecycle, the value perception also changes, and in turn, the pricing and packaging must also change in order to maximize the benefits of value-based pricing in SaaS.

INTERLUDE

Arnab Mishra, Chief Product Officer at Xactly, is an 18-year SaaS veteran who's run the gamut of success from smaller startups to enterprise software companies. He also brings an interesting perspective given his experience in investment banking and private equity. He knows both ends of the spectrum.

I met Arnab during my tenure in private equity when he joined a portfolio company I was working for at the time. He quickly catapulted into being one of the star product leaders in the portfolio. He was graceful enough to share his thoughts with me on pricing to value.

MARCOS: *Thanks for doing this. I love chatting with a fellow "Quant" about pricing. My first question is how did you get into pricing?*

ARNAB: Absolutely. I think there are several ways I could answer this question. I consider myself a commercial product leader and think a lot about how the product interfaces with the marketplace, what is the willingness to pay, what is our competitive differentiation, and that's where I live.

And in a lot of ways, monetization is the end product of all that work. And if you're doing a good job at all those things, understanding the willingness to pay and the pain your customers have, you should be able to deliver value that you can monetize.

I have a second view that in the software industry, pricing is what you make of it in the sense that software has an effectively zero marginal cost and there's a natural gravitational pull to bring down your prices. So you can price at whatever you want and cover your marginal cost, but you can't think of the world that way. You have to think about it from a value perspective. I think pricing becomes this exercise that forces you to think about the value you are delivering and how to articulate that value, which has other ramifications to the business.

MARCOS: *That is a very intriguing point of view. You almost have these two opposite forces tugging at each other. On one hand, the low marginal cost and race to get market share, and on the other hand, the high pace of innovation and desire to capture new value delivered. My*

CONTINUED →

next question is where do you see SaaS companies struggle the most with pricing?

ARNAB: I think one is understanding the importance of pricing. There's a mindset in software that pricing is whatever we can get from customers, and it is not a discipline. The second is making pricing a continuous process. Having a cadence of reassessing your pricing and packaging is super important and a source of competitive advantage. Another thing is being rigorous around quantifying the value, whether it's cost savings from efficiencies or driving some top-line result. I think companies are bad at that because it takes a lot of work in pulling the information out of your customers and understanding it.

MARCOS: *That's a great summary, and it's awesome you think of pricing in that way. So what is the best and worst pricing advice you ever heard?*

ARNAB: Oh man, the worst one is when I had a sales leader say to me, "Don't worry about the price. The customer will tell you the price."

And then the best pricing advice came when I was at an early-stage company. Realize that over time your product will evolve, and you can charge more later. It's like you're building a rocket ship and you naturally want to charge for X for the rocket ship out of the shoot, but the reality is that you start with one thruster and charge X for one, then change the pricing when you add the other thrusters. And just being okay with growing into higher prices over time. At one of my previous companies, our first version was only a fifth of the price we were charging after building out the product over four to five years.

MARCOS: *I love the rocket ship analogy; many startups feel like they need to figure it all out on day one and find the magic number to charge.*

ARNAB: And, they think if they charge X then when it comes up for renewal, they'll never be able to raise the price, so we should convince them to pay more now. And the reality is that you need to get your renewal people to articulate the value you've added since their last contract.

MARCOS: *Yes, it's important to avoid the fallacy around "they will never pay more."*

ARNAB: Yes and going back to my comment about letting customers dictate the price, you'll just end up with bad customers or losing your shirts on bad deals. And if you reach a certain point of maturity, you'll end up renegotiating or firing these customers. So, why even go through this churn process? Why even go there?

MARCOS: *Yeah, why even dig the hole in the first place, right? Next question: What is your favorite pricing success story?*
ARNAB: I don't know if this falls into the category of a pricing story, but I love the story of Domino's Pizza. They played in a commoditized market, and they were very clear that the value they were delivering wasn't necessarily the pizza, it was delivery—30 minutes or it's free. So, they differentiated not on pizza, but on service and generated greater market share. It doesn't touch on pricing, but it touches on understanding the value.
MARCOS: *I totally agree with you, it's hard to do value-based pricing without differentiation or an understanding of your value proposition and how it is differentiated. Do you have a pricing model that you admire the most?*
ARNAB: I like the razor versus blades model. In the SaaS world, there's a notion of consumption-based pricing and that's truly utility-based pricing. I would argue that is why Twilio has grown so fast, so when economic rents are due, Twilio can share in a percentage of those rents because they share the risk of the downside, but that risk is low since they have low marginal costs.

I always think about who's taking the inventory risk. In traditional SaaS models, the inventory risk is pushed on the consumer. I'm buying 500 seats and I'm committed to this inventory for the next year. Whereas in the Twilio model, Twilio is taking on the inventory risk and therefore can charge higher economic rents. If I'm the customer and I am taking on the inventory risk, I naturally want to push the price down to make up for whatever underutilization scenarios in my head.
MARCOS: *That concept of inventory risk is present in SaaS pricing today and I don't think too many SaaSletes out there realize it or think about it in that way.*

Congratulations, you are now better at pricing than 90 percent of the B2B SaaS companies out there! Tell your friends. Take a bow.

Let's recap what you learned from **PART TWO: PLAY:**

- How to detect pricing signals and run a baseline analysis to understand your pricing.

- The 5Q framework to structure your approach to monetizing value.
- Useful techniques to segment your audience, package your product/services, and price your value.
- The ins and outs of building your pricing muscle in house to help you get better over time.

I know, I know, it's crazy to think you were in business and pricing your products without this knowledge. But that's all in the past now.

Your chances of success just went up! How did that feel? You now have a pricing playlist to guide you through your monetization journey.

Let's fast-forward and take it a step further. In the next section, we're going to tackle a few of the toughest and most top of mind topics in B2B SaaS pricing.

We're going to start up with two dope boys in a Cadillac.

PART THREE: FAST FORWARD

Knowledge is worthless standing still; you have to run with it. In the final four tracks, we **FAST FORWARD** things to address the most critical obstacles and challenges to monetization and clear the path toward growth and prosperity. Damn skippy!

SO FRESH, SO CLEAN

PRICE NEW PRODUCTS TO LEARN, THEN EARN

WE FORGED A SOLID PRICING FOUNDATION BY REWINDING INTO MY PAST EXPERIENCE IN PART ONE.

In **PART TWO**, we dove into my 5Q framework and a step-by-step instructional playlist to help you price and package your product like a pro (try saying that five times fast). In **PART THREE**, I'll share some perspective on a three scenarios that SaaSletes face on the road to finding that successful monetization model.

These three scenarios call for specific pricing tactics and deserve their own set of rules: New Product Pricing, Enterprise Deal Pricing, and Pandemic Pricing. There is no doubt you will find yourself dealing with these scenarios at some point during your SaaS journey, so we should think ahead and lay out a game plan for how to monetize under these conditions. In this track, we are going to tap into the confidence it takes to price a new product.

Speaking of confidence, André 3000 and Big Boi may have been one of the most popular and respected hip-hop groups of all time, but they earned those accolades in their own way. The 1992 dynamic duo, OutKast was an example of an untapped market breaking through in spite of the suppressive treatment the southern region received from the music industry in the nineties.

Their fourth studio album, *Stankonia*, released in 2000 was arguably the most spellbinding album in hip-hop history, allowing the pair freedom to tinker with experimental musical aesthetic and pushing us beyond the box of what hip-hop music is supposed to sound like. In the frame of a Dirty South-orientated context, OutKast channeled their entrepreneurial spirit and fused everything from rave and funk to gospel into their pre-party anthem, "So Fresh, So Clean." With its inspired collages of rap, electronica, psychedelic rock, and funked-up soul—the jam sounded like nothing else at the time.

And it's that type of daring, bold, and fresh new thinking that inspired me to use this classic to represent a track dedicated to startup entrepreneurs, solopreneurs, and intrapreneurs alike. You see, launching a new product into the world is a big event, riddled with a mix of excitement and anxiety, adorned with all eyes watching, and laced with so many eager questions to answer. You need hella confidence to put your product, and yourself, out there naked and ready for judgement. You have no idea if they will love it or hate it, let alone what to charge people for it. Starting up is a leap of faith!

This thinking should resonate with any SaaSlete who has launched a new product from the ground up. What you think, see, feel, and wish could be very different and punctuates the need to stay nimble with pricing in the early days as you iterate your way to higher confidence.

PRICING TIP

Pricing is about confidence.

GIT UP, GET OUT

The first question will always be, "Did we build the right thing?" The elusive answer to that question is what keeps SaaSletes up at night. But a follow-up question that is just as pertinent as the first is, "Are we pricing it right?"

Remember that SaaS is a relationship, an exchange of long-term, ongoing value between you and your customer for ongoing payments. In this relationship, you as the SaaS provider have to both create and capture value over time.

In the early days of innovation, the startup should be more concerned about finding product-market fit before nailing down product-market price fit. Consider it as Step 1A when introducing new value to the world. You will find it hard to price to value when the value itself is not known yet.

PRICING TIP

As a startup or new product, you must price to learn before you earn.

Instead of wasting time and effort pulling things out of thin air (or somewhere else), acknowledge that you don't know what you don't know and go about it in a way that's designed to intelligently fill those knowledge gaps.

I simplify the concept of a startup lifecycle into three phases in **FIGURE 13.1.** Check it out.

FIGURE 13.1: PHASES OF A STARTUP

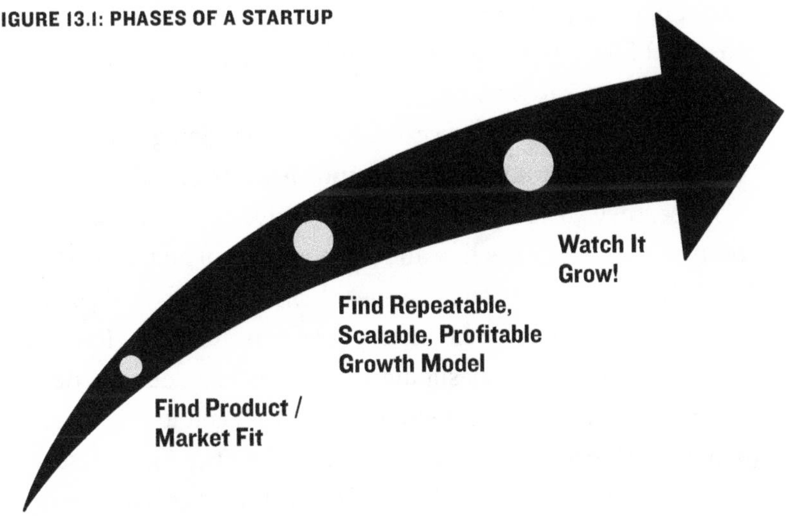

When I ask SaaS founders how they produced their pricing, I typically hear one of three answers:

1. **"We made it up."** The price was plucked out of thin air and the customer said yes, so that became the price going forward. Sometimes, for many years to come. Funny enough, I find this group to have the most misaligned price-to-value of all the clients we work with, meaning some customers are paying way too much and others are paying way too little. Not good if you want to scale.

PRICING TIP

Pricing without data, structure, and purpose is dangerous at worst and reckless at best.

2. **"We made it low to get customers."** This one is not too far from making it up, except they had a clue that it was on the cheap side of the table. They picked a number so low that price was not part of the sales conversion. It was a "no brainer;" they just wanted customers to buy. This type of market penetration strategy helps to grease the skids and bring in business, but it also sets a dangerous anchor of value perception that will be tough to climb if it works too well. I find this group to be woefully underpriced in magnitudes anywhere from 2 to 20 times. They are leaving real money on the table, and again, it's hard to scale when you are doing that.
3. **"We charge a premium for our ground-breaking innovation."** In this case, they go and price on the expensive side to signal the technology is top of the line and a premium tool on the market. This type of approach usually leaves them with high deal sizes and revenue per user, so no money is left on the table. However, they are losing deals they should win. In SaaS models, you need to grow your subscriber base in order to cross and upsell your way to lower CAC expansion revenue. One of the little-known truths about capturing so much value up front is that it gets harder to grow over time.

The statistics are bleak but deserve to be repeated. Ninety percent of startups fail, according to an in-depth analysis of 3,200 companies as part of the *Startup Genome Report*. The researchers blame "premature scaling" as the root cause, pointing out that 70 percent of startups in the study scaled before they were ready and that startup founders underestimated how long it takes to validate their market.

Product-market fit (PMF) is a critical prerequisite to scale and produce long-term value for customers and shareholders. PMF is when a startup or company introduces a new product that meets a real customer need in a way that's better than the status quo and in a market that can support a profitable standalone business.

PRICING TIP

Like pricing, product-market fit tends to be a spectrum rather than a discrete milestone and typically takes continued, sustained effort to improve over time.

First Round Capital recently researched the most common mistakes made by startups who struggle to raise capital. Compared to peers who breezed through the fundraising process, those who struggled were:

- Three times more likely to say they monetized too late.
- Two times more likely to pursue the wrong business model.
- Four times more likely to say they botched their go-to-market strategy.

Certainly, we can agree that picking the right go-to-market strategy is a part of finding product-market fit. But, deciding when to monetize and which pricing model to pursue seem to be afterthoughts, despite clearly fundamental to a startup's success. We should be seeking for not just product-market fit, but rather produce-market-price fit.

The "price" in product-market-price fit factors in a startup's ability to scale their value, which is based on their pricing power in the market, the attractiveness of their pricing model, and the health of their unit economics.

PRICING TIP

Product-market-price fit is when a startup offers a new product that meets a real need customers will pay for at a price that can support unit economics to scale.

"But Marcos, how do you figure out prices this early?" you ask.

In short, you have to put something out there to start the learning cycle. But don't pull a number out of thin air; pull it out of well-oxygenated and rich air. You'll have to make assumptions, generate a hypothesis, prove or disprove it, learn, and move on to the next. You guessed it: It's the old scientific method you learned in grade-school problem solving.

A classic marketing 101 framework to help you think about the initial price is the *Value-Price Thermometer*, published by Harvard Business School in 2014. To give you the Twitter version explanation, this tool plots four numbers to suggest incentives to buy and sell a product.

You start with the costs, which for SaaS is negligible, then the perceived value, then the true value. **FIGURE 13.2** is a common graphic used to express the value-price thermometer.

FIGURE 13.2: VALUE-PRICE THERMOMETER

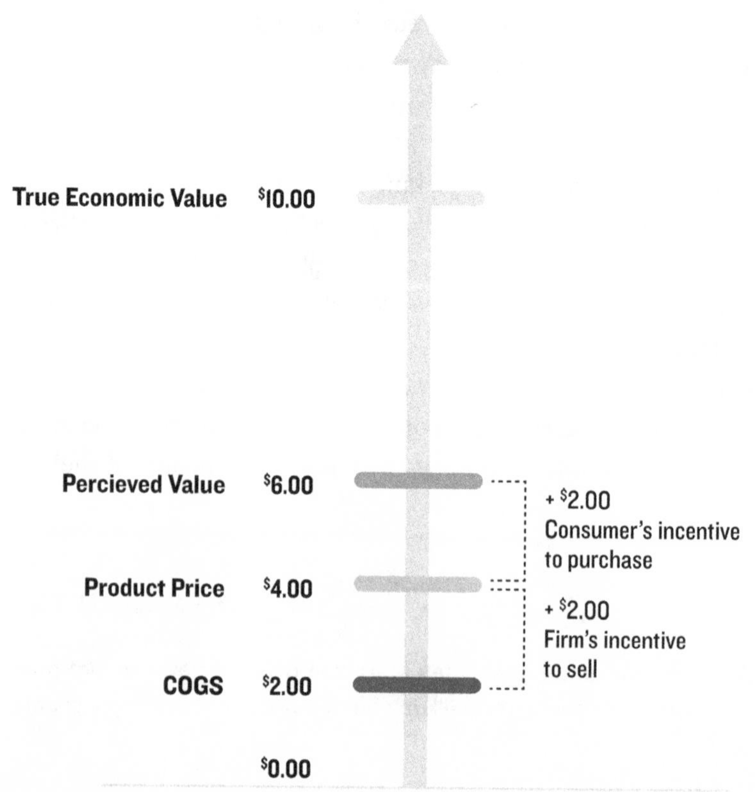

PRICING TIP

Pricing Tip. Startups and new products need to consider pricing during the initial stages of finding potential customers and product-market fit.

The basis is simple. Sell stuff above your costs and below the perceived value for a win-win. The hard part is how to figure out the perceived value. The truth is, you can't until real customers tell you what value they perceive. And even after that, the perception could be influenced by factors completely outside of the product.

But the good news is that I will give you shortcuts to focus in on the perceived value in the early days. Let's start with the old rule of thumb famed and acclaimed by Silicon Valley, the old rule of **10-5-20**.

THE 10-5-20 RULE

The Valley is full of rules of thumbs, tips, and tricks. Some are noteworthy, and some are a complete waste of time. The incubators and investors are famous for pitching to their cohorts the 10-5-20 rule to help with initial pricing of startups in the early years. I view it as the cousin of the 10X ROI we just stepped through earlier in **TRACK 11**, but here is how it works:

- Most buyers won't push back if they are getting 10 times the value for the price. Ten times, as an order of magnitude, is easy to digest and reasonable to expect. It is not at all accurate, but is safe, fair, and a decent place to start to see where on the spectrum your product's true and perceived value falls. If they do not immediately understand the 10 times value of the price, it's going to be hard to get them to move. Their incentive to buy might be too low, and potentially not a good fit customer as an early adopter.
- Once you have a few early adopters, you can start practicing raising prices. The rule of thumb is raising prices by 5 percent, but 10 percent is acceptable as well. My rationale is that most early adopters aren't buying your new product because you are cheap,

they are buying your new product to solve a problem in a new or better way. My view is that customers will not like the frequent bumps of 5 percent, and it signals that you are guessing. To shift from guesswork to framework, reassess your value and your price quarterly and update specific prices for specific packages to capture the value from specific buyers. A blanket 5-percent bump is a waste of time, but be thoughtful, be focused, and get a 10-15 percent bump instead, as an example. There is a time and place to do more frequent and incremental price uplifts, and we'll talk more about that in the next track.

- The third part of 10-5-20 is to keep raising prices until you're getting about 20 percent of your customers pushing back on the price. This was born as a derivative of the surprisingly accurate and applicable 80/20 rule.

Determining pricing for mid-market and enterprise in the early days of a SaaS product presents its own set of challenges. I've heard stories from founders about closing a deal, and afterwards the customer revealing they would have paid double. Nod your head if this has happened to you, too.

Use your sales process and cycle to gut check your pricing and average deal size to find a general order of magnitude. For example, you want a fully ramped sales rep to book at least five times their full cost in ARR in a year. If a rep costs $150K, ideally, they should book $750K or more in new ARR in a year (5 x 150 = 750). Given your average sales cycle, how many deals do you think a rep should close in a year?

If it takes about two weeks to close a deal, then a rep can close 25 deals a year (50 week divided by 2). To reach $750k, the average deal size needs to be around $30K (30K x 25 deals). This serves as a starting point but remember my rule from **TRACK II** in this next pricing tip.

Never make a price decision off one data reference point.

If you are on the fence, it's always better to start with a higher price and when buyers negotiate; use that as an opportunity to ask for other things in exchange for a discount. For instance, a longer-term contract, more money up front, a case study testimonial, or whatever is most valuable to you at this stage of your business.

The fear in most startups is that you might risk losing the deal if you ask for a higher price or concessions in return. But more often, it sets the tone for the relationship going forward based on the rule of reciprocity in human psychology. You should always think of price negotiations in terms of "something for something" rather than "something for nothing."

Prospects and customers often give signals on their willingness to pay during your sales and service conversations, and you can glean how they are thinking about your product. Think about these questions to spot the signals:

- Are they comparing it to other products they currently use or used in the past? If so, how were those products priced?
- Do they talk about the impact they think your product can have on their KPIs?
- Are they telling you how cheap or expensive you are?
- Are they raving about a specific feature or service you thought wasn't that impactful?

Pay special attention to these conversations and use the intel to refine your pricing and packaging model.

"So is the 10-5-20 rule the only path for startups or new products?" you wonder.

Nope, there is one piece of advice that I recommend in the early stage of any company or product: the **4 Count** approach.

THE 4 COUNT

Over the years, I've seen the inner workings of how 200 software products set their prices. And in my prior roles as a product leader, I've launched and priced over 40 new products to market.

No doubt, value-based pricing for new products is harder than existing for all the reasons we've talked about thus far. But it is not impossible. I've produced an easy-to-understand way to figure out how to price your products in the early days.

To start, you have to let go of any attempts to be precise, accurate, or perfect. Your goal should be to land prices that are directionally correct, influence the right behavior, and grow as value becomes sharper and clearer in both your mind and your customers' minds.

Now you're ready for the four steps to price your startup business or new product:

1. Begin by pricing one specific target customer segment or Ideal Customer Profile (ICP). Focusing on the customer you understand the best will increase your chances of success with identifying the price-value equation in their minds. Use this to learn and create a reference price point for the other customer segments.

   For example, maybe your product works across various customer sizes and verticals. Choose the one you know the best. Like many entrepreneurs, this might be the customer that was once you!
2. Craft two package options to price: one lead option and one backup. Having two plans allows you to pivot quickly and avoids knee-jerk reactions to a price. My suggestion is to have a standard and premium option.

   More often than not, you want to start with the premium option to test the higher-end prices and fall back on the standard option to close in case you run into resistance. The premium version doesn't need excessive new features, use value-builders like higher limits, additional support, faster access to new features, and hands-on implementation and training services to differentiate premium in the initial stages.

   Here is the non-intuitive part: You close the sensitive customers by telling them you will upgrade to the premium plan for the standard price as a gesture of goodwill and token of appreciation for being an early adopter. In this scenario, the customer feels like they get a bargain, you win the revenue and data, and in the process are anchored to a higher number to allow room to grow later.

3. You want to have at least three reference points before setting a price (remember the sources we talked about in **TRACK 11**). Set your two package options, standard and premium, to be about five times apart. For example, if your standard price is $50, then set the premium price at $250.
4. This is where we tie in with the 4C framework from **TRACK 6**. To narrow in a reference price, get scrappy with the data you have and can access within each of the 4C categories.

Each section of the 4C framework will continue to evolve as you gain traction with your new product. Use the strategic questions listed in each of the four phases in **FIGURE 13.3** to focus in on gathering whatever evidence is available to answer the strategic questions. Start with information on hand in the Capture and Context category to build up assumptions, then prove/disprove these assumptions with what you learn from Competitors and Customers.

Remember our thesis for this track: Learn before you earn. This will boost pricing confidence over time with every data point that you collect along the way.

Once you are comfortable with where you've landed in the value spectrum, plan to increase the price once a year, every year. The increase should align with how much additional value you've added over last year, how you stack up vs. the competition, and how your reputation grows. A bump of 5 percent to 10 percent is typically acceptable if you've made modest updates, but a price increase of 15-50 percent of the additional

PRICING TIP

Never stop reevaluating you're pricing. Build a repeated habit around assessing the price to value equation.

FIGURE 13.3: 4C CATEGORIES

CAPTURE

- Dissect every deal that you win and lose to uncover any patterns
- Look closely at who is buying more and who is not

Sales and Conversion Metrics
Incentives and Exceptions
Services Attach Rate

COMPETITORS

- Peruse competitor websites and testimonials for ROI and reconcile it with your market and value proposition
- Check software review sites for any price or package intel
- Ask your friends who have either worked at or purchased the competitor offering
- Analyze one competitor below, at, and above your position in the market

SWOT and Positioning
Loss Analysis
Competitive Threat Score

CONTEXT

Product Roadmap and Priorities
Feature Value Scores
Revenue Roll and Margins

- Ask for their budget or range
- Probe on how much they pay for the current solution
- Poke around their annual department budget
- Dig into how much the problem is costing them now

CUSTOMERS

Target Segmentation Attributes
Feature Preferences and NPS
Account Billing and Product Usage

- What is the pain you're solving?
- What price gives the customer a 10X return on buying product?
- What order of magnitude deal sizes do you see in this space?
- Are prices in this market growing or shrinking?

PRICING TIP

As they unlock more value, you unlock more revenue. That's the beauty of good monetization.

value you created is acceptable only if you've released game-changing updates that boost the value notably.

Figuring out pricing in the initial stages of a business or product poses crazy challenges for any SaaSlete. But pricing complex deals for enterprises introduces an entirely new set of obstacles.

The more money you want for your product, the more human interaction and psychological aspects come into play. It's like the bigger the deal, the bigger the art and the smaller the science when it comes to pricing. It's like the more money you come across, the more problems you see!

MO MONEY, MO PROBLEMS

PRICE ENTERPRISE DEALS, NOT ENTERPRISE PRODUCTS

NO SONG ANNOUNCED HIP-HOP'S ENTRY INTO THE MAINSTREAM LOUDER THAN "MO MONEY, MO PROBLEMS."

The video, directed by Hype Williams, literalized that flight. It featured Mase and Puff Daddy floating in a chamber of pressurized air like astronauts, then jigging ecstatically in a black tunnel lined with fluorescent lights, all while wearing reflective jumpsuits.

The song is a refusal of the desperation that an entrenched economic disparity and the crack epidemic had imposed on Black communities, and a paean to the kind of wealth accumulation often unattainable for these communities. "You'd rather see me die than see me fly," Puffy rapped at his verse's start. Built on a sample of Diana Ross' "I'm Coming Out" and a refrain sung by the R&B artist Kelly Price, "Mo Money" harnesses disco in order to transmit the song's insistence on rapture and the possibility that utopia can be found. It was an archetypal nod to the concept of "go big or go home!"

In the last track, we covered the ins and outs of monetizing new products or startups, where it is more about building up your pricing confidence and experience than the actual price itself. In this track, we'll dive into another scenario where the price itself is not as important as how you manage the natural pitfalls that come with going big.

In B2B SaaS, "going big" translates to going upmarket and selling to enterprise companies. Pricing becomes multiplexed as your average deal size grows. But when it comes to selling to enterprises, it's more about the deal than the product, more about relationship than the price, and more about art than science.

THE SSSS ENTERPRISE

The enterprise buyer can seem unfamiliar and daunting to some SaaSletes. The stakes are high, and the deals are large enough to make or break your year. To help demystify the enterprise buyer for you, I want to share four key attributes of enterprise software sales that I learned throughout my career (the largest deal size I was involved with was a win for a $50M contract over five years). To paint a complete picture of the enterprise SaaS buyer, I like to frame enterprise deals in terms of the four Ss: **Size**, **Safety**, **Scale**, and **Selling**.

SIZE

Enterprises tend to house thousands of employees, customers, or partners. This means a large population of people will be accessing your software and driving mega traffic, potentially around the clock. The vast quantity makes charging by the user tougher because they'll want deep discounts for the high volume. To prepare for this common scenario, you should have a well-defined discount matrix designed for high volume deals.

If your pricing model uses more than one value metric (as we discussed in **TRACK II**), I prefer to give the enterprise unlimited users and meter them on usage. This will remove a lot of friction in the sales process and avoid revenue obstacles like fractional user types and ramp-up schedules that slow down your revenue recognition.

> **PRICING TIP**
>
> When discounting for volume, start with five tiers of volume and about a 10-15 percent discount from tier to tier.

SAFETY

Remember that you are selling software to a living and breathing ecosystem and your solution needs to fit with little or no disruption. This means you need to help the client implement, train, and roll out the new solution. Enterprise deals will often include some level of professional services, so be prepared to include implementation and training as part of the offer mix.

PRICING TIP

Don't write a blank check for your "people power," instead, put guardrails around it and include the appropriate number of services for the size and software.

The other element around safety is security and privacy controls. Enterprises might demand a vulnerability scan of your software, a special privacy policy, or an incredible amount of privacy assurances. Be prepared to address these concerns in your enterprise package. Big companies have targets on their backs from hackers and fraudsters, both from inside and outside their organization.

SCALE

Enterprises require everything to function at scale. This will force you to keep innovating at a pace that keeps up with the organization, but conversely makes it tougher for them to absorb large amounts of change at one time. Because of this, you'll need to balance innovation with configuration to gain flexibility in how you release, or not release, new capabilities. As enterprises scale, they will also demand reports and analytics to monitor and prove the business is running more efficiently.

And over time, the enterprise organization will gain more scale, and hence more value, every year. This is where renewal uplifts come into play. Include a clause in the primary services agreement that gives you the right to raise prices annually. High-caliber legal teams will typically negotiate this clause out of the deal, but my advice is to fight for an inflation increase of at least 3 percent per year.

SELLING

Enterprises are too big and busy to buy software quickly, and they need convincing and consensus across the organization, which means your sales rep needs to shepherd the deal from cradle to grave. Be prepared to invest in this process with high-powered, relationship building account executives (AEs) who are well compensated for their trouble, because they

PRICING TIP

Enterprises don't buy software; they are sold software. Prepare to own the sales cycle from end to end.

will run into a lot of it. Deals are riddled with highs and lows. My advice is to not fight the sales cycle but own it, control it, and refine it over time.

Large enterprises don't know how to buy software despite their greatest efforts. In a false attempt to maximize value, they minimize it. In a high-stakes environment, nobody wants to make a final decision for fear of losing their job, promotion, or reputation. They also tend to come to the table with a warped view of the world shaped by their exaggerated cultured lens of how things work or get done.

Still interested? Well, I can't blame you as even one enterprise deal can change the course of any annual ARR goal. Let's take a look at how big deals are made.

THE BIG DEAL WITH BIG DEALS

Enterprises like to throw around their weight because they can. They have large-scale operations with large-scale problems that demand large-scale solutions. They know you want their large-scale checks, so they naturally use this as leverage. All negotiations come down to leverage, one way or another.

Enterprise buyers are stewards of the business trying their best to represent the needs and best interests of the company. The delegate buying the software is also representing his or her personal career needs as well, adding another dimension to the deal. You have to appeal to both the business and personal needs in order to win.

Like an absurdly priced one-bedroom apartment in New York City, you pay a close-ended subscription to access your place for a defined period of time. In subscription software, you are also charging for access (think Netflix or Spotify). When it comes to enterprise deals, the emphasis is more on usage over access, but in a subscription plan, you may be charging for access as well as usage. Therein lies the rub.

Enterprise deals with implementation and training will push you to defer SaaS license fee until you go live. They'll ask you to defer fees until full go-live or impose some complex ramp up schedule so you get paid slowly as they roll out the solution to groups of users.

One way around is to offer a step-up fee structure by offering a reduced SaaS license fee during implementation and have them step up to the full cost at a pre-negotiated launch date. Both sides need skin in the game.

As mentioned in earlier tracks, you can deploy other tactics to negotiate such as using "gives and gets" but you can avoid trap doors by implementing the 3Cs of contracts (clarity, consistency, and controls). Clarity helps you understand the risk profile you are signing up for in the deal, such as excessive SLAs or longer payment terms. Consistency measures how often you are holding to your policies, and Controls is all about implementing the right checks and balances. See the table in **FIGURE 14.1** for how to score your enterprise deals using the 3C method:

FIGURE 14.1: THE KEYS TO GOOD CONTRACT HYGIENE

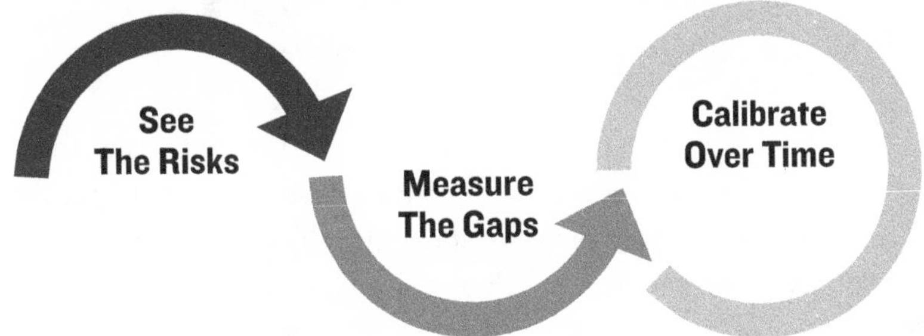

YOU DESERVE A RAISE

Why ask for a raise? Assuming you're a rational person, the trigger is the sensation that you've increased your value to the company, and therefore, would like to adjust your share in the price-value exchange.

Enterprise deals are typically multi-year and long-term relationships, but they are not static. Your software is changing and getting better, faster, and smarter. The enterprise customer is ideally consuming and benefiting from increased value every year.

So yes, it is appropriate to adjust your share of the price-value exchange as well.

But how do you go about doing that without disturbing the relationship? I like to think about it like a game of pool.

The whole purpose of the white ball in billiards is to cue another ball into motion. If you've ever played pool, then you know the positioning of the cue ball makes all the difference.

Your sales or CS team is your cue ball. Position them for success with a script to highlight the meaningful value of your product and navigate the price increase conversation. Include objection handlers and escalation paths.

Be sure to define the most suitable options for your client, a "one-size-fits-all" approach is a no-go if you want to pull this off. It is best to segment your customers and offer different options to each segment while giving customers a path to stay, upgrade, or downgrade.

The glossy white ball is lined up with the last sphere on the table, the eight ball. You draw back your blue-tipped stick and gently thrust it forward putting your cue into motion.

This is your team's strategic engagement. Your sales or success script should include a list of value boosters in three ways:

1. The value the customer has used to date (Hint: Tell them the number of users, messages, or contacts used so far this year.).
2. The biggest releases in the past six months (Hint: Choose big and noticeable enhancements they can see and feel.).
3. The new value coming in the next six months. (Hint: Talk about new goodies that are already in beta or close to finished. Avoid high level roadmap ideas or early concepts.).

Remember that investing in better support, faster onboarding, and more services boosts value as well. Make clear what you want the customer to do by giving them a specific call to action such as choosing a plan or confirming an option.

If the contract value is small, you may opt to take a passive approach (auto-renew, nothing for you to do, etc.) but always give the customer a

PRICING TIP

After a price increase, look for signs such as reducing user seats, asking for escalation, or a sharp drop in usage. Have a remedy in place for each scenario.

choice to accept the change or switch to a different plan. Identify churn risk by defining signals that your customers may not accept the new plan or price change.

Clack! The eight is in motion to the corner pocket. The kinetic energy is guiding that last ball to the goal, the price increase.

Reframe the pricing change by offering a time-bound promotion. Something like renewing in the next 30 days to get one month free or getting a free upgrade for three months. Ensure that all promotions have a condition and expiration date in order to sink the eight without scratching.

Another technique to ease customers into the new pricing plans is to define milestones that qualify for discounts, credits, or other terms. For example, when customers reach a certain amount in transaction volume by a specific period, they'll receive a credit equal to 10 percent of their contract value. Let them use the credits to buy services or purchase add-ons that could yield more value. If you want to get fancy, boost up the value of the credits so they get more when they buy selected products or services. Should you choose this route, be sure to track and enforce the milestones closely.

Grandfathering should be offered very selectively to accounts that fit a defined set of conditions (tenure, size, strategic value, LTV). Give them a path to full or near-full price over the next one to two years. In some industries, word travels, and others may demand the same rate. In other cases, some people leave organizations to join new companies and will demand the same rate. Too many grandpas lead to both financial and operational headaches, so be careful (check back to **TRACK 2** for mistakes to avoid when grandfathering customers).

Getting the raise you deserve takes discipline and systematic approach. If you follow these steps, you'll increase the chances of raising prices on enterprise deals to correspond with all the increased value they receive. As your customer base grows, so does the financial impact of a well-executed annual price uplift campaign.

INTERLUDE

Great success in winning SMB or mid-market customers does not guarantee you will be successful selling into the enterprise space. I'd like to share a true story about a high-rising SaaS company that ran into major headwinds moving up to serve enterprises.

This SaaS business was growing 100 percent year over year through their phenomenal viral coefficient. They had a freemium plan that worked well in spreading the word around. And growing up in the B2C space taught them a lot about being client-driven and designing intuitive and simple user experiences.

The line between B2B and B2C can become blurry. Users started to blend personal with business productivity, which in hindsight is natural evolution given that most of us spend the majority of our week working, either at home or at the office.

The company was not prepared to sell to enterprises. They lacked the right sales process and it showed. SDRs were thrusted into large deals and would say yes to anything. It was like watching a bad cha-cha on *Dancing with the Stars*; you could tell this company was completely out of their element.

From an enterprise-ready software perspective, they were woefully behind on robust privacy, SSO, and integration features required by enterprises. They also were far behind development of their reporting, analytics, and central administration tools, things that were not as important when serving small or micro-SMB clients. They flipped their roadmap upside down to get these feature gaps closed as quickly as possible. But wait, what about the tens of thousands of users already using the product and asking for updates. Do you see the dilemma?

It took almost two years to make the shift, but they did it! They soared past $50M in ARR last year and continue to climb. It took a serious investment in people, process, and product, but they did it and now enjoy the fruits of skyrocketing deal sizes, ARR, and valuation. I love it when the little guy comes out on top!

Navigating enterprise deals is reaching the next level when it comes to monetization, so congratulations for pushing the pace. But given the unpredictable world we live in, the environment can change on a dime, making pricing strategy and decisions even more audacious than ever before.

What happens when things go to hell in a handbasket? An economic downturn hits you out of left field. Think about the dotcom bubble circa 2001, the financial crisis around 2008, and then the COVID-19 pandemic we are living through right now!

The world will have its cycles, so it's best to be ready with a strategy for how to react when downturns inevitably happen to your business.

So what you supposed to do? Well, you gotta keep ya head up.

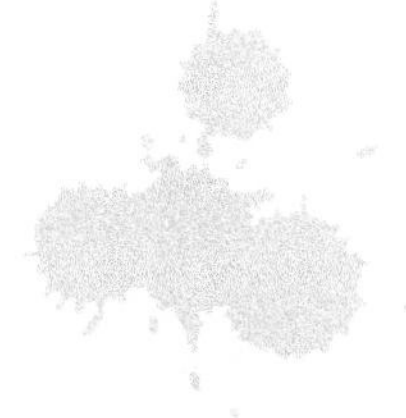

KEEP YA HEAD UP

MONETIZING IN HARD TIMES

TUPAC SHAKUR'S EVERGREEN CLASSIC "KEEP YA HEAD UP," RELEASED IN 1993, CARRIED A MELLOW AND SOBERING MESSAGE TO THE WORLD TO STAY STRONG IN THE FACE OF ADVERSITY.

The song chorus features R&B singer Dave Hollister as he melodically delivered a sample from "O-o-h Child" by The Five Stairsteps.

The song timing was no coincidence, surfacing in a time of high racial tension, wealth inequality, and feelings of hopelessness in the minority community, particularly among Black women. Released not too far after the Rodney King riots and inspired by a wrongful shooting death, the song became a beacon of hope for those who felt hopeless in hard times.

In this third and final part of our journey, I've exposed you to tried-and-true ways to deal with high uncertainty, such as with new products, and high complexity, such as with selling into large enterprises. In this track, I want to share my point of view of how to price when you're dealing with high uncertainty and high complexity at the same time.

From economic collapse and natural disasters to civil unrest or pandemics—your technology business must be ready to weather the storm if you want to survive. You can't predict or guarantee an outcome in an uncertain world, but you can do things to pull the odds in your favor. For one, you can shift and adapt your business by how you monetize value. However, this is only feasible when you have a clear monetization strategy and high pricing confidence.

How you price to value matters, and more so if conditions abruptly change. This book was written during the COVID-19 pandemic that took a stranglehold on the world economy in 2020 and 2021. I witnessed SaaS businesses flourish and perish, and for full transparency, it was not solely due to poor pricing. But I did see a pattern of pricing behavior that emerged among B2B subscription companies who navigated the crisis better than others, and therefore, would like to share what I observed to help prepare you for the hard times that undoubtedly will come your way.

PRICING IN HARD TIMES

Let's face it. None of us saw the pandemic coming. As we were all planning budgets and forecasts for the 2020 fiscal year, we had no idea our plans would evaporate as the world economy wore a KN95 surgical face mask.

Before you navigate a crisis, you must understand that there are three phases of a downturn and how to respond during each phase, as shown in **FIGURE 15.1**. In a time of uncertainty and fear, it is having clear goals mixed with speedy execution that gives you a fighting chance.

FIGURE 15.1: THREE PHASES OF A CRISIS

MARKET DEMAND	COLLAPSE	BOTTOM	RECOVERY
CONSUMER BEHAVIOR	**Panic & Pessimism**	**Logic & Realism**	**Caution & Optimism**
	Preserve cash	Resurgence of procurement	FOMO (Fear of missing out)
	Shut down of procurement	Uncertainly and opposition	Lockdown long-term advantages
	Expect top value at bottom price	High sensitivity to loss	Will pay premiums for convenience
	Time sensitive	Little sensitivity to anchoring	Pay for quality
	Weak loyalty	Zero loyalty	Total value focus
	"Wants" create friction	Bargain hunting	
	"Needs" are priority	Options become emphasized	

PRICING TIP

Adjusting to an economic downturn is not a single change, but a series of changes as the crisis goes through the three phases. Prepare for a long and bumpy ride.

Each phase comes with its sets of challenges and opportunities. Most businesses will over-index on reacting to the collapse phase but forget that eventually things bottom out and recover in a crisis.

As we come to grips with the reality that we are in a crisis, the most natural reaction is to discount heavily to save customers and close deals. While this may seem like a prudent tactic on the surface, panic-induced deep or mass discounts can have serious consequences and long-term implications.

There have been numerous studies on discounting's impact on LTV and churn. Deals acquired with discounts exhibited far more churn in the first three months and one-third the amount of LTV compared to customers not acquired with discounts. Keep in mind that subscription-based models already come with a revenue trough you need to climb out of to pay back your invested costs to acquire new customers. Discounts make this trough deeper and longer.

If you have to do it, put conditions around it, such as time limits or specific criteria to qualify for the discount. Be much more precise around how you discount if you go down this route.

To help you prepare for the next crisis, I've put together a simple framework to help you think through your options. You have to be product-led, precise with what you do, and present for the customers who need you the most.

THE 3P FRAMEWORK

Monetizing is hard enough without a crisis on hand. No one can prepare for the entire world being under mandatory curfews and lockdown, or strict constraints around business hours and max occupancy.

You'll be scared, you'll be nervous, and you'll be frustrated. These emotions can lead to less-than-ideal decision-making—something you can't afford to do during a crisis. The 3P Framework was designed to help you stop and think about your options from a product, sales, and process perspective. We want to keep things quick and actionable, but more importantly, be more product-led versus dollar-led in your actions.

In a quick poll I did with about 100 SaaS companies, over half of them were concerned about keeping the acquisition going during a crisis over expanding and retention.

In the first phase of a crisis, the collapse, people and hence, businesses, will clam up and pause any new purchases due to the uncertainty. While this opens up in the bottom and recovery stages, it can rattle any SaaS company. Be patient and stay diligent; the demand will return naturally. The 3P Framework shown in **FIGURE 15.2** will guide your thinking as you weather the storm.

FIGURE 15.2: 3P FRAMEWORK FOR MONETIZING IN A CRISIS

	PACKAGING	SALES EXECUTION	IMPLEMENTATION
PRODUCT LED	Redefine the experience	Fund the value machine	Guide step downs with data
PRECISE	Focus on the right segments	Revisit buy assumptions	Flex payment options
PRESENT	Pay more attention	Relearn and rebuild	Pause but don't stop

Let's touch on each of the 3Ps in the framework from a packaging perspective:

BE PRODUCT-LED

This means to think about looking deeper into your product or service for how to adjust and plan your counter measures during a crisis. Don't fall victim to becoming dollar-led and making decisions based on slowness in growth, drops in conversion rates, or delays in billing. The key is to redefine the product experience.

WHAT TO DO FIRST?

- Study product usage patterns compared to pre-crisis levels.
- Include features/professional service/support usage patterns as well.
- Categorize and score changes in usage by depth and breadth.
- Separate global vs. local responses; as well as proactive vs. reactive tactics.

WHAT TO DO NEXT?

Try offering more value in the form of a "1UP." A 1UP is giving the customer more value in the form of more access to a feature that is made critical during a crisis or an upgrade to the next package for a limited time. The good thing here is that the 1UP is not only helping the client, but it is helping you in the form of a future upsell opportunity if they enjoy the new access.

BE PRECISE

For this to work and be most effective, you need to focus on the right segments. All customers are important, but not all are created equal in terms of impact to them and impact to your business. Focus your efforts on the group that you need the most, and who needs you the most.

WHAT TO DO FIRST?

- Use product-led usage data to filter segments.
- Identify new use cases as a result of the crisis to filter segments.
- Score segments using dimensions such as risk, profitability, strategic value.
- Design a crisis-specific version/package to address crisis use cases.
- Define entry and exit criteria.

WHAT TO DO NEXT?

Try offering a "treemium" product, as shown in **FIGURE 15.3**.
A treemium product is a free offering designed to monetize later while

keeping you relevant during the hard times. Unlike a freemium (you read about this earlier), which is designed to monetize as a core part of your acquisition plan and convert as soon as the customers see value, a treemium is intended to be more patient, offer a specific solution to a specific segment, and wait out monetization until after the recovery phase of the crisis.

Zenput did an incredible job using this tactic. They offer a SaaS platform for restaurants, who were among the hardest hit during the Covid-19 pandemic of 2020-2021. They had to act swiftly as new restaurant sales halted. They shifted their strategy to offer a free version of their software that helped restaurants adjust and cope with all the new health regulations imposed by the new climate. It was a genius pricing and packaging move that resulted in hundreds of new customers as they moved into the bottom and recovery phases. It was a move that saved their business.

BE PRESENT

The last of the 3P Framework from a packaging point of view is to pay more attention. This means to give more face time to customers needing more training, knowledge, and assistance during turbulent times.

WHAT TO DO FIRST?

- Assess services and support capacity.
- Design crisis-specific resources and business-as-usual responses.
- Leverage a multi-channel strategy from passive to active, including knowledge base, communities, webinars, onboarding, training, and support.
- Define a ramp up and ramp down plan.

WHAT TO DO NEXT?

Try to offer a "visible hand" when helping your customers.

Playing off the old Adam Smith theory from economics class, the visible hand gives more attention to customers in a time when they need it the most. This means extending your customer service and success hands to just be there and listen to customers. Your customers will remember you for this, and therefore is a great way to build up your brand and future trust.

FIGURE 15.3 shows two examples of the visible hand similar to those offered by Salesforce and Pipedrive:

FIGURE 15.3: EXAMPLES OF THE VISIBLE HAND

At the end of the day, shifting your response to be more product-led, precise in your action, and paying more attention to real people and real needs will increase your chances of survival. I've summarized the key points and actions in **FIGURE 15.4**. Use it as a guide.

FIGURE 15.4: THREE STEPS TO PRICING IN HARD TIMES

THE 1 UP

Give more value instead of discounts

- Offer a service or capability that is highly valued during the crisis
- Close new deals or save renewals by offering the next level plan for the price of the current level for a limited time

2

THE TREEMIUM

Give a solution that plants seeds

- Offer a freemium of free trial version that directly solves a problem triggered by a crisis
- Use the solution to plant seeds to upgrade or convert after the crisis has passed (be strict with definition and qualifying criteria)

3

THE VISIBLE HAND

Give attention in a time of need

- Offer extended onboarding, training, or customer support to impacted groups of the base
- Delight new accounts during a crisis with a surprise upgrade (use as a retention tool or leverage as an intelligence tool)

I had the pleasure of speaking on this topic and framework in more detail in a recorded webinar. If you are interested in the full recording, reach out to us at pricingio.com.

When the going gets tough, the tough get going with 3P. How you react to a crisis will shape your company's character. Avoid the knee-jerk reactions and be deliberate and in the driver's seat and you will navigate and come out on the other side stronger, faster, and better. As the song goes, things are gonna get easier, ooh, things will get brighter.

But don't wait for a crisis to take your monetization into your hands. Take all the great knowledge you've acquired and put it to good use. And now we head into the last Track of *Street Pricing*—and remember, it's all good, baby, bay-beh.

AND IF YOU DON'T KNOW

PLAN THE WORK AND WORK THE PLAN

"JUICY" IS SYNONYMOUS WITH HIP-HOP'S AMBITIOUS ETHOS.

It's become such a staple that every hip-hop head is expected to know the first verse by heart. Biggie's life and career were cut tragically short in 1997. However, Diddy helped bolster the mythology of "Juicy" with the next generation by making it a key plot device in 2002's reality show *Making the Band*. Contestants were made to recite the song's bars aloud in order to prove their musical chops.

There's a universality in "Juicy" that enables it to stand the test of time, whether you grew up in the belly of Brooklyn's Bed-Stuy neighborhood, or you experienced your own daily struggles. Twenty-five years later, Biggie's uplifting message of perseverance, of better days, still resonates. We don't have him around anymore, but the music he left behind continues to inspire many of us today.

And now as we walk into the final track of this book, I want to shift the tone from teaching to inspiring. The Notorious B.I.G. transitioned from a dead-broke, starving, cold, and desperate urbanite whose birthdays were the worst days, to becoming a legendary hip-hop icon, beacon of hope, and reminder that anyone can make their dreams into reality with hard work, smart moves, and a killer product. Now armed with your newly acquired pricing skills, you'll be similarly unstoppable as you monetize your way to the top!

And you know very well who you are: a SaaSlete looking to make your dreams into reality via a technology product. Don't let them hold you down and reach for the stars!

IT WAS ALL A DREAM

I want to start my ending with a question: Why did you read this book?

As with many great entrepreneurs, chances are you're motivated by a dream. Whether you are after a $100 million payday from an exit or helping change the lives of 100 million people, or both, you are driven to make a difference. Inspiration can come from anywhere, as in this next story.

It was 1999. Dial-up internet with speeds up to 56k was the norm. A Wharton MBA student named Gregg Spiridellis, who was planning for a career as an investment banker, was surfing the world wide web (that's what we called the internet back then). Here's what he said:

> *"I stumbled across a site called shockwave.com, and on there, I clicked on one of the pieces of content and all of a sudden, streaming at me, was a giant dancing piece of poop ... and it was this hilarious 60 second video with an animated dancing piece of poop and I said, 'Oh my god, this is the future. Dancing poop!'"*

Excited by his epiphany, Gregg called his younger brother, Evan. Evan was an animator, artist, and independent filmmaker who was waiting tables in New York while trying to break into television. And Gregg told him:

> *"Stop thinking about TV ... look on the internet. You're banging out horseshoes while the Model T is rolling off the line. You can actually produce things and distribute them all around the world without having to go through any big media conglomerate and get some development exec to sign off."*

Within a few weeks, the two brothers had launched an animation studio named JibJab, positioning themselves at the forefront of an enormous shift in media consumption that was going to forever change the world and make them incredibly rich (of course, after five gut-wrenching years of figuring things out).

I hope that by reading this book, you're able to figure things out for yourself a lot faster than five years. My purpose in writing *Street Pricing* is to give you the deep insights into pricing and monetization in its rawest form, with real examples and real-world implications to cut down the learning curve (notice I said cut down, not eliminate).

As a SaaSlete, a startup founder, mature CEO, CPO, product manager, or just a hustle-and-bustle SaaS enthusiast, you have to keep things real. Yes, there is a lot of fluff out there, much of which is designed to make you feel good and give encouragement. Encouragement is good, right?

For me, nah. You have enough encouragement. What you need is real information and frameworks to figure this stuff out and get the job done. I hope this book is enough to encourage you to take these lessons forward.

PRICING TIP

It's not glamorous. You need to get "street" when running a SaaS business.

And with that, let's move into the final step of our journey. All the knowledge you just learned is begging for you to do something with it. The best thing you can do for your business after you put down this book is to pick up a plan.

THINKING OF A MASTER PLAN

Okay, we stepped through everything you need to know in this book. I hope it was helpful and a rewarding journey. As I said before, you now have more knowledge about monetization and pricing than 90 percent of the SaaSletes out there.

So, I ask again: What are you going to do?

For the ultimate playback exercise, I want you to put together a plan to outline what you want to do with your pricing and get cracking.

First, I suggest you start small. For example, focus on a small product, or a smaller segment you know well. Keep your first moves focused on familiar territory.

Next, I suggest you get some help from your team members, and remember, don't change pricing in a vacuum.

You should grab team members from sales, product, marketing success, operations, and spend 30 minutes on a brainstorming session to collect pricing ideas and opportunities. You'd be surprised with all the good ideas your own colleagues may have around pricing.

Now do something. For inspiration, check out **FIGURE 16.1** for eight ways to get started and apply your new knowledge. Don't overthink or overdo it, just start somewhere!

FIGURE 16.1: EIGHT WAYS TO GET STARTED WITH PRICING

Price Renewal Increase Analysis

Updated Packaging and Bundles

Define a Pricing Committee

Customer Research and Feedback

Redefine Value Segmentation

New Pricing Tiers or List Prices

Pricing Baseline Analysis / Findings

Updated Value and ROI Definition

And if you decide none of these projects make sense for you, then do something else, but do something.

If you need help from PRICING I/O, my team and I are here if you need us. Just let us know by going to **pricingio.com**.

Because you are now among the precious few SaaSletes out there who know how to price, you can't stop the learning momentum now. Follow us on LinkedIn to learn more pricing tips and tricks to get better at monetizing your value. I love sharing fresh thinking, relevant examples, and actionable techniques you can use.

If you are interested in more tools and templates, such as a typical pricing transformation plan or a quick checklist to make sure your packages make sense, reach out and let us know. Why waste a lot of time for no reason when there are templates to help you get started, copy and make your own?

I will leave you with this final pearl of wisdom:

PRICING TIP

Pricing is an immensely powerful lever of value creation but if you want it, you have to earn it. And by reading this book, you now have the confidence to take the necessary steps.

You've invested a lot of time and energy into learning how to get real with pricing and the 5Q framework. Don't let this knowledge go to waste. You've found a market that needs your value, you've spent countless hours learning more about that value, and even more hours to build that value.

Now go out there and capture that value!

PRICING TIP

The wise listen (as you did in **REWIND**).
The smart learn (as you did in **PLAY**).
The winners act (as you will after **FAST FORWARD**).

Congratulations—you just shifted your pricing from guesswork to framework!

Peace out! (Drops the mic)

HIGH-SPEED DUBBING

In the sound recording industry, dubbing is the transfer or copying of previously recorded audio material from one medium to another.

To help transfer as much pricing knowledge over to you as quickly as possible, I added this section to quickly reference the pricing tips. I like things that I can scan with little effort, so this is my way to make sure you have all the pricing wisdom from this book at your fingertips.

TRACK 1: STEP INTO A WORLD

- Understand the language of numbers in business. Understand how people behave. Understand the technology in order to understand the value to price.
- If you are looking to put someone in charge of pricing, it helps if they have a financial analysis background.

TRACK 2: LET ME CLEAR MY THROAT

- If you have data and observations to back it up, then go right ahead and double your prices.
- SaaS models are built on relationships, and relationships are built on trust. You can't build trust with guesswork.
- There is no such thing as an average value to someone, so don't use an average price as your anchor.
- The straight average price is usually the straight wrong price.
- If a salesperson cannot explain the pricing calculation to a 10-year-old, then go back to the drawing board.

- The best approach is giving customers 90 days or more notice for a price increase, along with solid value proof points to justify the new price.
- Highlight three to five of your most compelling value drivers and give the customer an option to go deeper into details.
- Offer a few packages, metrics, or add-ons to capture different values from different segments.
- No discount clock, then no revenue lock.

TRACK 3: WITH MY MIND ON MY MONEY

- Your pricing strategy should support moving the North Star metric in the right direction.
- For me, PE doesn't stand for Private Equity, it stands for "Potential Equity."
- The probability of selling to an existing customer is 60-70 percent, while the probability of selling to a new prospect is 5-20 percent. Existing customers are 50 percent more likely to try new products and spend 31 percent more, when compared to new customers.

TRACK 4: DON'T GO CHASING WATERFALLS

- B2B buyers are not as price sensitive as many may imagine, so don't hesitate to charge for your value.
- Stick to charging for the value you can prove with real customer feedback and understanding the operational constraints to capture value over time.

TRACK 5: KILLING ME SOFTLY

- The best packaging lineups result in customers buying more or upgrading between 2 and 9 months after the first purchase.
- Buyers don't want more value; they want the right value.
- Effective pricing pages build confident buyers. Design your pricing page with the right amounts of information and guidance.

TRACK 6: CHECK YO SELF

- Check your pricing before it wrecks your growth!

- You have to think of pricing as a living and breathing system ... not just a number.
- Gather data to understand what is working and not working in how your pricing model captures value. From there, you can plan what to do about it.
- You don't watch competitors to copy or define your strategy. You watch to understand your position in the value landscape.
- When it comes to good pricing analysis, let the numbers do the talking.
- It's better to work with a small data set that is accurate versus a large data set that is questionable.
- It is easier to focus a pricing baseline analysis on a single product than expand to other products once you have a chance to work out the kinks with the first one.
- Many say that pricing is both Art and Science. I say pricing is really Art informed by Science.
- Don't enter a sales negotiation or update your pricing page without understanding the playing field you're in.

TRACK 7: I GOT 5 ON IT

- To figure out how much to charge, you first need to understand what you're charging for.
- Pricing is much more than finding the dots—it's about connecting the dots.
- Pricing is the product of the product. And like any product, it has its own life cycle that demands research, innovation, and good execution.

TRACK 8: NUTHIN' BUT A "G" THANG

- Customers don't care about what you think your value is. They buy based on their perception of it.
- Value is a lot like love. You know when you have it; you know when you don't, and no one knows how to measure it.
- Numerical anchoring is a powerful and inescapable way to frame value.

- Fast value makes fast friends! The quicker path to value, the more value you can capture.
- Stop guessing and know your value with concrete proof—it is what separates the good SaaS businesses from the great ones out there.

TRACK 9: MY PEOPLES COME FIRST

- It is okay to start with firmographics, but as soon as you gain more customers and are headed toward product-market fit, you should quickly evolve from this form of segmentation.
- The closer you get with the customer, the closer you will be to realizing your full potential to deliver and capture value.
- Ask customers about price to get a lie; ask them about value to get the truth.
- As a shortcut, send the customer value survey to the same audience as your Net Promoter Score (NPS) survey to keep things simple.

TRACK 10: THE CHOCE IS YOURS

- Don't follow the pack when it comes to packaging. The choice is yours to decide which value to include for which customers. You are in control.
- When designing an offer mix, think about the entire customer experience, not just the feature set.
- Services exist to shorten the path to value for your customer; and by shortening the path to value, you enable more recurring revenue.
- A package without a purpose is pointless. Always assign a theme that links what you sell to how you plan to grow.
- Value drivers with specific or limited use cases or carry a variable cost are ideal for add-ons. If less than 20 percent of your audience uses a feature, consider it an add-on.

TRACK 11: CASH RULES EVERYTHING

- In the tiered pricing model, you are monetizing across a spectrum.

Charge customers a fair price for where they are today and progressively charge more as they move up the spectrum.

- Choosing not to monetize something is a form of monetization strategy, mainly because you are doing this in an effort to monetize something else.
- It's better for B2B SaaS companies to go with a Free Trial. The conversion rates from free to paid are 14 percent compared to 7 percent for Freemium. The execution risk is lower, and the cost is easier to contain.
- Your sales team will prove your pricing model right or wrong, whether or not it's really right or wrong.
- Customer success should be compensated to grow accounts, not sell to them.
- Ideal value metrics are easy to understand, grow as customers use the product, and get more value from that usage.

TRACK 12: THIS IS HOW WE DO IT

- Building a pricing function is a lot like building muscle—you need form and repetition
- You don't need a superhero; you need a system.
- A superhero will save the day! But a good system will pave the way.
- The best way to unify your team behind pricing is actually not to rally behind pricing but rally behind value.

TRACK 13: SO FRESH, SO CLEAN

- Pricing is about confidence.
- As a startup or new product, you must price to learn before you earn.
- Pricing without data, structure, and purpose is dangerous at worst and reckless at best.
- Like pricing, Product-market fit tends to be a spectrum rather than a discrete milestone and typically takes continued, sustained effort to improve over time.
- Product-market-price is when a startup offers a new product

that meets a real need customers will pay for at a price that can support unit economics scale.

- Startups and new products need to consider pricing during the initial stages of finding potential customers and product-market fit.
- Never make a price decision off one data reference point.
- Never stop re-evaluating your pricing. Build a repeated habit around assessing price to value equation.
- As they unlock more value, you unlock more revenue. That's the beauty of good monetization.

TRACK 14: MO MONEY, MO PROBLEMS

- When discounting for volume, start with five tiers of volume and about 10-15 percent discount from tier to tier.
- Don't write a blank check for your "people power." Instead, put guardrails around it and include the appropriate number of services for the size and software.
- Enterprises don't buy software; they are sold software. Prepare to own the sales cycle from end to end.
- After a price increase, look for signs such as reducing user seats, asking for escalation, or a sharp drop in usage. Have a remedy in place for each scenario.

TRACK 15: KEEP YA HEAD UP

- Adjusting to an economic downturn is not a single change, but a series of changes as the crisis goes through the three phases. Prepare for a long and bumpy ride.

TRACK 16: AND IF YOU DON'T KNOW

- It's not glamorous. You need to get "Street" when running a SaaS business.
- Pricing is an immensely powerful lever of value creation but if you want it, you have to earn it. And by reading this book, you now have the confidence to take the necessary steps.
- The wise listen (as you did in Rewind); The smart learn (as you did in Playlist); The winners act (as you will after Fast Forward).

WHAT'S THE SCENARIO? HOW I PRICED THIS BOOK

And one more thing...

I can't talk about the golden age of hip-hop without mentioning the epitome of energizing posse cuts, the 1992 shout-along anthem, "Scenario."

Spitting fire like a dungeon dragon, this hot track was brought to us by an intricate collaboration between A Tribe Called Quest and Leaders of The New School (notably the 19-year-old newcomer Busta Rhymes) exhibiting comradery at its finest. The team-vocal chorus was bursting with energy along with a voracious drumline percussion.

I love this song for many reasons: the retro battleship gray browser interfaces in the video remind me of how far technology has come; the word "Scenario" also means framework and schema, the essence of 5Q; and last but less obvious, this song integrated five verses from five talented artists to unify in both message and direction: another nod to the 5Q framework.

We've walked through 16 tracks together, building pricing confidence along the way. You've already graduated from guesswork to framework, but I figured one more demonstration using a real-life "scenario" in this bonus track will give you that final nudge. So here we go yo, here we go yo:

What's the scenario when it was time to price this book?

Let's start with the first factor in the 5Q framework we learned in **TRACK 8: NUTHIN' BUT A "G" THANG**, the **Why**.

My goal with this book was not to maximize my profit from book sales or generate tons of revenue as an author. From the get-go, the purpose of Street Pricing was to extend my voice to impact as many

Saasletes as possible. I wanted to change the narrative on pricing, lift the confidence of the scores of software entrepreneurs who aspire to capture value, and fuel the momentum of technology innovation that is changing our world.

So with this goal in mind, I needed a price that would not inhibit virality while still signaling to the prospective reader that the content is high quality and of high value. This meant leaning toward penetration pricing, as opposed to a neutral or skimming strategy. As this book is my first published body of work, my secondary goal was to infuse personal symbolism to deepen my connection with the content. Case in point, in addition to lacing each track with my favorite hip-hop jams growing up in the Bronx, I wrote 16 tracks because I was born on the 16th, and it happens to be my favorite number!

Let's move to the next factor in the 5Q framework that we learned in **TRACK 9: MY PEOPLES COME FIRST**—the **Who**.

This book is not for everyone, however from the over-caffeinated and sleep-deprived workhorses to the effervescent visionary savants, I wanted every SaaSlete to have a copy of this book in their hands. To avoid casting a net too wide, I decided my target audience falls into three specific demographics:

1. Tech Founders and Entrepreneurs
2. Technology Investors and Executive Leaders
3. Product Management, Growth, and Marketing Professionals

Using my experience and anchoring on feedback from 32 customer interviews, I formed a hypothesis that these three audiences have one major thing in common. Most of my readers will come from SaaS companies at the growth stage; and further, want to experience quick wins from applying the techniques showcased in this book. Initial feedback also suggested that price was not a major factor in their purchase decision because the book can be expensed.

With a sharp focus on my goal (the Why) and audience (the Who), here's how I thought about the **What** using the lessons we discussed in **TRACK 10: THE CHOICE IS YOURS.**

Packaging a book is a lot easier than packaging different flavors of SaaS software. So while my target audience could consume content in hardcover, paperback, ebook, and audiobook formats, knowing that most of my target audience travels more than the average person, I suspected that the paperback version would be the dominant format. Therefore, I needed to get the price right for the paperback format, then address the others.

Now that the What has been defined, I can move to the enthralling part of the pricing process: determining the **How**, which we covered in **TRACK II: CASH RULES EVERYTHING**.

Armed with the answers to the first three questions in the 5Q framework, I am ready to build a pricing envelope to determine how much to charge for the paperback book. Here are my inputs for the envelope:

- I reviewed my competitive landscape and narrowed in on pricing-related books that could potentially be alternative reads to *Street Pricing*. Based on page numbers, formats, and depth of coverage on the topic of monetization, the US dollar price levels ranged between \$19.99 and \$29.99.
- Going back to the 32 customers I interviewed and narrowing down to the buyers in growth-stage SaaS businesses interested in the paperback format, I noticed a high concentration of suggested prices between \$20 and \$25, as the book started to feel expensive (at face value) above \$25, and the quality started to come into question as the price fell below \$20.
- By polling the feedback of publishing experts, I learned that positive differentiation for books due to style and novelty can be worth up to a \$10 premium.

With these inputs, and my earlier decision to optimize for market share rather than profit, I began gravitating towards the lower half of the pricing spectrum with a safe zone of \$20 to \$25 for the paperback format.

To pin down my pricing even further, I wanted to position the price of the book just before the slope of the reference anchor price started to change, landing on \$24. Being mindful of the easy-to-read style and novelty of the mixtape approach, I started feeling confident that the $24 price point would resonate with my target buyer.

And finally, I wanted to introduce another symbolic reference. By reducing the price by an immaterial one cent from $24 to $23.99, not only do I improve the optics with a charm price, but also, I breathed in another part of my persona. With this book, I am sharing 23 years of pricing experience that began in 1999. To pile on, the number 23 is sacred in hip-hop culture, adorning jerseys of revered basketball legends Michael Jordan and Lebron James. A final nod to the genre.

Now let's wrap up with the final factor in 5Q, the **Which**, covered in **TRACK 12: THIS IS HOW WE DO IT**. Going back to the point about having a North Star metric, I decided to measure not only the obvious metric of total book sales but also virality metrics such as the number of mentions, shares, and referrals, that will be tracked from the various buying channels. If my pricing decisions are working, I should see these numbers move up.

You have now peeked into the mind of a pricing aficionado. Tackle monetization step by step, be clear on what you want and why, get some data together, and then follow the 5Q framework to price with confidence, just like I did.

And that's the scenario!

PROPS TO MY PEEPS

It took me a year to write this book and about another year to make it into a useful body of work. During that time, I took the entrepreneur's plunge, survived a global pandemic, reclaimed my health, and poured my soul into two little blessings, Tiago and Dahlia. The fact that this book made it out the door was entirely thanks to my amazing wife, Melanie, for being my biggest champion and for her unwavering support and commitment throughout this crazy journey. Can I get an amen?

I'm also grateful to all the brilliant, thought-provoking SaaSletes for sharing their knowledge and perspective along with their contributions to the field of SaaS, technology, and the subscription-based economy. I (we) owe a great debt of gratitude to each and every one of you.

By name, I need to express my gratitude to a few of my favorite pioneers of the SaaS model—Jason Lemkin from SaaStr, David Skok from Matrix Partners, Nathan Latka from FounderPath, James Wood from Insight Partners, Neil Patel and Hiten Shah from Crazy Egg, Lincoln Murphy, Tomas Tungus from Redpoint Ventures, Steli Efti from Close, Mark Suster from Upfront Ventures, and a special thank you to Patrick Campbell from Profitwell for making the topic of pricing cool again.

I'm eternally grateful to the scores of superstar SaaSletes who unselfishly shared their time and thoughts in interviews across a variety of pricing and SaaS topics. I want to thank SaaS growth mastermind Dan Martell from SaaS Academy, the savvy SaaS CEO Ajit Viswanathan from Doctible, the smarty-pants SaaS superstar Arnab Mishra from Xactly, the unstoppable CEO Alice Deer from GatherContent, the oracle of pricing

Dr. Dwight Porter for his unmatched support and thought leadership in the areas of SaaS, growth, and pricing, I want to give an epic-sized shout out to Kyle Poyar from OpenView.

I was lucky enough to have a great team in helping me side-by-side with design and content, which admittingly was a fun part of the journey. Special shout out goes to Andy Drogo for contributing his design vision that led to a fresh-looking book jacket, to Nita Payno and Kristi Seaver for turning boring words and images into interesting infographics for my readers. I also need to thank the tenacity and creativity of the Broad Book Group team and their efforts in making the book a reality.

And finally, a major thank you to the hundreds of followers and members of my "book club" for providing honest feedback to inspire me and keep the book real. I got nothing but love for ya.